Harmony
from
Discords

———————

JOHN DENHAM

The only known depiction of the poet is the
kneeling figure on the monument to Judge Denham's
wives in Egham Parish Church which represents him at about
four years of age. The inscription in English reads:
"Here lye buried the Bodies of Lady Cicile Denham
first Wife of Sr. Iohn Denham Knight and formerly
the Wife of Richard Kellefet Esquire deceased and of Lady
Ellenor Denham second Wife of the sayd Sr. Iohn Denham
and one of the daughters of Sr. Garret Moore Knight
Lord Barrone of Mellefont in the Kingdome of Ireland
whom he married during his Seruice in Ireland in the
Place of Cheife Iustice ther and by whō he had issue
a Sonne now liuinge and a Daughter interred here
with her of whom shee died in Childbed." The shield
above the monument impales the arms of Denham,
on a field gules three lozenges ermine,
with those of the first Lady Denham.

Here lye buried the Bodies of Lady Cicile Derham first Wife of Sr. John Derham
Knight and formerly the Wife of Richard Kellett Esquire deceased and also
of Lady Ellenor Derham second Wife of the said Sr. John Derham and one
of the daughters of Sr. Garret Moor Knight Lord Barone of Mellefont in
the Kingdome of Ireland whom he married during his Service in Ireland in the
Place of Cheife Justice ther and by who he had issue a Sonne now liveing
and a Daughter interred here with her of whom shee died in Childbed
ERGO ERAS MITIS ET MANSVETA PLUS TVMULO TV MOESANATION PRIVALES
ECCE NON HABES VITAE GLORIOSAE SED TERRAE CHRIS

Harmony

from

Discords

A LIFE OF

SIR JOHN DENHAM

BY BRENDAN O HEHIR

UNIVERSITY OF CALIFORNIA PRESS

BERKELEY AND LOS ANGELES 1968

University of California Press
Berkeley and Los Angeles, California

© 1968 by The Regents of the University of California
Library of Congress Catalog Card Number: 68-27162
Designed by Wolfgang Lederer
Printed in the United States of America

For Andrew: *fuit*; *futurus est*.

Preface

"Sir *John Denham*, in his *Coopers Hill* [has written] a Poem which your Lordship knows for the Majesty of the Style, is, and ever will be the exact Standard of good Writing." So wrote John Dryden in 1664, near the beginning of his career. At the end, in 1700, he expressed yet once more the undeviating admiration for Denham which he had voiced also several times in the interim. To Dryden's admiration may be added that of Herrick (the first publicly to praise *Coopers Hill*), of Addison, Garth, Goldsmith, and Johnson. Pope and his antagonist Dennis disagreed over Denham only as rivals in lauding the beauties of *Coopers Hill*. These are names only of the better known today of countless seventeenth- and eighteenth-century admirers of Denham. Perhaps hundreds of obscurer men committed their adulation to writing, while thousands were content to marvel in silence. Yet though Pope wrote that "On Cooper's Hill eternal Wreaths shall grow, / While lasts the Mountain, or while Thames shall flow," it is possible that at present even Dennis is more widely known than the man Dryden denominated one of the "fathers of our English poetry."

Recent critical studies of *Coopers Hill* as a prime document for the understanding and elucidation of English Augustan poetics, canons of taste, and even cosmology and social doctrines, have made manifest the necessity for a new critical edition of that poem. In developing such an edition it became clear to me that the two principal texts of that poem are products of two distinct periods and sets of circumstances in Denham's life, set apart by more than a decade. In attempting to convey the very different flavor and quality of those separate historical moments for Denham I encountered the obstacle of severe inadequacy and distortion in all the published accounts of Denham's life. No full-length biography of John Denham has hitherto been written, and all the briefer biographies and epitomes are largely inaccurate. The present life attempts for the first time to put the discoverable details of Denham's career in perspective, and to connect his poetic canon with the episodes of his experience. *Coopers Hill* itself, the stimulus for this effort, was first written when Denham was twenty-six, before the outbreak of the Civil War; the major revision was made when he was thirty-eight or thirty-nine, the war lost, and Cromwell lord protector; he published the final version as the fifty-three-year-old surveyor general to the restored King Charles II, and even thereafter continued to tinker with the text. In this biography I endeavor to find the threads in Denham's life which connect these episodes and times, and connect the considerable body of Denham's other poetic production with these revisions of *Coopers Hill*, and with his life.

Acknowledgments

Only when faced with the actuality of attempting to return some crumbs of gratitude for the banquets of help of which I have been the beneficiary am I made aware of the inevitable perfunctoriness of all such listings as this. The people who have helped me, at any rate, are almost too numerous to name, and the help they have given too vast to specify. Of some of those who have contributed materially to this book I do not even know the names: without, for instance, the friendly and intelligent staffs of the Bodleian Library and the Public Record Office I might still be hopelessly embogged in documents; certainly the work would have been much less pleasurable without those gracious and busy people. Other names I have doubtless forgotten or overlooked, but to everyone so slighted I can only add my sincerest apology to my equal gratitude. Nor, though certain persons are named only in this present list, others only in the companion study of *Coopers Hill* (to be published in 1969 by the University of California Press), would I willingly imply that anyone's contributions can be arbitrarily isolated within a single one of the two books.

Because contributions of these first to be named are recognized, however inadequately, within the body of this present work, I beg them to accept this brief listing here as a token of my unrepayable indebtedness: Professor Thomas G. Barnes, Department of History, University of California, Berkeley, for citations, information, and advice; Professor Ephim G. Fogel, Department of English, Cornell University, for a stimulating correspondence about attribution; Michael B. Hutchinson, Esq., Vaud, and Mr. F. C. Tighe, city librarian, Nottingham, respectively, for permission to use the Lucy Hutchinson commonplace book, and for facilitating that use; Professor George deF. Lord, Department of English, Yale University, for his personal courtesy in face of my assault on some of his scholarly conclusions; Professor Gerald A. Mendelsohn, Department of Psychology, University of California, Berkeley, for informative discussions of psychopathology; Mr. James M. Osborn, Department of English, Yale University, for favors, scholarly and personal, too manifold to catalogue.

Next, but equally sincerely, I would thank all those who have helped in my task who are not specifically acknowledged within the book, and especially, for aid in my pursuit of Caroline pictorial iconography, Mr. R. J. B. Walker, curator of pictures, H.M. Ministry of Works; Mr. M. Randall, Publications Department, National Gallery, Trafalgar Square; Dr. M. Poch-Kalous, Direktor, Gemäldegalerie der Akademie der Bildenden Künste, Vienna; and, for criticism, advice, and special encouragement, my good friend Professor Ralph W. Rader, Department of English, University of California, Berkeley.

Last, I thank all my students who have taught me.

B. O H.

Contents

Abbreviations

For sources that appear repeatedly in the footnotes I have habitually used the following abbreviations and short titles:

Aubrey, *Brief Lives* — *"Brief Lives" chiefly of Contemporaries set down by John Aubrey, between the Years 1669 and 1696*, ed. Andrew Clark. Oxford, 1898. 2 vols.

Banks, *Poetical Works* — Theodore Howard Banks, Jr., *The Poetical Works of Sir John Denham*. New Haven, 1928.

Bentley, *Jacobean and Caroline Stage* — Gerald Eades Bentley, *The Jacobean and Caroline Stage*. Oxford, 1941–1956. 5 vols.

BNYPL — *Bulletin of the New York Public Library*

C.Cl.S.P. — *Calendar of the Clarendon State Papers.* Vols. I–IV, Oxford, 1869–1932; Vol. V unpublished, bound proofs on file at Bodleian Library.

C. Com. Comp. — *Calendar of the Proceedings of the Committee for Compounding*, ed. M. A. E. Green. London, 1889–1892. 5 vols.

Clarendon, *History of the Rebellion* — Edward Hyde, Earl of Clarendon, *The History of the Rebellion and Civil Wars in England*. Oxford, 1707. 3 vols.

Clarendon S.P. — State Papers of Edward Hyde, Earl of Clarendon, in the Bodleian Library.

Commons Journal — *The Journals of the House of Commons*

C.S.P.D. — i. *Calendar of State Papers (Domestic*

Series) *of the Commonwealth* [1649–1660], ed. M. A. E. Green. London, 1875–1886. 13 vols. ii. *Calendar of State Papers (Domestic Series) of the reign of Charles II, 1660 to 1685.* London, 1860–1947. 28 vols. Citations are limited to Vols. I–X (1660–1670), ed. M. A. E. Green. London, 1860–1895. The two *Calendars* compose in effect a single sequence.

C. Treas. Bks.   *Calendar of Treasury Books.* London, 1904 ——. Citations are limited to Vols. I–III (1660–1672), ed. William A. Shaw. London, 1904–1908.

DNB   *The Dictionary of National Biography*

Expans'd Hieroglyphicks   Brendan O Hehir, *Expans'd Hieroglyphicks: A Critical Edition of Sir John Denham's* Coopers Hill. Berkeley and Los Angeles, 1969.

Foster, *Alumni Oxonienses*   Joseph Foster, *Alumni Oxonienses: The Members of the University of Oxford, 1500–1714.* London and Oxford, 1891–1892. 4 vols.

"Four Scarce Poems of George Wither"   J. Milton French, "Four Scarce Poems of George Wither," *Huntington Library Bulletin*, II (1931), 91–121.

Johnson, *Lives of the Poets*   Samuel Johnson, *Prefaces Biographical and Critical to the Works of the English Poets.* London, 1779–1781. 10 vols. Reprinted as *The Lives of the Most Eminent English Poets.* London, 1781. 4 vols. Frequently republished.

Lords Journal   *The Journals of the House of Lords*

Manning and Bray,   Owen Manning and William Bray, *The*
Hist. Antiq. Surrey   *History and Antiquities of Surrey.* London, 1804–1814. 3 vols.

      MLN   *Modern Language Notes*

      MP   *Modern Philology*

   N & Q   *Notes and Queries*

Nicholas Papers   *The Nicholas Papers: Correspondence of Sir Edward Nicholas,* ed. George F. Warner. Vol. I, 1641–1652, Camden Society Publications, 2d ser., 40 (London, 1886); Vol. III, 1655–1656, Camden Society Publications, 2d ser., 57 (London, 1897).

Pepys, *Diary*   *The Diary of Samuel Pepys,* ed. Henry B. Wheatley. London, 1894–1910. 9 vols.

Pepys MSS   *Report of the Historical Manuscripts Commission on the Pepys Manuscripts preserved at Magdalene College, Cambridge.* London, 1911.

  PMLA   *Publications of the Modern Language Association*

    PQ   *Philological Quarterly*

  RES   *Review of English Studies*

Sixth Report   *Sixth Report of the Royal Commission on Historical Manuscripts.* London, 1877.

S.P. Dom.   State Papers Domestic in the Public Record Office. (Eight series are cited: ser. 18, Interregnum, 1649 to 1660; ser. 19, Committee for the Advance of Money, 1642 to 1656; ser. 20, Committee for the Sequestration of Delinquents' Estates, 1643 to 1653; ser. 23, Committee for Compounding with Delinquents, 1643 to 1660; ser. 25, Council of State, 1649 to 1660; ser. 29, Charles II, 1660 to 1685; ser. 38, Docquets, 1549 to 1761; ser. 44, Entry Books, 1661 to 1828.)

S.P. Thurloe   *A Collection of the State Papers of John Thurloe, Esq.,* ed. Thomas Birch. London, 1742. 7 vols.

Surrey Arch. Coll.   *Surrey Archaeological Collections*

Vic. History Surrey   *The Victoria History of the County of Surrey,* ed. H. E. Malden. Westminster, 1902–1912. 4 vols.

Wood, *Athenae Oxonienses*   Anthony Wood, *Athenae Oxonienses: An Exact History of all the Writers and Bishops Who have had their Education in the most Antient and Famous University of Oxford . . . The Second Edition, very much Corrected and Enlarged.* London, 1721. 2 vols. in 1.

the harmony of things,
As well as that of sounds, from discords springs.
— *Coopers Hill*

I: Youth

Oh happiness of sweet retir'd content!
To be at once secure, and innocent.

A WRITER'S BIOGRAPHY often illuminates his work; just as often, on the contrary, the work glows as the only sign of life in the dry sticks displayed in the biography. Although the career of John Denham is much more amply documented than is sometimes realized, the documents show a public man — ineffective warrior, temporizing conspirator, uninspired surveyor general, and dutiful Member of Parliament — rather than private man, lover, or poet. Even his private afflictions come to us as public events: between 1665 and 1667 Denham filled variously the roles of public madman and public cuckold. The relationship between his biography and his work may therefore seem to be of the second kind: only the poems show that those bones really lived, that Denham was not a mere puppet on the Restoration stage.

Nonetheless Denham's public life, when examined at length, reveals not only a glimpse or two of the private man, but explains much about his poems, even about his best effort, the famous *Coopers Hill*. For Denham's character was a peculiar blend of weakness and strength which finds its correlative exactly in his poetic work. Like all his contemporaries, he lived through trying times; his reactions to the pressures of those times reveal his character, and his character reflects itself in his verse. Every version of *Coopers Hill* contains, at the end of Section II ("London"), a couplet that expresses Denham's inmost desire, in a context that demonstrates his awareness of the impossibility of its attainment:

1

Oh happiness of sweet retired content,
To be at once secure, and innocent!

He could not be at once secure and innocent, but in attaining
security he gave up innocence with reluctance. Almost throughout
his life we find him forced into involuntary compliance with the
desires of others; but he always resented his position, and developed in himself a devious underhandedness by which he could
attempt to assert his own integrity. Consistency and loyalty were
principles he genuinely respected, and when he failed to honor
either in the observance he failed through weakness and under
compulsion; unlike Waller he never turned his coat or openly toad-
ied to his superiors. He had perhaps no great compensatory strengths,
but his weakness at least was the weakness of a Peter, not of a
Judas. The sort of resilience Denham showed in fact is hard to cate-
gorize. A weak man's stubbornness may often resemble a strong
man's discretion: Would it have been more admirable in Galileo to
shout from the stake or the gallows rather than murmur under his
breath, "eppur si muove"?

The politic temporizing typical of Denham's career may be seen
also, for instance, in his revisions of *Coopers Hill*. After his own
initial composition of the poem he was able to absorb into the text
the emblematic value of St. Paul's Cathedral thrust upon him by
Waller's poem on its renovation. A decade later, the utter defeat of
Royalism having rendered ludicrous the tenets of the original poem,
Denham had the resilience to recast it, so that a new statement,
appropriate to the change in times, arose from his warping or from
his sacrifice of parts of the original. Not only did the new text comply with the times, however — deleting the person of Charles I
and acknowledging the outcome of the war — or even speak with
a new apparent universality that guaranteed the poem's continued
fame for a further century, but it contained, I believe, a number of
covert gibes at the new order established in the land. While out-
wardly complying with the state, while altering his poem in a way
that seemed superficially to make it comply also, while living

under the protection of a member of Cromwell's Council of State, Denham covertly vented his discontent. If it shows nothing else, a survey of Denham's life will show how typical of him is the *sotto voce* defiant rejoinder; at best such a survey may clarify the nature of his poetic work, and so of *Coopers Hill*, and go some way toward an explanation of its genesis and its extraordinary power, now vanished, to move other poets to eulogy and imitation.

The remoter ancestry of John Denham is of little relevance to his career, and in any event cannot be readily determined. He himself seems to have regarded himself as of western stock, or at least of stock derived from the neighborhood of Winchester, but his father and his grandfather were both born in London, and all three generations established particular associations with the area about Egham in Surrey.[1] His grandfather, William Denham (d. 1583), a wealthy goldsmith of London — apparently one of the Tudor new rich — was the first to remove to the vicinity of Egham, and was buried in the parish church of the nearby village of Thorpe. Yet whatever the true history of family connections, Denhams of high and low degree occur in the county records of Surrey from the fourteenth century onward.[2]

---

[1] Every life of Denham must start from the biographical memoranda of John Aubrey, set down in his *Brief Lives*, I, 216–221. This work may be cautiously supplemented by the sketch of Denham, largely derived from Aubrey, in Anthony Wood's *Athenae Oxonienses*, wherein the note on Denham constitutes entry no. 286 in "The History of Oxford Writers" (II, cols. 301–303).

Most later biographers until Sir Sidney Lee in *DNB* derive uncritically from Wood. Lee adds from original sources material not to be found in Aubrey or Wood, but he is frequently careless or incorrect. He confounds events widely separated in time, and adds to his own errors an occasional flat misrepresentation of his authorities.

The best biography of Denham offered hitherto is that of Theodore Howard Banks, Jr., in the introduction to his edition of Denham's *Poetical Works*, pp. 1–26. In spite of a great deal of research, to which I am heavily indebted, Bank's life of Denham is marred by a too-ready acceptance of the statements of earlier writers, by a signal failure to observe the chronology of recorded events — a failure that often invalidates his discrimination between causes and effects — and by what I see as major errors in the interpretation of evidence.

[2] Pedigrees of Denham's family appear in *Surrey Arch. Coll.*, XXX (1917), 11, and in Banks, *Poetical Works*, App. C, p. 332. The family's connections are dis-

John Denham's father was the eminent judge Sir John Denham (1559–1639), who at the time of his only son's birth was serving as lord chief justice of the King's Bench in Ireland. His mother was Eleanor, daughter of Sir Garret Moore, Baron Mellifont and Viscount Drogheda in the Irish peerage; she was his father's second wife, whom Judge Denham met and married during his Irish service (1609–1617). Denham was born at Dublin, and although no known documents attest the year, the commonly accepted date of 1615 is probably correct.[3] This date is deduced from the fact that his age in 1631, upon matriculation at Oxford, was given as sixteen; it is somewhat supported by a pathetic event of 1619. Sir John Denham, having been created a baron of the English Exchequer, removed his family to England in 1617, and two years later Eleanor Denham died giving birth to a daughter who also died. In the parish church at Egham the Judge erected an alabaster monument to his two wives and his infant daughter. Within an oval frame two busts and a small reclining figure portray respectively the women and the child. Outside the frame, modeled on a much smaller scale, kneels the tiny figure of a little boy dressed in ruff and scarlet cloak. This depiction of a four-year-old orphan is perhaps the best authenticated representation in existence of the poet John Denham.[4]

cussed by Frederic Turner, "Notes on Some Surrey Pedigrees," *Surrey Arch. Coll.*, XXX, 1–12; some of his errors are corrected by Mill Stephenson in "A List of Monumental Brasses in Surrey," *Surrey Arch. Coll.*, XXXIII (1920), 4–7. The coat of arms confirmed to the poet's grandfather, William Denham, in 1572, seems to assert connection with the baronial house of Dinham or Dinaunt of Devon and Somerset, the legitimate male line of which became extinct in 1501. William Denham's father was virtually certainly one of the three brothers of Sir William Denham, Merchant of the Staple of Calais — perhaps of John, draper and citizen of London (d. 1532). The four Denham brothers were born in Devonshire toward the end of the fifteenth century, and so at least were neighbors of the noble house, which was descended from an eleventh-century Geoffrey, Sire de Dinan in Brittany. This incidentally shows that the name Denham, despite its Anglo-Saxon appearance, is really of French derivation (see my discussion, "The Family of Denham of Egham," *Surrey Arch. Coll.*, LXV [1968; in press]). Other genealogical notes on Surrey Denhams and their relatives may be found via the indexes to that journal.

[3] For the career of Sir John Denham the judge see *DNB* (contains errors, but is slightly more reliable than on his son the poet). Details of Denham's birth and parentage are offered by Aubrey, Wood, *et al.*

[4] The monument may still be seen (see frontispiece). The photograph of it has

Especially in view of his later attack of temporary but severe insanity, a knowledge of Denham's childhood, during which his personality was formed, might be invaluable for the fullest understanding of his career both as poet and as public man. But aside from the glimpse into his infancy supplied by the Egham monument, Denham's boyhood is almost a blank. He was motherless at four, yet what woman or women attended thereafter to the practical details of his rearing cannot even be readily guessed. His father was fifty-six years his senior, and so is unlikely to have been his son's close companion, even if his duties as a judge did not call him away frequently to Westminster or on circuit through the country; nor did Judge Denham marry again, to provide his son with an obvious mother substitute. Under the conditions of sixteenth- and seventeenth-century mortality it is not strange that most of the Judge's contemporaries, including his sister Sarah Morley, who might naturally have mothered the orphan, had already died before the poet was born. In effect John Denham was separated from his father by the distance of two generations, rather than one, and though his boyhood may well have been tranquil it can hardly have been warmly blissful. The exact state of his relationship with his father cannot be known. Later reports suggest a constant sense of strain between the older Denham and the younger, yet on the surface John seems always to have been anxious to please his father,

---

been previously published by the Urban District Council of Egham in *Egham: Runnymede* (Egham, 1951), p. 7. (For a copy of that very interesting little book I am indebted to the late A. E. Villars, clerk of the council.) The monument is described by Manning and Bray in *Hist. Antiq. Surrey*, III, 251. This work additionally describes Denham's home, "The Place," as having been at the time of writing "totally decayed, and become a very poor house" (*ibid.*, p. 249). The *Vic. History Surrey*, III, 420, records that "The Place" "was pulled down about forty years ago." Although the family home has vanished, the name of Denham is still honored in Egham: aside from the monument to Judge Denham's wives, the parish church retains also a monument to the Judge himself. Denham Almshouses, founded by the Judge in 1624, also survive. Nor has the town forgotten the poet of Cooper's Hill. Photographs of the hill and the view from its summit celebrated in the poem are accompanied by lines both from *Coopers Hill* and from Pope's complimentary reference in *Windsor Forest*, not only in the booklet already mentioned, but also in the *Egham Official Guide*, likewise published by the Egham Urban District Council.

and even to have been emotionally dependent upon him. When he married he brought his bride home to share his father's household. Almost certainly Judge Denham is the original authority figure with whom the poet strove to cope all his life, placating and obeying him while at the same time carrying on covert sedition and sporadically breaking out into open but fainthearted rebellion. His demeanor at the age of about sixteen, as others later recalled it, consorts well with this view of his fundamental character — his habitual dreaminess was sometimes interrupted by bouts of energetic irresponsibility.

The circumstances of Denham's preliminary formal education are unknown, since his name has not been found among the records of any of the great public schools. Yet, by whatever means, he had received before he went to Oxford the fundamentals of a gentleman's training. That he had already mastered Latin is unquestionable, and that he had already attained facility in French hardly less so. No doubt also he already knew something of mathematics, and sometime either before or during his stay at the university he acquired at least a gentlemanly acquaintance with architecture.

A detail of Denham's childhood almost as obscure as the question of where he received his schooling is where exactly he grew up. His father owned extensive estates in Essex and Buckinghamshire and elsewhere in England, in addition to his holdings in Surrey, and probably owned land in Wales also. Although "The Place" in Egham, which he built about 1622, served Judge Denham as a family seat or favorite residence, his son the poet was entered at Trinity College, Oxford, on November 18, 1631, as from Essex: "filius Johannis Denham de Horseley parva."[5] Certainly both Denhams are almost as often identified with Little Horkesley as with Egham. When John Denham entered Trinity College as

---

[5] Aubrey received from Anthony Wood a copy of the entry in the matriculation book, which he reproduces thus: "Johannes Denham, Essex, filius Johannis Denham de Horseley parva in com. praed., militis, aetat. 16, 1631" (*Brief Lives*, I, 216). Foster, *Alumni Oxonienses*, I, 393, lists "Denham, (Sir) John, s. John, of Horsley Parva, Essex, militis. Trinity Coll., matric. 18 Nov., 1631, aged 16."

a gentleman-commoner he intended or expected to follow ultimately his father's profession of the law. So much is clear from the
prior recording of his name, on April 26 of the same year, in the
registers of Lincoln's Inn, where his father's name had first similarly appeared fifty-four years previously.[6] It is therefore in
1631 — his sixteenth year — that Denham's recorded life may be
said to have begun.

A contemporary of Denham's at Trinity reported him afterward
to have been "the dreamingst young fellow" from whom "he never
expected such things . . . as he haz left the world."[7] His career
at Trinity was not academically distinguished, and was marked
chiefly by a public reprimand in chapel from Ralph Kettel, president
of the college, and by the first manifestations of the compulsive
gambling that was to mar at least the first twenty years of Denham's career. The two marks of distinction were not unconnected.
The chapel reprimand occurred on one of the Tuesday mornings
for which Kettel was famous, when any undergraduate who had
committed a fault "should be sure to heare of it in the Chapell
before his fellow Collegiates." Denham, it seems, had borrowed
money of the recorder, a man named Whistler — perhaps to meet
his gambling debts — and had laughed at Whistler's attempts to recover it. For this insolence Kettel denounced him in chapel, pro-
claiming, "Thy father haz hanged many an honester man!"[8]
During his Oxford days also, we are told, Denham "would game
extremely; when he had played away all his money he would play
away his father's wrought rich gold cappes."[9] How these last came
to be at his disposal nobody explains.

In the year 1634 Denham left Oxford. Although he had been
examined in the public schools for the degree of Bachelor of Arts

---

[6] *Records of the Society of Lincoln's Inn: The Black Books* (London, 1898), II,
350.

[7] Josias Howe, as reported by Aubrey, *Brief Lives*, I, 217.

[8] Aubrey, "Ralph Kettel," in *ibid.*, II, 422; Kettel was president of Trinity from
1599 to 1643. This anecdote is not reported in Aubrey's memoranda on Denham.

[9] *Ibid.*, I, 217.

within that year, there is no record that the degree was ever conferred on him.[10] On June 25, at the early age of nineteen, he
married Anne Cotton, daughter and heiress of Daniel Cotton,
Esq., of Whittington in Gloucestershire, at St. Bride's Church,
Fleet Street. By her, according to Aubrey, Denham received an income of £500 a year.[11] The new household was established with
Denham's father at "The Place" in Egham. During the same
year Denham entered upon his legal studies at Lincoln's Inn, where
he is described as having been "as good a student as any in the
house." Here also, although he was "not suspected to be a witt,"
his career as a poet, and possibly also as a prose writer, almost
certainly began.[12] Almost as certainly, his addiction to gambling
continued through the years at Lincoln's Inn, and became the occasion for what is perhaps his earliest literary production. Although
Wood places the episode firmly in the Lincoln's Inn period, Aubrey, Wood's source, is completely indefinite as to the time (except as
it necessarily preceded the death of Baron Denham in 1639). To free
the story from Wood's embroidery, Aubrey may be allowed to speak
directly: "He was much rooked by gamesters, and fell acquainted
with that unsanctified crew, to his ruine. His father had some suspition of it, and chid him severely, whereupon his son John . . .
wrot a little essay . . . *Against gameing and to shew the vanities
and inconveniences of it*, which he presented to his father to let
him know his detestation of it." [13] This treatise was printed many

---

10 Wood reports the examination but mentions no degree. Foster, *Alumni Oxonienses*, also lists no degree awarded, which presumably means he found no indication
of it in the university records.

11 *The Marriage, Baptismal, and Burial Registers of . . . Westminster*, ed. Joseph
Lemuel Chester (London, 1876), Publications of the Harleian Society, X (1875), 170.
Aubrey's information was fragmentary: "His first wife was the daughter and heire
of . . . Cotton, of . . . in Glocestershire, by whom he had 500 *li*. per annum, one
son and two daughters" (ellipses Aubrey's).

12 The characterization of Denham at Lincoln's Inn was provided to Aubrey by
Judge Wadham Windham.

13 Readers have often been cautioned against the reliability of Aubrey's gossipy
fragments, but for the life of Denham at least the judicious reader will find much
less palpable fiction in Aubrey than in the smoothly plausible narratives of Anthony
Wood and his successors. Except in the matter of dates, where Aubrey is usually

years later, in 1651, during Denham's political exile, by a London bookseller into whose hands it had fallen, under the title *The Anatomy of Play*.[14]

This little tractate — a mere thirty pages in octavo — was published with the names of both the author and his officious editor suppressed, but the text is preceded by a dedicatory letter "To my Father" signed "Your most dutifull Son." If, then, *The Anatomy of Play* is indeed Denham's essay presented to his father, it can perhaps afford us a hasty glimpse into the young man's mind. The contents of that mind as they are revealed in the work are for the most part commonplace: allusions to Horace, Cicero *In Catilinam*, Plutarch on the laws of the Thebans, and platitudinous examples from classical history. More out of the ordinary, perhaps, are quotations from the Koran and citations of decisions of the Sixth Council of Constantinople and of the Council of "Ausburgh." Of genuine personal thought and experience there is little, although that little is enhanced in value by its scarcity. In one place Denham apparently hints that a suicide occasioned by gambling occurred within his own acquaintance, yet the episode, if a real one, serves but to

---

defective and Wood seems to have made a conscientious effort to be accurate, the orderly outline of events in Wood is almost purely factitious; Wood weaves the raw material of Aubrey into a consistent and specious texture, whose resemblance to the underlying body of facts may, however, often be remote. A reader may accept or reject Aubrey's disjointed anecdotes as their veridicality is tested by what he otherwise learns about Denham. The reader of Wood has no such option; every detail is inexorably knitted into the whole, and the narrative proceeds with a confident sobriety that conceals a total lack of authority for its ordering, harmonizing, and embellishing of Aubrey's fragment, except for Wood's own sense of the fitness of events. Creative imagination being a more valuable attribute of the novelist than of the biographer, I have therefore, contrary to precedent, always allowed more credence to Aubrey's version of an event (including his silences) than to Wood's, provided exterior evidence fails to corroborate one against the other.

The ludicrous distortions of reality conveyed to later biographers through the derivative succession of Aubrey-to-Wood-to-Johnson are illustrated below in the successive accounts of Denham's part in the loss of Farnham Castle in 1642 (see chap. iii, p. 61 and n. 14; App. A, pp. 259–260).

[14] *The Anatomy of Play: Written by a worthy and Learned Gent.: Dedicated to his Father, to shew his detestation of it*, by G. P. for Nicholas Bourne (London, 1651), 8vo (Wing D989). George Thomason dated his copy of this pamphlet April 28, 1651.

point his moral, and seems not to have affected his soul. Two remarks in the work, however, do seem to have some biographical bearing. Although he expressly writes out of his own experience of the vice of gaming he insists, as a defense against possible imputations of vengeful malice to his attack, that "I have not lost any so great summes either of mony, credit, or times, as to sharpen my pen." If to his own mind he is speaking truth here, we are left perhaps with the alternatives of believing that Aubrey and others have much exaggerated the recklessness of Denham's youthful gambling, so that we may feel that Judge Denham was able to retain safely his wrought rich gold caps (cups?); or that Denham was so irredeemably sunk in the vice, despite his protestations, that he did not regard his losses, even including the gold caps or cups, as large enough to be provoked about. Another remark that may well enter our evaluation of Aubrey's accuracy is the one to the effect that no "wise Parent will trust a son either with the fruition of a present or the possibility of a future estate, whom he sees addicted to Gaming, unless he be willing to behold the utter subversion and ruine of his family and estate, and the fruit of all his labours and cares vanish into nothing." Perhaps it was this passage that led, by a rather familiar process of misapprehension, to Anthony Wood's allegation that Baron Denham threatened to "cast off" his son if the latter did not forbear gambling. In real life fathers disinherit their only sons with somewhat less alacrity than they do in melodrama.[15]

John Denham in the later time of his own maturity was reputed

---

[15] For the present episode Wood's embroidery upon Aubrey and its dangers may be seen not only in the certainty with which Wood places Denham at Lincoln's Inn at the time of his "rooking by gamesters," but in his description of Baron Denham's reaction. That Denham's father "chid him severely" is all that Aubrey notes, whereas Wood writes, on what can only be his own authority, that Sir John "took him severely to task, *with many threatnings to cast him off if he did not forbear*" (my italics). Sir Sidney Lee, in *DNB*, converts this warning to an explicit threat on the part of the father to disinherit the son, and even Banks, who has gone back as far as he could to original sources for his biographical notice of Denham, still yields to the insinuation that one of Denham's motives for writing *The Anatomy of Play* was "to make sure of his patrimony" (*Poetical Works*, pp. 5–6).

a wit and an anecdotist. That judgment of his contemporaries is not readily explicable to us, for we can recover but pallid traces of the witticisms and anecdotes upon which it presumably was based. In *The Anatomy of Play*, however, we can discern the fairly substantial lineaments of an anecdote that may at some time have entertained his friends, although here it is rather dismally flattened, perhaps to edify his father:

I was wont to accompany a Gent. to the house of a great Lady, where commonly meeting other company they fell to play, the Gentleman upon winning was very free and open handed to the servants, so that if they sat up all night, not a servant would go to bed, but when they broke up Play, the Butlers would be ready to present him with wine or beere, the Pages and Lackies one would hold up the hanging, another hold open the door, another light him down the staires, and be ready to do all offices expecting their reward.

But if the Gentleman were a looser, and like to continue so, they all get them to bed, and he might stumble and break his neck down the staires, for any help he should have of them, not one of them being to be seen, making good that of the Poet.

Nullus ad amissas ibit amicus opes, so that a mans winnings are as it were in jest, but his losses alwayes prove in earnest.

(pp. 18–19)

If *The Anatomy of Play* belongs to the Lincoln's Inn period, so too probably does Denham's earliest known venture into verse. Although late in life he was to assert, in effect, that he had lisped in numbers — "the inclination which I have to [Poetry], came to me by Nature from my Infancy" [16] — nothing of his survives which can be surely dated before about 1636, which would seem to be the time he attempted a verse translation of at least part of the *Aeneid*. No original poetic composition by Denham can be dated with security earlier than about 1641.

---

[16] Preface to *A Version of the Psalms of David . . . By the Honourable Sir John Denham, Knight of the Bath* (London, 1714), composed about 1667.

11

Consideration of the *Aeneid* translation perhaps throws some oblique light on Denham's social life at Lincoln's Inn. One of his coevals at Trinity College had been Allen Apsley, son of Sir Allen Apsley, sometime lieutenant of the Tower, and Apsley likewise undertook the study of law at Lincoln's Inn. Apsley and Denham were to be vaguely associated during the Civil War, and were certainly united in Royalist conspiracy around 1659. Both were knighted consequent upon the Restoration, and together entered the Cavalier Parliament in 1661. It is safe, then, to assume an acquaintance approaching friendship between the two men, to date the beginning of that acquaintance to their undergraduate days at Oxford, and to assume a fellowship between them at Lincoln's Inn. Another student of law at Lincoln's Inn between 1636 and 1638 was John Hutchinson, the future Parliamentary colonel, governor of Nottingham, and regicide. Although Hutchinson found the law "unpleasant and contrary to his genius," he became a frequenter of the Apsley household at Richmond, where he met and fell in love with Allen's younger sister, Lucy. On July 3, 1638, he married her at St. Andrew's Church in Holborn, and retired with her to Nottingham. Unquestionably Denham and Hutchinson must have met, and an acquaintance between Denham and Lucy is also likely, on the grounds both of Denham's presumptive friendship with Allen Apsley, and that Richmond could have served as a convenient way-stop on his journeys between Egham and London. The significance of these suppositions resides in the fact that Lucy Hutchinson commenced a commonplace book, probably in the 1650's, and in that commonplace book transcribed what she identified as Denham's translation of *Aeneid* II–VI.[17] This transcript is the only surviving exem-

---

[17] The evidence for Denham's 1636 partial translation of the *Aeneid* is twofold. First is the ascription to Denham by Mrs. Hutchinson (who is of course celebrated in her own right as the memorialist of her husband, Colonel Hutchinson) of the translation in her (unpublished) commonplace book. The unique survival of Denham's on the whole fairly crude and unfinished translation among the effects of that relatively secluded Nottinghamshire lady further suggests a date for its creation antecedent to the end of the conjunction of Hutchinson, Apsley, and Denham at Lincoln's Inn — that is, before 1638. Second is that Denham during his lifetime pub-

plar of what appears to be Denham's 1636 translation, and one may speculate that it came into Lucy's hands in some way as a fruit of the temporary conjunction of her husband, her brother, and Denham at Lincoln's Inn.

The significance of this *Aeneid* translation in Denham's poetic career is various. For one thing, it provided him with experience in the extensive deployment of poetic diction and in the composition of heroic verse (Denham's Vergil runs to more than 3,500 lines). For another, it made available to Denham a specifically English Vergil to preside as genius over Denham's georgic, *Coopers Hill*. A nice metaphysical problem is posed, however, by the attempt to distinguish between Denham's English Vergil and Denham himself. Denham's Vergil in fact grows in poetic maturity *pari passu* with his translator. In the Hutchinson transcript of *Aeneid* II, for instance, Vergil is made to say that the Greeks from the Horse "the guards with sleep & wine / Surprizd, surprize" (translation of lines 265–266), a turn of phrase parallel to the kind of juvenile wit displayed by Denham in the earlier versions of *Coopers Hill*: "the Christall floud / Dying he dies, and purples with his bloud." By the 1655 *Coopers Hill* and the 1656 *Destruction of Troy*, respectively, both these felicities had been refined out of existence. Nevertheless phrases and lines from this early translation of the *Aeneid* continue to echo even into the last versions of *Coopers Hill*.

Meanwhile Denham's personal life went on. On one occasion at

---

lished two translations of portions of the *Aeneid*: in 1656 and 1668 *The Destruction of Troy*, covering approximately *Aeneid* II.1–558; and in 1668 "The Passion of Dido for Aeneas," covering approximately *Aeneid* IV.276–705. Comparison of these two translations with the equivalent portions of the Hutchinson MS reveals them to be the work of the same pen, thus confirming Mrs. Hutchinson's ascription. But the 1656 edition of *The Destruction of Troy* asserts that the translation was made in 1636. The most convincing interpretation of that statement is to understand that the 1656 publication was in fact a revision of an earlier translation originally made in 1636, and that the 1636 translation is the one represented in the Hutchinson transcript.

The relationship among the translations can be clarified only by a comparative edition of the texts. Through the kindness of Mr. Michael Hutchinson I have acquired a photographic reproduction of Mrs. Hutchinson's transcript, from which I hope to publish such an edition.

least he found relief from the tedium of his lawbooks in a gambol more lighthearted than recourse to dice or cards, and less elevating than poetry. Aubrey recounts it thus: "He was generally temperate as to drinking; but one time when he was a student of Lincolne's-Inne, having been merry at the taverne with his camerades, late at night, a frolick came into his head, to gett a playsterer's brush and a pott of inke, and blott out all the signes between Temple-barre and Charing-crosse, which made a strange confusion the next day, and 'twas in Terme time. . . . This I had from R. Estcott, esq., that carried the inke-pott." By 1638, too, Denham's wife had borne him at least one son, John, who went the way of most seventeenth-century infants, and was buried on August 28, 1638, in Egham parish church. Shortly thereafter, however, she seems to have produced another John, who lived until after 1654.[18] Denham's two surviv-

---

[18] Aubrey credits Denham with only one son, John, but has him survive until at least 1654. Aubrey says that Denham had by Anne Cotton "one son and two daughters. His son did not *patrem sapere*. He was of Wadham College in Dr. Wilkins's time: he dyed *sine prole*, I thinke, there." Aubrey has in mind the John Denham who matriculated at Wadham on July 20, 1654, having been received as a fellow commoner on July 8. Little more is known of this young man, except that he is noted in the register to have been "*arm. fil.*" This relatively rare condition would fit exactly a son of John Denham, but of no other identifiable Denham. The term *armiger* as used in Oxford registers did not signify, as might be supposed, merely one entitled to heraldic coat armor; such a designation would be applicable to almost any gentleman, but a gentleman was designated merely *generosus*. *Armiger* was used strictly as a translation of the title "Esquire" (see F. Madan, *Oxford Books*, III [Oxford, 1931], 35). John Denham is frequently and properly designated "John Denham, Esquire," that designation not being as meaningless in the seventeenth century as it has since largely become. *Esquire*, as a title of honor, was restricted to certain classes of men, such as the younger sons of noblemen (there were no remaining noble Denhams); the eldest sons of knights (as John Denham was); barristers-at-law (as John Denham was); and the holders of certain offices of state. If the John Denham of Wadham College was not the son of John Denham, Esquire, the poet, he was necessarily the son of some other Denham, Esquire, and that means his father was necessarily either a Denham who was the eldest son of a knight named Denham, or a barrister or officer of state named Denham. Such a person has not come to light.

There is also an oblique connection between this younger John Denham and the poet through another matriculation on the same day in 1654. R. B. Gardiner writes in apparent unawareness of Aubrey's assertion: "It is to be observed that the next name in the [matriculation list] is Samuel Woodford. Now Samuel Woodford wrote verses in commendation of 'A new Version of the Psalms of David by Sir John Denham 1668': whence it may possibly be inferred that the above John Denham was

ing daughters appear to have been born during the course of the subsequent five years.

Denham's father's official position in the state had in recent years involved him more and more in the great events that were about to overwhelm England, but no record survives of any intrusion by Denham himself into politics in these years or for some time later.

related to the poet of Cooper's Hill, and that his residence at Wadham brought him into connection with Samuel Woodford" (*The Registers of Wadham College, Oxford . . . 1613 to 1719* [London, 1889], p. 203). Gardiner has nothing to say either of this Denham's death, indicated by Aubrey, or of his further career. If this John Denham was sixteen at matriculation, like the poet Denham, his birth would have occurred in 1638, the same year as the burial of Denham's known infant son. Samuel Woodford, his fellow collegian, was born April 15, 1636, at a time when the poet also might have had a son, having been married since 1634. Whether Aubrey meant, in saying that the young Denham did not *patrem sapere*, that he did not take after his father in appearance or in character, remains undeterminable.

The relative vagueness of the Wadham College entry may also be advanced as a sort of negative argument in favor of Denham's paternity of this young man. Although the son of an esquire, he is listed without his father's name, without his own age, and without a place of origin. Denham's children had been under guardianship since the Civil War because of his Royalism, which also cost him his estates except for one-fifth for the support of his family reserved in the hands of the guardian. Denham's own legal position in 1654 was very ill defined, and he was certainly not functioning parentally toward his children, nor was he capable of directing their education.

That Denham had a son still living both in 1650 and in 1652 is also indicated by the records of litigation that took place in those years concerning an estate of which he was nominally possessed, "his sonne being right Heir" (see S.P. Dom., ser. 23, Vol. 104, pp. 595–608). The estate had passed in 1643 to Anne Denham, entailed upon her and the heirs of her body, from the deceased infant son of Anne's deceased sister. Therefore it could never have been inherited by the infant Denham son who died in 1638. Anne herself had died by 1647, leaving as we certainly know two daughters. Yet depositions made in 1650 and also in 1652 speak invariably of a son as the heir of her body, not of her daughters, making the inference inescapable that she was survived by a son. Moreover, the son must have remained alive throughout those years, for otherwise, barring issue of his own (he may have been fourteen in 1652), his sisters would have succeeded him in the inheritance. If then Denham had a son alive in 1652 he may very well have had the same son still alive in 1654, and that son appears very likely to have been the John Denham of Wadham College.

Biographers later than Aubrey continue to reckon Denham's offspring as a son and two daughters, but usually understand the son to have been the infant buried in 1638. Clearly Aubrey's reckoning would not be the same; he would either not know or not care about the dead child. John Denham's will makes certain that no son of his survived him, but every reason encourages us to believe Aubrey's assertion of his paternity of the youth who apparently died at Oxford sometime after 1654.

As a baron of the Exchequer, Judge Denham was required in his eightieth year to submit judgment in the crucial case of John Hampden. While on circuit duty — shortly after the death of his infant grandson — he had contracted an ague which delayed his submission in Hampden's case until he was the last of the twelve barons to report.[19] He returned a brief opinion concurring with the four other judges in the minority favorable to Hampden, and on January 6, 1638/9, died at Egham, where he followed his grandson, his brother, his daughter, and his two wives to burial in the parish church.

John Denham succeeded to his father's estates, and was himself called to the bar on January 29, 1638/9, within a month of his father's death. He did not, however, inherit his father's gravity; according to Aubrey, he now in fact committed himself once more to heavy and reckless gambling and, having played away some £1,500 to £2,000 of his cash inheritance, sold his father's plate to continue his rake's progress. Not merely is there no reason to doubt this story, since Denham's inveterate gaming has still other attestation, but he appears to have been even more profligate than Aubrey knew. Transactions of the parliamentarian committees of sequestration later revealed that much of Denham's estates had either been sold off or encumbered before the outbreak of war in 1642, less than four years after he had inherited them.

In 1639 and 1640, at the age of twenty-four or twenty-five, Denham must already have come largely to match his physical description as given by Aubrey, who did not meet him until some years later: his skin "was unpolished with the small-pox: otherwise a fine complexion. . . . He was of the tallest, but a little incurvetting at his shoulders, not very robust. His haire was but thin and flaxen, with a moist curle. His gate was slow, and was rather a stalking (he had long legges). . . . His eie was a kind of light goose-gray,

---

[19] Prior to his minority judgment in the Hampden case, Baron Denham had ruled for the Crown, with the majority, during the controversy in 1636–37 about extending the ship money imposts to inland counties.

not big; but it had a strange piercingness, not as to shining and glory, but (like a Momus) when he conversed with you he look't into your very thoughts." Aubrey, moreover, unkindly confesses that Denham's stalking gait put him in mind of Horace's mad poet striding with head held high into a well or ditch (*De Arte Poetica* 457–459). This unprepossessing portrait rather resembles Alice's White Knight, and lends some point to Aubrey's marginal comment on Denham's mother: "She was a beautiful woman . . . Sir John, they say, did much resemble his father." Nonetheless the tall lanky Englishman with thin, flaxen hair and pale-blue eyes is neither an uncommon nor an unattractive physical type. Aubrey's description probably corresponds most closely to Denham's appearance in his thirties; he aged rapidly, and at fifty was taken for very much older. He seems never to have been athletically inclined, although it is not at all surprising to learn that "he delighted much in bowles, and did bowle very well."

The years 1639 and 1640 were years of national crisis in England: the two Bishops' Wars were fought and stalemated; the Short Parliament was called and dissolved; the policies of Laud and Strafford divided Englishmen into factions more and more hostile to one another. No record reveals any participation by Denham in the Bishops' Wars; he served in neither the Short nor the subsequent Long Parliament. His one political gesture of the period is of so negative a character that it cannot clearly be interpreted. In April of 1639 he was one of twenty-five Middlesex gentlemen (he had estates also in that county) who made no answer to the King's request for a contribution to support the fight against the Scots in the North.[20] Whether his abstention reflected an adaptation of his father's judgment in the Hampden case, or merely a pecuniary embarrassment occasioned by his gambling (in June of the same year he was to sell his manors of Barholt Sackville and Woodhall in Essex, to realize the sizable sum of £4,390 payable in install-

---

[20] John Rushworth, *Historical Collections*, III (London, 1702), 914. I owe this reference to my friend, Professor Thomas G. Barnes of the Department of History, University of California, Berkeley.

ments over the following two years),[21] there is no sure way to determine. Although relatively soon he was to be drawn deeply into political engagement, for this period imagination may safely choose to picture him dividing his time between Hogarthian gambling hells and village bowling greens. What is really important for us about Denham's life at this time is that he must have been turning his attention more and more to poetry, and that the poetry he turned to was of a singularly political cast. With Denham it remains a nice question whether it was his poetry that drew him into politics or his political involvement that determined the tendency of his poetry.

Political poetry was no new thing in Denham's England, or in Europe. Yet under the Stuarts a new *kind* of political poetry evolved in England, quite distinct on the one hand from the doggerel satires and broadsheet ballads of traditional Opposition and popular political expression, and on the other from the merely ornamental or fulsome royal eulogies embodied in court masques and pageantry, although it had noticeable affinities with both. This new sort of poetry, which may never have been consciously recognized by its practitioners as a unique genre, owed something to the political verse of Ben Jonson, who may, both in his masques and in his *Epigrammes* addressed to King James (to say nothing of his "localization" of political discourse in *Penshurst*), be regarded as its real founder. It depended upon a kind of wit (in the seventeenth-century sense) somewhat akin to the wit of the so-called metaphysical poets, but really closer to the kind of "wit" displayed in the emblem books: the wit required to disclose concealed and latent significance in emblem and lemma. Above all this poetry was written in the afterglow of Roman political poetry, particularly the *Georgics* of Vergil and the political *Odes* of Horace. Some of the greatest of this kind of poetry in English was later to be written by Andrew Marvell: the three poems on Cromwell and the poem *On Appleton*

---

[21] S.P. Dom., ser. 23, Vol. 88, pp. 1013, 1017–1026.

House. In its own time Denham's *Coopers Hill* was the most celebrated instance of the kind; yet preceding Denham, and of demonstrable influence on his early work, came Edmund Waller's *Upon
His Majesties Repairing of Pauls,* an excellent short example of the
new political poem.

St. Paul's Cathedral in London had never been adequately re-
paired after the disastrous fire of 1561 in spite of feeble good inten-
tions expressed by both Queen Elizabeth and King James. The truth
was that the Church, impoverished by Henry VIII's sequestrations,
could no longer afford the vast capital outlay to build or rebuild a
cathedral as it could in the Middle Ages, and the state had little
difficulty in finding other uses for its money. Not until the pious
reign of Charles I, under the instigation of William Laud — at
the time bishop of London — was a determined effort made to rebuild the dilapidated fabric. Work actually began, under the
supervision of Inigo Jones, in April 1633. Laud, now archbishop of
Canterbury, by his strong-willed persuasions managed to bring in
the sum of £101,330 4*s.* 8*d.* before collections for the repair fund
came to an end in 1643. The main structural renovations seem to
have been completed, and Inigo Jones's new Corinthian portico
added, by October 25, 1639, when the books were audited; thereafter work slacked off considerably as the attention of King and
Archbishop was directed to religion in Scotland and politics at home.
Nor was the repair of the cathedral popularly approved of; money
for the work was raised during the same period in which Charles
was levying tonnage and poundage and ship money without grace
of Parliament, and by what seemed to be analogous means. To the
Puritans St. Paul's, as a cathedral church, was a prelatical abomina-
tion, and its patronage by Laud served only to incense them further
against it: Dugdale reports that on March 13, 1640, Robert Greville,
Lord Brooke, "passing by Water, upon the *Thames . . .* with
three other Lords, said concerning this famous Cathedral . . . *That
he hoped, that one of them should live to see no one Stone left*

upon another of that Building." [22] (The allusion to the Temple at Jerusalem is particularly interesting in the light of Waller's poem.) The businessmen of London were rendered equally unhappy by the fact that the shops and houses that had been allowed to spring up within the precincts, and close to the west end of the cathedral, were pulled down, and Laud at his trial was indicted for this aesthetic and sensible act, even though some £11,080 16s. 8d. are recorded as having been paid in compensation.[23]

All this is background to Waller's poem *Upon His Majesties Repairing of Pauls*, which was almost certainly written at the time of the Bishops' Wars, when King Charles was being widely accused of putting through by Laud religious innovations that were indistinguishable from popery. Against this background Waller's verses appear as somewhat of a tour de force. In thirty-two couplets Waller manages to identify the former wreckage and obliteration of St. Paul's Cathedral with the Apostle Paul's shipwreck, his shackles, and his snakebite; to identify Charles's repair of the church with Solomon's erection of the Temple at Jerusalem (not to mention with the foundations of both Thebes and Troy); to associate all these events with Charles's shipbuilding program for which the ship money was levied; to demonstrate both the private and the public benevolence of the King; to prove that Charles's religious policy is "To frame no new Church, but the old refine"; and finally to warn the King's opponents that his reserved powers of punishment and destruction are far greater than his mildness has deceived them into believing.[24]

Denham came to know this poem not very long after it was written, although it was not printed until 1645, and its effect upon him seems to have been immense. Although its influence on Den-

---

[22] Sir William Dugdale, *The History of St. Paul's Cathedral in London, from its Foundation* (2d ed.; London, 1716), p. 147.

[23] *Ibid.*, pp. 135–148; E. F. Carpenter, "The Reformation: 1485–1660," in *A History of St. Paul's Cathedral and the Men Associated with It*, ed. W. R. Matthews and W. M. Atkins (New York and London, 1957), pp. 141–161.

[24] This poem is reprinted with annotations as App. B in *Expans'd Hieroglyphicks*, my edition of *Coopers Hill*.

ham's poetic growth is not easily calculable, something of its effect can be traced and annotated. In what may be the earliest surviving version of the first of Denham's poems which can be associated with a dated event, *On the Earl of Strafford's Tryal and Death*, the last line echoes the fourth line of Waller's poem.[25] The first published version of *Coopers Hill* (August 1642) contains an open complimentary allusion to Waller and his poem, emphasized by a shoulder note, although this reference appears not to have been part of Denham's original conception of *Coopers Hill*.[26] In truth the poem *Upon Repairing Pauls* seems more to typify the strength attributed to Denham than the sweetness ascribable particularly to Waller's earlier verse: all the rhymes are masculine (giv'n/heav'n at lines 55–56 hardly constitutes an exception), and if the couplets are not in fact closed, or all the lines end-stopped, they *appear* to be so. In only four instances do the divisions between couplets fail to correspond to syntactical divisions, and three of these four constitute what may be called the pseudoclosed couplet as found sometimes in Ben Jonson and frequently in Thomas Carew:[27]

> Not ought which SHEBA's wond'ring Queen beheld
> Amongst the works of SOLOMON, excell'd
> His ships and building. . . .
>
> (lines 43–45)

These characteristics are also in a general way typical of Denham's early versification, but Denham hardly needed Waller's poem to teach him prosody. What he learned from the poem on St. Paul's, if anything, was a particular sort of vision and a tone in which to

---

[25] Compare "Our Nations glory, & our Nations hate" with Waller's "Our Nations glory, and our Nations crime." Banks has already drawn attention to this parallel (*Poetical Works*, p. 153).

[26] See my *Expans'd Hieroglyphicks*, "Critical Readings," II.

[27] This couplet is typified by a transitive predicate verb that appears at first to be intransitive, so closing the sense of the couplet. The transitive nature of the verb is made plain by a continued predication within the next couplet. The reader experiences a momentary feeling of closure at the end of the first couplet, and is then slightly jarred to discover that the couplet is really open.

express that vision. The sort of vision was the emblematic view: the capacity to see in a concrete object, whether made by God or man, both a specific history and a universal significance. The tone had something of the quality of Roman public statement, and owed something to the "strong lines" of the turn-of-the-century Senecan reaction. Both *Upon Pauls* and *Coopers Hill* begin with the utterance in a completely impersonal manner, as the formulation of a public truth, of what in fact is a subjective conceit of the poet's. Waller's opening conceit might be engraved on a monumental plaque:

> That shipwrackt vessel which th'Apostle bore
> Scarce suffer'd more upon Melitas shore,
> Then did his Temple in the sea of time
> (Our Nations glory, and our Nations crime.)

The opening of Denham's first surviving draft of *Coopers Hill* betrays somewhat more the presence of a musing mind, yet the enthymeme expressed reflects public, not private, reasoning:

> Sure we have Poets y^t did nevr dreame
> uppon Pernassus, nor did tast ye Streame
> of Hellicon, And therefore I suppose
> those made not Poets, but ye Poets those.

All the same, despite the impression Waller's poem made upon Denham, it is possible that he learned no more from it specifically than the emblematic possibilities of St. Paul's Cathedral which, once introduced into the gestating *Coopers Hill*, grew more and more important with each successive draft. The vision and the tone he may have discovered for himself, and his approbation of *Upon Pauls* may have been the product of his recognition of a successful exemplification of the new mode rather than of the revelation to him of the mode itself. The question of influence here involves itself naturally with the question of when Denham and Waller became personally acquainted.

Because Denham and Waller have been so frequently twinned in

22

commentary upon the development of English Augustan "numbers," it has been usual to assume that the two poets knew each other early, that is to say, before the Civil War. Yet the evidence that they actually did so is far thinner than it has been made to appear. That evidence has been of two kinds: indications of likely crossings of their paths, and indications of their familiarity with each other's writings. Of the first kind is the evidence derived by Banks from Thorn-Drury that Waller and Denham's first cousin George Morley, later bishop of Winchester (son of Baron Denham's sister Sarah), were on close terms around 1635. Against this evidence must be set the facts that Waller was ten years older than Denham, Morley eighteen years (born in 1597, he graduated from Oxford in 1618, when Denham was only three years old).[28] Waller, moreover, was a Cambridge man rather than an Oxonian, had been a precocious M.P. in 1621 and a member of every Parliament since, and already a courtier in the days of James I — all of which put him in a world of experience separate from Denham's. By contrast, in 1635 and for some time to come, Denham was a youth nobody had heard of, and although the gap between him and his illustrious elders was not insuperable, solid evidence that he crossed it early is lacking.

The second kind of evidence for acquaintance between the two poets is that which may be inferred from indications of their knowledge of each other's works. That Denham had read Waller's poem on St. Paul's prior to the August 1642 publication of *Coopers Hill* is beyond dispute; the only question is how long before that date he first encountered it. The title page of the 1655 edition of *Coopers Hill* asserts that the poem was "Written in the year 1640." The factuality of this statement may legitimately be doubted, but even acceptance of 1640 as the date of a first essay at the poem would not constitute evidence of Denham's awareness of Waller's piece at

---

[28] Inasmuch as Sarah Denham Morley and Francis Morley, her husband, George Morley's parents, both died several years before John Denham was born, occasions for interfamily visits of Denhams and Morleys in John Denham's childhood would seem to have been minimal, and it is at least possible that Denham never met his cousin George at all, until they were brought together by the chances of later life.

the time. The transcript of the earliest surviving draft of *Coopers Hill*, whether or not it represents the actual first draft, does not yet contain the allusion to Waller. An evidential date for Denham's knowledge of Waller's poem depends therefore on the dating of the second surviving draft of *Coopers Hill* — the first to contain the allusion — and on the dating of a manuscript version of Denham's elegy *On the Earl of Strafford's Tryal and Death*. Since no firm date can be established for that second draft of *Coopers Hill*, the resolution hangs entirely upon the determination that the version of the Strafford poem containing the Waller echo is in fact the earliest version of that poem.[29]

In his later career at least, Denham could be a very rapid writer. His elegy *On Mr. Abraham Cowley his Death and Burial amongst the Ancient Poets* (1667), justly considered one of his most felicitous productions, was licensed for publication within nineteen days of the death and twelve of the burial that it celebrates. If this speed of composition was an attribute of Denham's from the beginning, he may have been echoing Waller's poem within perhaps the month of Strafford's execution, which took place on May 12, 1641.[30] That

---

[29] The relationships among the respective drafts of *Coopers Hill* are discussed in *Expans'd Hieroglyphicks*.

[30] The apparently original version of Denham's elegy survives in at least three manuscripts: British Museum MS Egerton 2421 (printed by Banks); National Library of Scotland Advocates' MS 19.3.8 (a copy made by Sir James Balfour of Denmilne apparently before April 1643; printed by H. L. Hamilton in *Times Literary Supplement*, Sept. 22, 1966); and Bodleian MS Locke e.17, pp. 81–82, which seems to have escaped other notice. This version of the elegy differs in several regards from the final version that Denham published in his 1668 *Poems and Translations*. The later version is ten lines longer than the earlier (thirty lines to twenty), it no longer contains the echo of Waller, and its tone is purged of all ambivalence toward Strafford. Four of the new lines have been interpreted as internal evidence that the revision was made after the reversal of Strafford's attainder after the Restoration, but they can hardly bear that interpretation:

> They after death their fears of him express.
> His Innocence, and their own guilt confess.
> Their Legislative Frenzy they repent;
> Enacting it should make no President. (lines 23–26)

"They" and "their" can refer only to the members of the Long Parliament which

Denham knew one poem of Waller's by early 1641, at least, may therefore be taken as established. That he knew it in manuscript is also a necessary inference from the fact that it was not printed until 1645, but knowing the poem in manuscript does not by any means imply that he knew its author. Unprinted poems in the seventeenth century often had very wide circulation, as most of the manuscript collections testify, and Denham could have seen a copy of *Upon Repairing Pauls* which had reached him through a series of transcriptions.[31] It has been asserted also, however, that *Coopers Hill* echoes three other Waller poems — *The Battle of the Summer Islands*, *Of Love*, and *On the Head of a Stag* — so that Denham must have been extensively acquainted with Waller's work by 1642.[32] But the supposed echoes of *On the Head of a Stag* will not stand up to close examination, and the echoes of the other two poems do not in fact enter *Coopers Hill* prior to the revised edition of 1655, ten years after the publication of Waller's *Works* had made those poems available to all the world.[33] The restriction, then, of Denham's verifiable knowledge of Waller before 1645 to a single poem

---

killed Strafford; it is inconceivable that Denham should have meant the pronoun to include simultaneously the members of the Cavalier Parliament (of whom he himself was one) which reversed the act of the Long Parliament. The sense is obviously that the (Long) Parliament, by seeking to reassure the populace that Strafford's was a highly special case which uniquely warranted overriding the common law, and that their attainder of him constituted no precedent for legislative abrogation of the rights of the subject, tacitly admitted Strafford's *de facto* innocence of the crime that was fastened upon him *de jure*. The argument that seeks to lump together the parliaments of 1640 and of 1661 under the single pronoun "they" betrays a modern frame of mind in which "Parliament" is regarded as a standing continuous institution, instead of as a generic name for a kind of formalized assembly representative of the estates of the kingdom which the monarch might convoke on emergent occasions.

As is shown later, however, internal evidence does suggest that Denham's revision of his Strafford elegy was effected certainly after the outbreak of civil war, and very likely after the execution of the King.

[31] Several manuscript copies of Denham's own poems are to be found among the papers of persons quite remote from him or his circle.

[32] See Banks, *Poetical Works*, p. 36 n. 170.

[33] See Brendan O Hehir, "The Early Acquaintance of Denham and Waller," *N & Q*, n.s., XIII (1966), 19–23.

might well suggest an argument that he did not know Waller personally at all.

For the other side of the relationship — indications of Waller's early acquaintance with Denham — Aubrey's often quoted report of Waller's remark on the success of Denham's play, *The Sophy*, must be considered.[34] Authorities customarily quote only Wood on this point, but Aubrey, Wood's source, should first be allowed to speak for himself: "At last, viz. 1640, his play of *The Sophy* came out, which did take extremely: Mr. Edmund Waller sayd then of him, that he *broke-out like the Irish Rebellion — threescore thousand strong*, before any body was aware when nobody suspected it." To this Aubrey adds the note: "His play came out at that time." Since the Irish uprising took place in 1641, not 1640, and word of it did not reach London until November 1 of that year, Wood incorporated a correction of the date into his rewriting of Aubrey: "In the latter end of the year 1641 he published the Tragedy called *The Sophy*, which took extremely much and was admired by all ingenious men, particularly by *Edm. Waller* of *Beaconsfield*, who then said of the author *he broke out like the Irish rebellion, threescore thousand strong, when no body was aware, or in the least suspected it*." Unambiguous as this little anecdote may seem, it gives rise to a mist of unanswerable questions, for the verifiable facts are not quite as given. At this moment, however, all that needs to be considered is what this story seems to indicate about the relationship between Denham and Waller. And the first question that must be propounded is that of Aubrey's authority for the content and the date of Waller's alleged remark. Despite the story, no other echoes of applause greeting the first appearance of *The Sophy* reach our ears. Even the date and the circumstances of its performance — assuming it really was performed — have been utterly lost. In 1641 Aubrey was a boy of only fifteen, and could scarcely have heard Waller's remark himself; therefore if Waller at that time did say

---

[34] *The Sophy* was first printed in August 1642. See following discussion, and chap. ii, n. 10.

something to the reported effect, Aubrey could have heard of it only years later, as transmitted through somebody's memory. No firsthand evidence therefore exists as to *when* Waller made the remark, and it is quite easy to imagine his making it at any distance in time after the event, in retrospect associating Denham's sudden emergence into the literary world with the roughly contemporary surprise of the Irish rebellion of 1641. Any conceivable version of the story, or none, may be the truth; the detail worth considering, however, is the suggestion of surprise. As Dr. Johnson shrewdly perceived, Waller's observation "could have had no propriety had [Denham's] poetical abilities been known before."[35] To this might be added, there could have been little impulse to the observation had Denham's abilities previously been known to Waller. This reported remark, therefore, which has sometimes been interpreted as significant of early familiarity between the two poets, may well indicate only that Waller had never heard of Denham until he "broke out" in 1641 or 1642 with *The Sophy* and *Coopers Hill*.

---

[35] Johnson, *Lives of the Poets*, "Denham."

II: Strafford

Great Strafford! *worthy of that Name, though all*
Of thee could be forgotten, but thy fall.

WITH OR WITHOUT BENEFIT of Waller's acquaintance, Denham preceded his service of the political Muse by playing a walk-on role in the greatest political drama of the day. On March 22, 1640/1, after a winter of preparation by his foes, Thomas Wentworth, Earl of Strafford, was arraigned of high treason by the House of Commons before the bar of the House of Lords. Serious proceedings began on the 23d, and from the 23d through the 29th Denham's name was listed among those of the very few witnesses for the defense.[1] The trial riveted the attention of all Englishmen, but Denham's most intense interest in it was assured as a spectator present at the event in which he was also called upon to play a part. The opening scene was indeed spectacular.[2] Strafford was islanded upon a raised platform in the center of Westminster Hall, behind him the tiered seats of the Commons and the spectators, before him, in two parallel rows, his peers of the House of Lords in their robes. In front of the peers sat the judges, and to Strafford's left, their backs to a little doorway, sat the committee for the prosecution. It was composed of John Pym, John Glyn, John Maynard, and Geoffrey Palmer, under the chairmanship of Bulstrode

---

[1] House of Lords Record Office, Main Papers (March 11–26, 1640/1), f. 97. This document was discovered by my friend, Professor Thomas G. Barnes of the Department of History, University of California, Berkeley, to whom I am immensely indebted for calling it to my attention.

[2] For the following narrative of the trial and death of Strafford, and the circumstances surrounding these events, I have relied chiefly upon C. V. Wedgwood, *Thomas Wentworth: First Earl of Strafford 1593–1641* (London, 1964), esp. pp. 337–399.

Whitelocke, and seconded by George Digby, the son of Lord Bristol. Confronting this pack of accusers, Strafford stood alone, dressed all in black, wearing for sole ornament his emblem of the Garter, that "Azure Rounde (Who Evill thinkes may Evill him confound) [which] The English Armes incircles," which Denham so lovingly dwells upon in *Coopers Hill*. The trial did not go well for the prosecution. The endless list of petty and dubious charges which it was hoped should amount to a sum of "constructive treason," delivered by impatient relays of prosecutors who failed to conceal their thirst for blood, led to some revulsion of feeling. "They have so banged and worried him as it begets pity in many of the auditors," an observer wrote.[3] Strafford, moreover, stood his ground with firmness and dignity, warding off accusation after accusation by appropriate and accurate citation of the law, suggesting to a modern biographer the image of "a proud, wily, dauntless beast whose powerful blows time and again sent the snarling dogs of the prosecution head over heels and sprawling."[4] This image seems to have been arrived at completely independent of reference to Denham's parallel image in *Coopers Hill*:

> Soe stands the Stagg among the lesser houndes
> Repelles their force, and woundes returnes for woundes.

The climax of the trial was Strafford's great speech in his own defense, filling two hours of the morning of Tuesday, April 13. No poet could have listened unimpressed to that stately speech, couched in language that since Elizabethan times had been particularly dear to the poets:

I have ever admired the wisdom of our ancestors, who have so fixed the pillars of this monarchy that each of them keeps due measure and proportion with other. . . . The prerogative of the Crown and the propriety of the subject have such mutual relations that this took protection from that, that foundation and nourishment from this;

---

[3] Quoted in *ibid.*, p. 342.
[4] *Ibid.*, p. 353.

29

and as on the lute, if anything be too high or too low wound up, you have lost the harmony, so here the excess of prerogative is oppression, of a pretended liberty in the subject disorder and anarchy. . . . the happiness of a Kingdom consists in the just poise of the King's prerogative and the subject's liberty and that things should never be well till these went hand in hand together.

These were sentiments drawn from the emblem books and spread at large throughout late sixteenth- and early seventeenth-century poetry.[5] The analogy of the lute was a commonplace that had already been used by Bacon. But the most illustrative commentary upon this paragraph of Strafford's is provided by the closing lines of all the early versions of *Coopers Hill*:

> Thus kings by grasping more then they could hould,
> First made their subiects by oppression bould,
> And popular sway by forcing Kings to give,
> More then was fitt for subiects to receave
> Ranne to the same extreame, & one excesse,
> Made both by striving to be greater, lesse:
> Nor any way but seeking to have more,
> Makes either loose, what they possest before.
> Therefore their boundles power lett princes draw
> Within the Chanell & the shoares of Lawe:
> And may that Law which teaches Kings to sway
> Their Septers, teach their subiects to obey.

Those critics, Edmund Gosse and others, who profess to see in the political tenor of Denham's poems of this period "the very doctrine of the neuters" — those who disapproved as much of royal high-handedness as of parliamentary aggression — by logic should

---

[5] The "pillars of the monarchy" keeping due measure and proportion may be illustrated by Juan de Solorzano Pereyra's Emblem XLVIII in his *Emblemata Regio Politica* (Matriti, 1653). This illustration shows two pillars bearing an arch and keystone with the lemma *Casura nisi invicem obstarent*. The lute is Emblema X in *Emblemata Andreae Alciati* (I have used the edition of P. P. Tozzi [Patavii, 1626]) as a symbol of *Foedera* (in the Italian version, *Confederatione o Leghe*). The emblem is addressed to Maximilian, Duke of Milan, as a potential uniter of Italy.

reckon the Earl of Strafford the arch neutral. Earlier during his trial he had advanced as a doctrine "which I learnt in the House of Commons . . . that the prerogative of the Crown and the liberty of the subject should be equally looked upon, and served *together*, but not *apart*." In seeking to determine Denham's political commitment from the sentiments expressed in his poems, the less hasty critic will bear in mind how many of the same sentiments could also be expressed by Strafford. And in Strafford's defense Denham discerned "wisdom . . . Joind with an eloquence soe great, to make / Us heare with greater passion then he spake."[6]

After the climax of Strafford's speech the tragedy began to hurry toward the catastrophe. Pym, facing judicial defeat, switched to a legislative attack, and on the same day introduced to the Commons a bill of attainder to enact by statute the guilt of Strafford which could not be proved in law. The bill reached its third reading on April 20, and was carried by a vote of 204 to 59. The one notable voice raised against it was, startlingly, that of George Digby, who had been vehement in the prosecution before the Lords but could not reconcile himself to murder by act of Parliament:

Let every man lay his hand upon his heart and sadly consider what we are going to do with a breath, either justice or murder. . . . I do, before God, discharge myself, to the uttermost of my power, and do with a clear conscience wash my hands of this man's blood, by this solemn protestation, that my vote goes not to the taking of the Earl of Strafford's life.

In 1667 when Denham publicly stated his admiration for the by then Earl of Bristol perhaps he retained some warmth of memory for that act of solitary courage. For the bravery of Digby was singularly lacking in most of his colleagues of the House of Commons. One anonymous craven spoke for who can say how many of his brethren when he insinuated to Strafford's friends the reason for his own damning vote: a great many gentlemen could not help

---

[6] "On the Earl of Strafford's Tryal and Death."

themselves for fear of Mr. Pym; they would not have voted for the bill, but they knew it would do no harm; the bill would be rejected by the Lords.

Gentlemen were correct to fear Mr. Pym, for on the 22d, in flagrant breach of parliamentary privilege, the names of the "Straffordians" in the Commons were placarded through the town. But they were quite unwarranted in hoping for the Lords to show less pusillanimity than themselves. The pace of events meanwhile accelerated. The King wrote to Strafford indicating that he could never employ the Earl again, but guaranteeing Strafford's life, honor, and fortune. Strafford immediately appealed to the Lords to accept such an arrangement, permitting him to retire to his private estates, debarred from all offices of state. On the same day a petition with more than twenty thousand signatures arrived in London, demanding Strafford's death. On April 26 and 27 the bill of attainder was read for the first and second times in the Lords, and on the 29th Oliver St. John urged before the Lords that Strafford deserved to be killed without process of law, as "a beast of prey," twisting the metaphor that dominates the case. On Saturday, May 1, King Charles delivered in person to the Lords an inept plea on Strafford's behalf which did much to alienate the sympathy the Earl in his own right had been garnering. The real peripety, however, occurred on Monday, May 3, and the fatal fault was largely that of the King.

During the late winter a number of harebrained and hotheaded young officers, some perhaps in the confidence of the Queen, had begun to concoct various half-baked plans to reestablish the royal supremacy, overthrow Parliament, and rescue Strafford by a military coup d'état. By the beginning of April, Pym was well apprised of the extent and personnel of these wild and formless conspiracies, and was quietly biding his time. Meanwhile, however, the King had contrived his own plot, and on April 27 attempted to occupy the Tower with loyal troops, and so both rescue Strafford and put himself in a position to overawe the City. His chosen instruments were inevitably some of the same officers who had been entangled in their own plots, and Pym was able to foil the attempted seizure of the Tower without revealing his own hand. On Monday, May 3, however, as the House of Lords prepared to engage in its final debate on the bill of attainder, Pym revealed the so-called Army Plot to a silent House of Commons. The result was shattering: plotters fled the country overnight, everybody feared and suspected his neighbor, and Strafford was doomed. On May 5, after a sufficient number of key Royalists had panicked and fled, Pym revealed the full extent of the complicated plots and counterplots he had uncovered:

> Some study plots, and some those plots t'undoe,
> Others to make 'em, and undoe 'em too,
> False to their hopes, afraid to be secure
> Those mischiefes onely which they make, endure . . .

These lines, although not in the first drafts of *Coopers Hill*, are contained in the first text of the poem to be printed, some fifteen months after the execution of Strafford. It is difficult to view them as anything other than exasperated allusion to the Army Plot, the only enduring result of which was the mischief it wrought, in precipitating the death of Strafford and destroying the public credit of the King.

On May 8 the Lords came to their final vote on the bill in an atmosphere of cowardice even more shameful than that demonstrated by the Commons. Five of the peers whom Strafford might have relied upon simply absented themselves. The bishops abstained en bloc from voting because "they had taken no part in the trial." The Earl of Bristol, less courageous than his son, abstained because he *had* taken part in the trial, as a witness for the defense. The Earl of Cumberland, Strafford's friend from boyhood, conceived that his close relationship with the accused perhaps disqualified him from voting. As the Commons had sought to shift the burden of saving Strafford to the Lords, so the Lords sought to shift it to the King. *Coopers Hill* once more accurately depicts Strafford's predicament:

He tryes his frends amongst the lesser heard,
where he but lately was obey'd & fear'd:
Safety he seekes, the heard unkindly wise:
or chases him from thence, or from him flyes;
(like a declyning Statesman left forlorne
To his frinds pitty & pursuers scorne).

The House of Lords voted twenty-six to nineteen to enact the bill of attainder. Only the King now remained between Strafford and the block.

The 9th of May was a Sunday, and all day King Charles in the inner rooms of Whitehall Palace deliberated in tears the fate of Strafford, while in the outward chambers a mob surged, clamoring for the Earl's life and hinting strongly that if it were not granted them they might seek the King's instead. As the dapper sentimental king trembled for the safety of his wife and children and agonized over the fate of his great and grim servant, it is difficult to guess if his decision was made harder or easier by Strafford's last and most enigmatic act of statesmanship. For on the preceding Tuesday, May 4, Strafford had written to release the King from his promise of April 23 that Strafford's life should be preserved; more, he had advised the King to sign the instrument of death:

so now to set your Majesty's conscience at liberty, I do most humbly beseech your Majesty for prevention of evils which may happen by your refusal, to pass this Bill; and by this means to remove I cannot say this accursed but I confess this unfortunate thing, forth of the way towards that blessed agreement which God I trust shall ever establish between you and your subjects.

Sir, my consent shall more acquit you herein to God than all the world can do besides; to a willing man there is no injury done, and as by God's grace I forgive all the world, with calmness and meekness of infinite contentment to my dislodging soul; so Sir, to you, I can give the life of this world with all the cheerfulness imaginable. . . .

Pusillanimity once more ruled Strafford's fate. Bishop Williams, who had persuaded the bishops not to vote in the Lords, now persuaded Charles that he could separate his conscience as a king from his conscience as a man. At nine o'clock in the evening Charles signed the bill, and Dudley Carleton, one of the royal secretaries, conveyed the news to the doomed Strafford, alone in his room in the Tower. In Denham's first drafts of *Coopers Hill* he describes an allegorical stag receiving his deathblow from King Charles — "glad & proud to die / By such a wound, he falls." By the version first printed in August 1642, however, Denham more obviously responds to the pathos of Strafford's letter to the King and the doomed man's acceptance of his fate:

> As some brave *Hero*, whom his baser foes
> In troops surround, now these assaile, now those,
> Though prodigall of life, disdaines to die
> By vulgar hands, but if he can descry
> Some Nobler foe's approach, to him he cals
> And begs his fate, and then contented fals . . .

One might wish to dispute the characterization of King Charles as a "Nobler foe," but Denham's purport is absolutely clear.

The Act of Attainder had stripped Strafford of all his titles and honors, and with the reverence for order and degree which shaped his life, in the few letters he wrote between the signing of the act and his execution on Wednesday the 12th of May, he gave himself no name or title but what was irreducibly his: Thomas Wentworth. In a brief, brilliant career of only a few years he had become Earl of Strafford, lord lieutenant of Ireland, lord president of the North, lieutenant-general of the King's forces, knight of the most noble Order of the Garter, yet he died a private man, "to shew how soone / Greate things are made, but sooner farre undone."

The fall of Strafford was both awful and mysterious, shrouded like the man himself in enigma. Poets could not fail to respond to it, and in different ways Fanshawe, Cleveland, and Denham tried to meet the challenge to their imaginations. Strafford had died as a traitor, yet no court of law could have convicted him on the evidence presented against him; even those who encompassed his death tacitly conceded as much. It was patent to all that Pym and his fellows had contrived a legal murder, but was not King Charles their accomplice? And how accommodate the fact that Strafford had advised his own execution? Cleveland succinctly formulated the mystery:

> One in extremes, lov'd and abhorr'd
> Riddles lie here, or in a word,
> Here lies blood and let it lie
> Speechless still and never cry.

But even with Strafford's goodwill his blood would not lie speechless; it continued to cry aloud, for one instance, in the King's conscience until the day when Charles, as he himself saw it, paid with his own blood for his part in that unjust sentence. No sensitive observer but must conclude that Strafford had been murdered; yet he had declared himself a willing victim. At the same time, a Royalist could not call down vengeance for that blood without invoking heaven's retribution on the King. Denham's first essay at a poetic response to Strafford's death was more overtly partisan than Cleveland's, yet remained frozen between the impulse to defend the dead man and a hesitancy in attacking those who killed him:

> Great Strafford, worthy of that name, though all
> Of thee should be forgotten but thy fall.
> How great's thy Ruine, when noe lesse a weight
> Could serve to crush thee then 3 Kingdoms hate?
> Yet (Single) they accounted thee (allthough
> Each had an army) as an equal foe.
> Thy wisdom such [at] once it did appeare
> Three kingdoms wonder, & 3 Kingdoms feare.
> Joind with an eloquence soe great, to make
> Us heare with greater passion then he spake:
> That wee forcd him to pitty us, whilst hee

Seemd more unmov'd and unconcearnd then we.
And made them wish who had his death decreed
Him (rather then their owne discretion) freed!
Soe powerfully it wrought, at once they greive
That he should dye, yet feare to lett him live.
   Farwell, great Soule, the glory of thy fall
Outweighs the cause, whome we at once may call,
The Enemy, & Martyr of the State,
Our Nations glory, & our Nations hate.[7]

The revision of this poem which Denham first published in 1668 is ten lines longer, but far more drastically altered than that addition alone accounts for. No trace of ambivalence remains; the original end, with its possible implication that some fault lay in Strafford, is totally expunged. In the new poem Strafford is viewed as "Crusht by Imaginary Treasons weight" when "Pretexts are into Treason forg'd by Law." More significantly, it is "*Legislative* Frenzy" that killed him — the King is not so much exculpated as effaced. Last, Strafford's choice of death before dishonor is made to arise directly from confrontation with his enemies, with no suggestion of reference to the King. An inescapable inference is that the revision was made after the Royalist inhibition against attacking Strafford's murderers had been dissolved by the polarization of King and Parliament through the outbreak of overt civil war, and perhaps even after the King by his own death had atoned for his share in the death of Strafford.[8]

   But Denham's two versions of his elegy *On the Earl of Strafford's Tryal and Death* did not exhaust his poetic response to the event. Throughout the foregoing narrative the text of *Coopers Hill* has often offered ready commentary on the trial and execution of Strafford, and many more lines might have been cited with equal suggestiveness. A modern critic has persuasively argued that

---

[7] The text is that of Bodleian MS Locke e.17.
[8] As argued above, there is nothing in the revised text to compel a post-Restoration date for it.

the long episode of the stag hunt that is so marked a feature of *Coopers Hill* was in fact developed by Denham as an allegory of the fall of Strafford.[9] The intimation now being advanced here is that not the stag hunt only, but the entire poem of *Coopers Hill*, is a product of Denham's extended meditation upon that great event and all its concomitant circumstances. A necessary corollary, of course, is that the date of initial composition of *Coopers Hill* must not be very remote from the period dominated by Strafford's case. The 1655 edition of *Coopers Hill* asserts that the poem was written in 1640, but that dating need be accepted only as an approximation. Moreover, for Denham the year 1640 did not end until March 24, 1641, by our reckoning, the third day of Strafford's trial and the second of Denham's recorded presence as a witness.

If the stimulation of Denham's political sentiments stirred him notably to poetry during 1641, it was not until the following year that, by publication, he was formally enlisted in the service of the Muse. In August 1642 the London bookseller Thomas Walkeley published *The Sophy* and *Coopers Hill* separately, possibly on the same day.[10] The play appeared in folio, the poem in small quarto. Since the title page of *The Sophy* bears the notation "As it was acted at the Private House in Black Friars by his Majesties Servants," it has sometimes been assumed to antedate the composition of *Coopers Hill*. The belief, however, that the indicated performance took place in October or November of 1641 is based on the airiest sort of evidence: a special interpretation of Wood's statement that "in the latter end of the year 1641 [Denham] published" his tragedy. The general assumption that by "published" Wood meant *performed* is idle; Wood meant nothing so precise. His word is a mere elegant synonym for Aubrey's "came out." And "the latter end of the year 1641" is a correction of Aubrey

---

[9] Earl R. Wasserman, *The Subtler Language* (Baltimore, 1959), pp. 35–88.

[10] On August 6 Walkeley entered in the Stationers' Register "two bookes vizt, *A Tragedy*, called *The Sophy* & a *Poem* called *Coopers Hill*, both of them by Mr. John Denham." George Thomason purchased a copy of *Coopers Hill*, on which he marked the date "Aug. 5."

based solely on the date of the Irish rebellion, not in the least on any special information about the performance of the play. It should not be forgotten that Aubrey compiled the principal part of his biographical jottings in the 1670's, and that Wood converted them to his own uses only in the following decade. It is vain to suppose, therefore, that Wood (working at Oxford, not London) should have acquired solid knowledge of a 1641 performance, forty or fifty years after the event, which Aubrey had not given him. That the play was performed at all, in fact, is supported only by three frail pieces of evidence: the first, the assertion of the title page, which would make an implausible lie; the second, that the play as printed is accompanied by a prologue and an epilogue in conventional style, to be spoken by or on behalf of the players. Although such addresses to the audience were frequently composed for specific performances, and did not constitute an invariable accompaniment of the text of a play, still their composition hardly serves as proof positive of a performance. The third piece of evidence is more remote: in 1660 "the Sophy" occurred as one of "some of the most ancient Playes that were playd at Blackfriers," which Davenant was granted permission to reform and make fit "for the Company of Actors appointed vnder his direction." [11] (There is no indication that Davenant availed himself of the chance to revive Denham's play.)

It is remarkable indeed that for this play, which during Denham's lifetime was almost always linked to *Coopers Hill* as a twin pillar of his fame, there should be so little evidence of performance, or of the early critical acclaim that the Waller anecdote suggests. Its success, indeed, such as it was, appears to have been as a closet drama, and the closing of the theaters in 1642, which forced critical attention to closet drama rather than to performance, may ironically have added not a little to the esteem in which *The Sophy* came to be held. Certainly the earliest datable allusions to *The Sophy* do not appear until the 1650's, the period of greatest

---

[11] Bentley, *Jacobean and Caroline Stage*, III, 276.

theatrical dearth.[12] Nor, even for reading purposes, does the play appear to have sold unusually well. Although printing rights to *The Sophy* changed hands twice during the interim, there is no trace or record of any edition between that of 1642 and that which appeared with Denham's collected *Poems and Translations* in 1668. Humphrey Moseley, who held the printing rights throughout the 1650's, seems never to have issued an edition of his own, although he advertised the play a number of times during the decade.[13] This may indicate that he continued to have on hand unsold sheets from the 1642 printing for Walkeley, from whom he acquired the rights in 1650.[14] During the same period Moseley brought out at least two, and probably at least three, individual issues of *Coopers Hill*.[15]

Although Banks prints with *The Sophy* a "Prologue at Court" which he says appears in the 1642 edition, and uses it as evidence for a performance at court, G. E. Bentley shows him to have fallen into unaccountable error.[16] In fact the "Prologue at Court" and accompanying "Prologue at the Fryers" belong to Habington's *Queen of Aragon* (1640), and apparently do not occur in any copies of the 1642 *Sophy*.[17] Hence the "evidence" for a court performance of *The Sophy* completely vanishes.[18]

---

[12] There are allusions to *The Sophy* in verses by Jo. Leigh prefixed to William Cartwright's *Comedies, Tragi-Comedies, with Other Poems* (London, 1651), and to Denham as a dramatist comparable to Beaumont and Fletcher in Thomas Pestell's "For the Author, Truly Heroick, by Bloud, Virtues, Learning," prefaced to Edward Benlowe's *Theophila* (1652), reprinted in *The Poems of Thomas Pestell*, ed. Hannah Buchan (Oxford, 1940), p. 84. See Bentley, *Jacobean and Caroline Stage*, III, 278.

[13] W. W. Greg, *A Bibliography of the English Printed Drama to the Restoration*, II (London, 1951), 752.

[14] Stationers' Register, Feb. 4, 1649/50: "Master Moseley. Entred . . . all the right & interest of the said Mr Walkeley in a play called *The Sophy, a tragedy*, written by Mr John Denham, Esqr."

[15] See below, pp. 88, 109, and B. O Hehir, " 'Lost,' 'Authorized,' and 'Pirated' Editions of John Denham's *Coopers Hill*," *PMLA*, LXXIX (1964), 242–253.

[16] Banks, *Poetical Works*, pp. 47, 232n; Bentley, *Jacobean and Caroline Stage*, III, 278.

[17] They do not occur in the copies at the Huntington Library and the William Andrews Clark Library, which presumably are additional to the four copies examined by Bentley and to Banks's own copy which he acknowledged to Bentley (*loc. cit.*) not to contain these prologues.

Such a performance, in the face of events, would seem anyway highly improbable if not impossible at any time during 1641, and absolutely impossible thereafter. The early months of 1641 had darkened life at court by the impeachment, trial, and killing of Strafford, and the summer was distressed by the Army Plot and by expectations of war. The royal circle was in no mood for theatrical evenings. On August 10 the King departed for Scotland, not to return until November 25, which meant that the court did not even exist in the interim. On August 7, three days before the King's departure, the Lord Chamberlain on behalf of the King's Men protected from publication a list of plays belonging to that company; *The Sophy* does not appear on the list.[19] If this means that the actors had not yet acquired the play, a date for a Blackfriars performance must be later than August 7, for a court performance later than November 25. The King's resumed residence at Westminster lasted just under seven weeks — until January 10, 1641/2, when, after the failure of his attempt on the Five Members (Jan. 4), he departed finally from the capital. A performance of *The Sophy* at court during those tense forty-five days seems therefore prima facie highly unlikely.[20] After January 10, 1641/2, there was no royal court at Whitehall until the Restoration.

What is truly remarkable about *The Sophy*, then, is not the dazzling immediate success usually attributed to it, but the fact that it should so often be regarded as having been successful in the face of so little evidence that it actually was.

Despite the haze of doubt about the first appearance and reception of *The Sophy*, the fact remains certain that it was written before August 1642, and therefore during the period of increasingly acri-

---

[18] With the evidence for a performance at court vanishes also the supposition that Denham himself might at the time have appeared at court, and so met Waller among the courtiers.

[19] Bentley, *Jacobean and Caroline Stage*, I, 65–66; III, 277–278.

[20] The presentation of "The King's Last Masque" — Davenant's *Salmacida Spolia* — at Christmas 1639 may in fact have been the last display of dramatics at court before the Civil War (see C. V. Wedgwood, *The Great Rebellion: The King's Peace 1637– 1641* [New York, 1956], pp. 310–313).

monious struggle between King and Parliament, but before the contest was transferred to the battlefield. The events that the play directly deals with were fairly recent happenings in Persia, as reported in England by travelers' tales.[21] Certainly it was easy to read into the play allusions or references to contemporary English persons and events, particularly if one was hostile to those persons. The wicked and misled King Abbas of Persia, who had opened his way to the throne by the murders of his brother and father, and who took a very exalted view of his royal prerogatives and his power over the purses (specifically in 1642, the "shops and ships") of his subjects, might easily seem to reflect the less amiable side of King Charles. Resentment of Charles's taxation methods was accompanied by the revival of rumors — ultimately to be formalized by Parliament at Cromwell's instigation in 1648 — that he had encompassed by poison the death of his father, James I.[22] Nor, though Charles could hardly be blamed for that, was it forgotten that his succession to the throne came by consequence of the premature death of his popular elder brother, Prince Henry. The evil Caliph, who cloaks with religion the sins of the Shah, could be identified with Archbishop Laud, and those so minded could see in the intriguing favorite, Haly, a representation either of Strafford, or of all the "evil councillors" about King Charles.

That Denham intended any such direct correspondences, however, must be judged unlikely in the extreme. His participation in Strafford's defense and the tone of his verses on Strafford's death, both openly in his elegy and covertly in *Coopers Hill*, run strongly counter to the notion that he could have intended to represent the Earl by the hypocritical schemer Haly; a general representation of "evil councillors" may be accepted, but general reference is

---

[21] It is usually assumed that Denham's source was Thomas Herbert's *A Relation of Some Years Travel Begun Anno 1626 into Afrique and the Greater Asia*, published in 1634, 1638, and 1639, but Bentley (*Jacobean and Caroline Stage*, III, 278) believes that Denham may have known a fuller relation than that given by Herbert.

[22] See Robert S. Paul, *The Lord Protector: Religion and Politics in the Life of Oliver Cromwell* (London, 1955), p. 161, and documentation there given.

the contrary of direct correspondence.[23] And that Abbas on the whole could be meant for a portrait of Charles is fantastically improbable: the main action of the play, the conversion of the Shah's love for his son, Mirza, through the machinations of Haly, to a murderous jealousy that destroys Mirza, Abbas, Haly, and the Caliph, could have no imaginable parallel in the life of Charles I. No distinct evidence can be found for Denham's feelings, if he had any, about Archbishop Laud, but his praise in *Coopers Hill* not only of Charles, but of Charles's religious policy, makes any extreme antagonism toward the Primate seem also unlikely.

Undoubtedly current events were on Denham's mind as he wrote his tragedy, but insofar as his political opinions are reflected in the text of the play, they are those not of an anti-Royalist, but of an advocate of moderation and the middle path between political extremes. In this regard there is no marked distinction from the views expressed in *Coopers Hill*, a poem that unambiguously sides with King Charles in the impending Civil War. Denham certainly rejected the extreme view of Stuart divine-right theorizing, that a king could literally do no wrong: history abounded with the evildoing of kings, and in *The Sophy* Denham could point to the example of Abbas of Persia, in *Coopers Hill* to that of Henry VIII of England. Denham would agree completely with his father in opposing the judgment set forth by Judge Robert Berkeley in the Hampden case, ruling for the King: "Rex is lex . . . lex loquens, a living, a speaking, an acting law. . . . But I never heard . . . that lex is rex." [24] To Denham this sort of language would appear foolish, for he regarded kings and subjects as bound — and bound together — inexorably, by the same laws. But paradoxically, at least from a modernist viewpoint, Denham seems to have regarded

---

[23] Any direct allusion to Charles I's "evil councillors" intended by Denham would in the event have been highly ironical, since within a few years he was himself to be officially listed by Parliament as one of their number.

[24] Among the more recent citations of this famous remark is that by Wedgwood, *The King's Peace*, p. 196.

Charles I as a monarch who, on the whole, confined his actions within the boundaries of the law.

To clarify Denham's view of the law it is necessary to remember the time in which he lived and wrote. Doubtless much of modern constitutional theory evolved out of the political controversies through which Denham lived, but in spite of his legal training it is doubtful that he ever saw the law in what would now be recognized as constitutional terms. It was not until after Denham's time that in the later seventeenth century, consequent upon the work of men such as Newton, Boyle, and Berkeley, a whole series of what our language likewise calls laws were formulated: the laws of optics, the laws of physics, the law of gravitation. To a man like Denham the distinction between such laws and nomic laws, statutory or constitutional, had not been made apparent and was by no means self-evident. Even in the eighteenth century it remained possible to view the mechanical laws as statutory in origin, the product of divine legislation. When Denham thought of the laws that governed kings, therefore, he did not think in terms of the British constitution or of the hereditary rights of Englishmen: the laws that bound kings and subjects were laws as neutral, as impartial, as inexorable, and ultimately of as divine an origin, as the law of gravity. And if the important law of physics remained to be formulated — that every action generates an equal and opposite reaction — Denham already could, and over and over again did, express his belief in the universal application of a law to the effect that every extreme begets an equal and opposite extreme.[25] An important corollary of this law, which was to dominate the thinking of Alexander Pope to an even greater extent than it dominated Denham's, is that every extreme is an evil. When the passages in *The Sophy* which seem to reflect upon King Charles or Archbishop Laud are excerpted in isolation, they present a dis-

---

[25] This law should not be conceived of as merely a political law, a social law, a physical or a mechanical law, but as a law that operated equally under each and all these categories; to Denham (or to Pope) it was a law that described an important characteristic of the total structure of reality.

torted picture of Denham's beliefs and his method of displaying them. In the first scene of Act IV, for instance, occurs a conversation between two just and judicious courtiers, Abdall and Morat. Beginning at line 16 of the scene, each is allowed a long speech, motivated by the Caliph's perfidy in prostituting religion to the flattery and deception of the king. To a reader predisposed to see in the Caliph a portrait of Archbishop Laud the twenty-three lines of Abdall's speech might seem to be a scathing attack upon Laud's supposed Erastianism, but Denham redresses the balance by giving to Morat twenty-eight lines, absolutely unmotivated by anything within the play, on the topic of the equal and contrary perfidy of the clergy who pervert religion to the service of the evil extreme *reaction* to royal tyranny. If the two speeches taken together make up a discourse on clerical hypocrisy, Abdall's speech has much less direct applicability to the career of William Laud than Morat's has to the fire-eating Puritan preachers. Morat's speech — which, to tip the bias the other way, is given here separately — might well be a passage from the last section of *Coopers Hill*:

> For if the many-headed beast hath broke,
> Or shaken from his neck the royal yoke,
> With popular rage, Religion doth conspire,
> Flows into that, and swells the torrent higher;
> Then powers first pedigree from force derives,
> And calls to mind the old prerogatives
> Of free-born man; and with a saucy eye
> Searches the heart and soul of Majesty:
> Then to a strict account, and censure brings
> The actions, errors, and the end of Kings:
> Treads on authority, and sacred Laws:
> Yet all for God, and his pretended cause,
> Acting such things for him, which he in them,
> And which themselves in others will condemn;
> And thus engag'd, nor safely can retire,
> Nor safely stand, but blindly bold aspire,
> Forcing their hopes, even through despair, to climb
> To new attempts; disdain the present time,

Grow from disdain to threats, from threats to arms;
While they (though sons of peace) still sound th'alarms:
Thus whether Kings or people seek extreams,
Still conscience and religion are their Theams:
And whatsoever change the State invades,
The pulpit either forces, or perswades.
Others may give the fewel, or the fire;
But they the breath, that makes the flame, inspire.[26]

As a piece of literary dramatic art, *The Sophy* is neither so good as its seventeenth-century reputation might indicate, nor so bad as it has been judged by more recent critics. Nor is it fair to interpret the line of the Prologue — "He did it when he had nothing else to do" — as a slight by Denham upon his own work; in the bantering context of a theatrical prologue such an attitude was merely conventional, as it was also in the ideal Renaissance concept of the gentleman. In the same prologue, moreover, Denham also slights the critical capacity of his audience, declaring:

He'll not be try'd by any, but his Peers;
He claims his priviledge, and sayes 'tis fit
Nothing should be the Judge of wit, but Wit.

Denham may very well have had little else to do at the time he wrote this play, but that fact would allow him to devote to its composition all the care and skill he was capable of at the time. The result has elicited at least one remarkably favorable verdict from a modern critic. What Alfred Harbage has to say about *The Sophy* may be allowed to stand here as a final judgment upon the play:

One is inclined to question Waller's testimony to the popularity of this play, not that it lacks desert, but that it stands so aloof from the fashions of the day. It is one of the most original plays of the Caroline era . . . simple, dignified, clear, and if notable

---

[26] Act IV, 41–46 (Banks, *Poetical Works*, p. 271). Both speeches were printed consecutively as a separate poem entitled "Verses," in Dryden's *Fifth Part of Miscellany Poems* (4th ed., 1716; 5th ed., 1727).

neither for prosody nor poetic delicacy, yet full of fine thoughts and eloquent lines. . . . Assailing our emotions delicately rather than through mass attack, Denham departs from the usages of his day, his play portending, in its restraint and reality, a type of classic tragedy which in England never materialized. Talent was not lacking; conditions in the reign of Charles were simply adverse to its development. The air was vitiated. . . . Like Cowley, [Denham] might have made a first rate dramatist.[27]

Practical obstacles more adverse than the air of Charles I's reign also stultified Denham's continued growth as a dramatist. Not the least of these was the closing of the theaters in 1642, which blocked one outlet for a talent that in any event the civil wars diverted to another direction. No practical opportunity for exercise of dramatic talent was to exist in England for another eighteen years, and Denham did not resume writing for the stage until 1667, and then only in a very minor effort, as will appear.[28]

If dating the composition of *The Sophy* is a problem that remains in the end insoluble, except within a vaguely definable span of years, the problem of dating the composition of *Coopers Hill*, even with more material to work with, is one that proves equally vexing. One other poem of Denham's, however, written during roughly this same period, can be tied by date to a specific event. This is his "Elegy on the Death of Judge Crooke" — a death that took place on February 16, 1641/2. The difficulty that arises with this poem is of a different kind: Denham never acknowledged it as his, and it does not appear in the *Poems and Translations* volume of 1668, although Denham then included several of his other early unpublished pieces. The poem in fact was not printed until 1790, although it appears in at least four seventeenth-century manuscript copies, two of which attribute it to Denham, while the

---

[27] *Cavalier Drama* (New York, 1936), p. 132.
[28] A possible exception is a prologue attributed to Denham composed for a recital at a performance of Jonson's *The Silent Woman* in 1660. It is improbably his; see pp. 160–161 below.

others make no attribution.[29] It may fairly safely be credited to
him, therefore, on a number of considerations, the least persua-
sive of which should be the highly subjective criterion of "evidence
of style." More to the point are the several independent ascriptions,
and the fact that no rival claimant has as yet appeared. Additionally, Sir George Croke was the chief spokesman for the five
minority judges who ruled for Hampden at his trial, and Denham's
father, as has been seen, made one of that minority. This fact
would equally account for Denham's interest in Croke, extending
to the writing of an elegy on his death, and for a decision to
omit the unpublished elegy from his collected works in 1668. That
Denham in 1668 would have suffered retaliation for printing among
the body of his works an elegy upon a judge who had in a court
case of 1638 ruled contrary to the interest of the king may be
supposed highly unlikely. But publication of the elegy would have
been somewhat tactless and relatively pointless, even if Denham
remembered that he had once written the poem and still retained
a copy after twenty-six years. The poem itself, it may be remarked
in support of the Denham attribution, is extremely tangential in
alluding to the ship-money dispute, but quite specific in attribut-
ing to Croke, not partisanship, but — Denham's highest praise —
consistent moderation and avoidance of extremes:

> [His] Zeal was warm when all to Ice did turn,
> Yet was but warm when all the World did burn.
> No ague in Religion eer inclin'd
> To this or that Extream his fixed Mind.
>
> (lines 33–36)

---

[29] It is highly likely that this poem is preserved in many more than the four MSS
mentioned. Banks used two, both in the British Museum, for his edition; one attributes
the poem to Denham, the other not. I have made no effort to seek out further copies,
but in the course of establishing the texts of *Coopers Hill* I have run across two others.
One in the Henry E. Huntington Library (MS EL 8849) is unascribed; it is a very
inferior copy. Another in the Folger Shakespeare Library (MS V.a.160, pp. 94–95)
corresponds fairly closely to the text printed by Banks; it is headed "An Elegie on the
Death of Judge Crooke by Mr. Denham."

In this passage may be seen the language both of *The Sophy* and of *Coopers Hill*.

Coopers Hill itself, Denham's greatest and most famous poem, is the last of his literary works certainly attributable to the interval of leisure that preceded the outbreak of civil war and his own involvement in the hostilities. The problems of dating its original inception and the subsequent versions of its text are examined separately in my edition of the poem, *Expans'd Hieroglyphicks*, and only the results of that examination need be summarized here. Some preliminary notion of the poem may have formed itself in Denham's mind as early as 1640, the date asserted by the 1655 edition as that of the composition of the poem, but any such preliminary notion could have had only slight resemblance to the *Coopers Hill* first printed in 1642. The hill from which the poem takes its name rises immediately upward from the meadow of Runnymede on the Thames, within the confines of the town of Egham, and so must have been known to Denham since early childhood. The view it provides — London to the east, Windsor Forest and Windsor Castle to the west, Runnymede directly at its foot — might quite early have suggested itself to Denham as symbolic of the chief antagonistic forces of the time, King and parliament (or populace), and of the possibility of a bloodless covenant between them. This symbolic interpretation of the landscape, fundamental to all versions of *Coopers Hill*, is not susceptible to rigorous dating, but some details of even the earliest surviving version of the poem may allude to events later than 1640. The year 1641 on the whole seems a much more acceptable date for the first writing of the poem, if not so late as 1642.

The earliest known version of *Coopers Hill* got into circulation probably well before the first printing in August 1642, perhaps as early as 1641. The fact that at least two copies of this version survive, in quite different collections, suggests that Denham did not regard it as a provisional draft, but as a completed poem, which he allowed to be "published" in a common seventeenth-century manner: by circulation and multiplication of manuscripts. Nonetheless, second thoughts occurred to him, and a revised draft, somewhat altered and slightly longer, followed the first into manuscript circulation. This was the first draft to allude to Waller's poem on St. Paul's. The third known draft of *Coopers Hill* is that which was published on August 5 or 6, 1642, by the London bookseller, Thomas Walkeley. This version of the poem, though longer than either of the two manuscript drafts, differs from both in showing a greater conciseness in many of the altered details. It is on the whole a much more finished version, both more elaborate and better balanced, and is in fact the best integrated of all the versions of *Coopers Hill*. A certain verbosity persisted, which was to be corrected later, but this "A" text of *Coopers Hill* remained the received text through almost two decades of increasing appreciation and influence before yielding at last to the "B" text which ultimately replaced it.

Walkeley's edition of *Coopers Hill* in most modern bibliographies is mislabeled a piracy, but there is in fact every reason to believe that Denham was a willing party to the publication of his poem.[30] The bookseller entered both *The Sophy* and *Coopers Hill* in the Stationers' Register on the same day, August 6, although the pamphlet collector George Thomason marked "Aug. 5" on his copy of the poem as the date of acquisition. *Coopers Hill* appeared as a quite small quarto of nineteen pages printed on three sheets. It was a fairly conscientious job of bookmaking for so slight a volume, but it contains both a number of small typesetting errors and a number of demonstrable compositor's misreadings of the manuscript copy text. The significance of these for Denham's biography lies in the fact that they form a link in a chain of reasoning which connects Denham with this edition.[31] The printing of *Coopers Hill*, therefore, indicates that Denham was at last willing to venture his poem before the disinterested eye of

[30] See pp. 62, 109, below.
[31] See pp. 62, 66, below.

the public. The printing of *The Sophy* at the same time, after its more restricted "publication" at the Blackfriars, followed an analogous pattern. Although both volumes were formally anonymous, the authorship seems never to have been a secret (Walkeley had in fact registered both works as "by Mr. John Denham"), and in August 1642, therefore, Denham may be said to have emerged finally from private life, into the light of literary history.

Denham's participation in the Civil War was shortly also to bring him onto the stage of political history, but one minor product of his pen belongs also to 1642, and may serve as preface to his direct action. "To the Five Members of the Honourable House of Commons: the Humble Petition of the Poets" is a partisan satire on the five members Charles had failed to arrest on January 4, 1641/2: Pym, Strode, Haslerig, Hampden, and Holles. The "Petition," which was not printed until the publication of *Rump Songs* in 1662, consists of twenty-eight couplets, seventeen employing feminine rhymes, accusing the members of usurping the poets' two special privileges of lying and of disposing of kings. The reference to the five members provides an antecedent date in early January, and the probable inference from the conclusion that warfare had not as yet broken out at the time of writing suggests the poem was finished before August. In these verses Denham is unreservedly Royalist.

More interesting both metrically and as an expression of orthodox Royalist views, however, is another exercise in the same genre, "A Speech against Peace at the Close Committee," also later to be included in *Rump Songs*. This belongs to the beginning of the following year, the period 1642/3 (by which time Denham had actually borne arms on behalf of the King), and appeared first as a broadsheet entitled *Mr. Hampdens speech occasioned upon the Londoners Petition for Peace*, of which George Thomason dated his copy March 23, 1643. The "Close Committee" appears to mean the Joint Committee of Safety set up by the two houses on July 4, 1642, of which Hampden was a leading member. The "Londoners' Petition" has a triple reference: (*a*) in mid-Decem-

ber, 1642, the Royalist merchants of London drew up a petition
for peace, which they were forbidden by the Common Council
to present to the House of Commons; (*b*) an authorized delegation of London aldermen, inspired and controlled by Pym as a
meaningless sop to the Parliamentary peace party, visited Oxford
at the end of the month to request a treaty with the King; (*c*) in
January an anonymous *Complaint to the House of Commons*,
purporting to be the work of those in London and Westminster
who desired peace, was widely circulated in London to coincide
with the King's answer to the aldermen's propositions.[32] In content, Denham's poem is a first-person discourse, the speech (needless to say, fictitious) of a Machiavellian Hampden, reviewing
the causes of the war, for which he candidly and proudly assumes
full responsibility. The stock Parliamentary accusations against
the King are all rehearsed, Hampden explaining how he and his
associates have contrived each of the instigating episodes — the
Irish rebellion, for example — in such a way as to bring about
war and cast its onus on the King. Hampden's argument against
peace is based on the twofold plea that peace would undo all
his destructive labors, whereas continued war opens endless vistas
of further deception and plunder. Especially interesting is the
basic motive Denham makes Hampden acknowledge for his overthrow of the established order:

> I would not Monarchy destroy,
> But as the only way to enjoy
> The ruine of the Church.

The meter of the "Speech against Peace" contrasts markedly
with the decasyllabic-line couplets, or blank verse (*The Sophy*),
Denham had chiefly employed hitherto, consisting as it does of
six-line stanzas rhyming *aabccb*, the couplets in tetrameters, the
b-rhymes in trimeters. Like the "Petition of the Poets," it abounds

---

[32] See C. V. Wedgwood, *The Great Rebellion: The King's War 1641–1647* (New
York, 1959), pp. 154–155, 163, 166.

in feminine rhymes. Neither a sudden uprush of lyricism in Denham, however, nor an untimely urge to experiment, accounts for this departure, but the practical fact that, like the bulk of the verses that were ultimately to be gathered in *Rump Songs*, the "Speech" was intended to be sung to a familiar air — in this instance, "To the Tune of, *I went from England*" — to facilitate its popular dissemination as propaganda. The new meter also really marks Denham's entry into a new medium, toward which the "Petition of the Poets," composed in decasyllabic-line couplets, was merely a transition: the political or occasional satire. During the seventeenth century his name became so firmly associated with this kind of writing that almost any anonymous piece of political doggerel with the least pretense to wit was at once ascribed to Denham. Many such items to which his name at one time or another has been affixed are certainly not his; but almost equally certainly he has not been credited with all in that line he actually wrote. For the "Petition of the Poets" and the "Speech against Peace," however, the attribution is in no doubt; both were published by Denham as his own in his collected *Poems and Translations* of 1668.

So much attention to two of Denham's minor political squibs must be justified by the change they show to have taken place in his mind during the critical year, both for England and for him, of 1642. Works published or written in that year reflect successively the mind of a peace-loving moderate from which some hints of disapproval of the King's more extreme acts are not absent (*The Sophy*, "Elegy on Judge Crooke"); that of a passionate believer in the virtuous mean, who nonetheless construes the path of King Charles to be in fact that middle way (*Coopers Hill*); and at last that of a committed partisan in the war. The isolation of Hampden as the begetter of the war, and his depiction as at bottom a fanatic enemy of the Church, may serve as a final commentary on Denham's previous feelings, whatever they may have been, about Hampden's ship-money trial of 1637 and 1638 and the religious policies of Archbishop Laud.

III: Civil War

For armed subjects can have no pretence
Against their Princes, but their just defence;
And whether then, or no, I leave to them
To justifie, who else themselves condemne.

WHILE DENHAM the writer was making himself known to the
world during 1642 as playwright, poet, and propagandist, Denham
the man and subject was also preparing his public emergence.
Although he was soon to leave it forever, he appears to have
genuinely enjoyed his life as squire of Egham. He continued to
live chiefly at "The Place," although Aubrey reports "he had better
seates," for he "did take most delight in" this one. Aubrey notes
certain pleasant features of Egham which seem irrelevant to the
life or writings of John Denham unless, as details in the notes
suggest, they represent the nostalgic reminiscences of Denham himself: "In this parish is a place called Cammomill-hill, from the
cammomill that growes there naturally; as also west of it is
Prune-well-hill (formerly part of Sir John's possessions), where
was a fine tuft of trees, a clear spring, and a pleasant prospect to
the east, over the levell of Middlesex and Surrey. Sir John tooke
great delight in this place, and was wont to say (before the
troubles) that he would build there a retiring place to entertaine
his muses. . . ." What children he had at the time cannot with
exactness be said; if his son was the later John Denham of Wadham
College, he would have been only a little boy in 1642. Of the two
daughters who survived Denham, the elder, Anne, must already
have been born, for although Denham's wife became pregnant
again sometime around August (from the fact of her confinement

the following May), it is difficult to discover any later occasion on which the couple may once more have lived together.[1] In any event, no specific indications of Denham's movements come to light until the very end of the year.

On July 11 a resolution of both houses of Parliament agreed that the King had commenced war against the Parliament. On August 22 the King formally reciprocated by raising his standard at Nottingham and declaring the Commons and their soldiers to be traitors. This was just two weeks after the publication of *Coopers Hill*, and although Denham's sympathies by now were patent, what he actually did nobody knows. Sometime during the autumn the King, having earlier acquired possession of the Great Seal, proceeded to prick sheriffs to serve the various counties for the following year. This procedure normally took place early in October, but 1642 was not a normal year.[2] Whenever the names were pricked, and whatever motivated the King to his choice, John Denham was pricked as sheriff for Surrey. Thus was inaugurated Denham's career as a public personage.

During the summer of 1642 as the two sides in the impending civil war grew more distinctly polarized, the struggle between the two factions went on at the local level all over England. As the county gentry took sides, the more industrious or the more numerous seized control of local strongpoints and avenues of communication. In some places, of course, other considerations beside local sentiment or diligence affected ultimate control of the situa-

---

[1] See below, p. 63 n. 17; p. 71 n. 32; p. 178 nn. 57, 58.

[2] If Clarendon's memory was accurate in this matter, pricking for sheriffs in 1642 apparently took place at the usual time. Writing of the Parliament's loss of the Great Seal he says "of this disadvantage the season of the year put them in mind: for the King now, according to course, prick'd Sheriffs" (*History of the Rebellion*, Vol. II, part 1, pp. 88–89). John Vicars might be construed as testifying to a later date for the appointments, but his reference is probably only to the time of the parliamentary reaction: "About the latter end of *November* 1642 the *Parliament* took into serious consideration a new plot on the Kings side . . . a list of new high Sheriffes of their owne picking and culling out, and to be confirmed and appointed by his Majestie for all the severall Counties . . ." (*Jehovah-Jireh: God in the Mount, Or, A Parliamentary Chronicle* [London, 1644], p. 220).

tion. It was inevitable, for instance, regardless of its particular balance of opinion, that Surrey, because of its proximity to London, should fall under the dominance of the Parliament. But Egham, in the extreme northwest of the county (the present urban district is bounded precisely by Berkshire on the west and Buckinghamshire on the north), was to remain throughout the first Civil War, regardless of which force actually occupied it, essentially a border area, only a few miles from the Royalist heartland of Oxfordshire. Farther south along the western edge of Surrey, near its border with Hampshire, the administrative center of Farnham, with its castle and arsenal, was also an object of concern to both sides during the opening moves of the war. The security of Farnham Castle, which had been stocked with royal armaments as early as January 14, was formally the responsibility of the sheriff of Surrey.[3]

Although Denham, in conjunction with his cousin, Denham Hunloke, and Wolley Leigh, the young squire of neighboring Thorpe, began raising all the money he could for the King in the Egham area, he is not likely to have entered active military service so early as October, as a timetable of events will show.[4] After raising his standard at Nottingham in August, King Charles with his forces had remained in the north. The Parliament proceeded meanwhile to consolidate its military position in the south, and to attempt to check the King as far distant from London as possible. As early as September 12 Parliamentary forces moving northward against the King had occupied Oxford in strength. A dedicated Surrey Royalist might certainly have made his way around the interposed enemy to reach the King's army, but that Denham did so seems very doubtful. Not until about October 15 did the

---

[3] *Commons Journal*, II, 379.

[4] See Frederic Turner, "Notes on Some Surrey Pedigrees," *Surrey Arch. Coll.*, XXX (1917), 5; and Denham's will, *Wills from Doctors' Commons*, ed. John Gough Nichols and John Bruce, Camden Society Publications, 83 (Westminster, 1863), 119–123.

King commence, from the neighborhood of Coventry, a determined march southward upon London.

Meanwhile Parliament, its eyes on the north, had not been able at first to pay attention to the relatively quiet though potentially dangerous situation in west Surrey: Farnham Castle lay unsecured in a Royalist town. But in the Royalist town of Farnham a very much older poet than Denham, George Wither (b. 1588), a determined Puritan, had acquired a retiring place to entertain *his* Muses. Wither had on his own initiative raised a troop of horse for the Parliament, and on October 14 the Parliament appointed him governor of Farnham Castle, which he proceeded to occupy and fortify. The date, it will be noticed, coincides not only with the beginning of the King's march from Coventry, but also approximately with the probable date of Denham's pricking as sheriff.

On October 23 the Parliamentary forces moving north from Oxford and London encountered the King's forces moving southward, at Edgehill in southern Warwickshire. Historians sometimes describe the ensuing battle as "indecisive," but its immediate results were a continued triumphant advance of the King, and a general falling back of the Parliament's armies. As the war drew nearer, Parliament became more apprehensive of the intermediate ground, and on October 28 garrisoned Windsor.[5] This action may have had some effect in keeping nearby Egham subdued. The next day, however, October 29, the King entered Oxford in triumph. It is possible that Denham made his way to the royal forces at this time, but still better opportunities were shortly to arise. Having reached the Thames at Oxford, the King now began to advance southeastward along the river valley toward London. On Monday, October 31, Abingdon was occupied, and on Friday, November 4, having administered another defeat to the Parliamentarians, the King himself was at Reading, about twenty miles from

---

[5] Windsor was occupied by a City of London band commanded by Venn. The castle remained in Parliament hands throughout the war, becoming in 1643 a prison for captured Royalists.

Egham, while Prince Rupert was already at Maidenhead, only ten miles away. By this time Wither had become alarmed for the fate of his little garrison at Farnham. He had still greater cause the following Monday, the 7th, for on that day Rupert established his quarters in Egham itself. Denham may well have been his host, and certainly now, if not earlier, Denham joined himself to the royal military effort. Farnham Castle was not a strong fortress, the townspeople were Royalists, and with the King's armies already in Surrey, Wither's position became desperate. In a grave breach of military discipline, motivated however by an amateur soldier's zeal rather than by cowardice, Wither left his command and rode alone to London for help; there, on the 8th or the 9th, he was told that the fortress must be evacuated. On the 9th, Wednesday, he rode back to Farnham, and that night managed to bring away safely most of his stores and men to the Parliament garrison at Kingston. The next day Rupert had returned once more to headquarters at Egham, whither the King himself had now arrived, and possibly on the same day John Denham, the new sheriff of Surrey, took possession of the abandoned Farnham Castle as governor for the King.[6]

Denham had with him a number of "persons of quality," among whom the names of Captain Hudson, Captain Brednoxe (identified as a brewer of Southwark and "a most desperate Malignant against the Parliament"), Mr. Jo. Tichborne, and Parson Keeley are on record, besides about "an hundred vulgar persons." For victuals they were extravagantly well provided, having 300 sheep and 100 oxen; in addition to arms and ammunition they were also said

---

[6] Details may be found in most histories of the war. Especially clear are H. E. Malden, "Political History," in *Vic. History Surrey*, I, 406–410, and "Farnham," II, 603–604; H. E. Malden, "The Civil War in Surrey, 1642," in *Surrey Arch. Coll.*, XXII (1909), 106; and C. V. Wedgwood, *The Great Rebellion: The King's War 1641–1647* (New York, 1959), *passim*. Wither's own version is set forth in his *Se Defendendo: A Shield, and Shaft, against Detraction . . . touching his deserting of Farnham-Castle* (London, 1643/4), and in his *Justitiarius justificatus: The Iustice justified* (London, 1646). It was this Royalist campaign against London which occasioned Milton's Sonnet VIII, "When the Assault Was Intended to the City."

later to have had about £40,000 in money and plate.[7] They may also have had "above 1000 weight of cheese, nigh 800 weight of Butter, many quarters of Wheat and Mault, sixe or seven Hogsheads of Beere and Cider, Bacon, Beef, and other necessaries," for Denham and his men were accused of an act of depredation before shutting themselves up in the castle which was to link his name with that of his predecessor at Farnham in a wearisome bondage of well over a decade. In the words of a resolution of Commons passed on Thursday, February 9, 1642/3, "Mr. *Denham* . . . did, in a hostile Manner, enter into the House and Grounds of Captain *George Wither*, in the County of *Surrey*; and did from thence carry and take away all his Books and Writings, with his Goods, Houshold-stuff, Cattle, Sheep, Corn and Hay, and his Teams, to the value of at least Two thousand pounds; as appeareth by an Inventory of the Particulars taken and estimated by his Neighbours, and others."[8]

How Denham managed to dispose of so much property beyond any recovery ever conceded by Wither is not easy of conjecture, for he had not long to enjoy the fruits of his pillage. No doubt its disappearance may be laid at the door of the Parliamentary troopers who eventually retook the castle, and "had good pillage for themselves."[9] The royal tide that had swept down the Thames in the first weeks of November exhausted its energy at the bloody victory of Brentford, on the western outskirts of the capital, on Saturday the 12th. On Sunday the 13th Prince Rupert's men were blowing up Parliamentary ammunition barges in the Thames, but the Earl of Essex had twice the Royalist numbers entrenched between Brentford and the city. Between the 12th and

---

[7] Vicars, *Jehovah-Jireh*, p. 223, is the source of the foregoing quotations, and of the evaluation of the plate. Vicars names Denham, Hudson, and "Brecknox"; Wither (source of the subsequent quotations) names Denham, Hudson, Tichborne, Brednoxe, and a Captain Andrews (*Se Defendendo*, pp. 10–13). The names occur on several other lists, particularly in *Commons Journal*.

[8] *Commons Journal*, II, 964.

[9] Vicars, *Jehovah-Jireh*, p. 223.

13th also, the Parliament withdrew its isolated garrison from Kingston to the main defenses, and with the garrison of course came Wither's dispossessed little troop from Farnham. Captain Wither himself was dispatched into Kent with orders to seize the horses of all who were disaffected to the Parliament.[10] The tide of movement now turned; faced with cold, hunger occasioned by extended supply lines, and a snugly dug-in enemy in superior numbers provisioned directly from London at his rear, the King's armies had no alternative to withdrawal. Protected by Rupert's cavalry, the royal forces retired slowly to Reading and Oxford. Feelings in London remained far from jubilant, however, and dismay and disaffection continued throughout the winter. The Parliament remained apprehensive, and on Wednesday, November 23, John Denham, though anonymously, figured for the only time in his life as a grave threat to the Parliamentary cause. On that day the House of Commons instructed the Lord General "not to omit any Opportunity of Advantage, in disposing of his Army for the Preservation of the Peace of the Kingdom, and keeping the People from being plundered; and particularly to have a Care of Farnham Castle." [11]

The Royalist troops began their withdrawal on the 18th, and by November 29 all were back at Oxford, except for a garrison left at Reading to command the approaches to London. Another exception, of course, was the tiny force left behind in Farnham Castle, under the command of John Denham. It was now Denham's turn to live through Wither's experience of isolation amidst a rising enemy tide. On balance it is hard to decide which of the two behaved more creditably. Wither lost his stronghold but saved his men by a timely retreat; Denham's decision to stay and fight might have had the credit of greater gallantry had the fight itself

---

[10] Wedgwood, *The King's War*, p. 143; *The Camden Miscellany III: Papers Relating to Proceedings in the County of Kent, 1642–1646*, Camden Society Publications, 61 (London, 1855), 5. See also *Commons Journal*, II, 920.

[11] *Commons Journal*, II, 864.

been more impressive. On December 1 Sir William Waller with a small Parliamentary force, consisting mostly of horse, and with absolutely no artillery at all, appeared before the castle. Waller managed to fix a petard to the gate, by which he blew it in, only to encounter a barricade of timber the defenders had erected inside. Nevertheless the Royalists seem to have made only token efforts to prevent the assailants from removing the barricade, which once effected, Denham surrendered. It was an inglorious moment for him, and one that Parliamentary accounts continued to gloat over. More cutting, however, than any sneers of Roundhead journalists, is this Royalist reference to the event, in Clarendon's *History of the Rebellion*: "Marlborough [taken by the King's forces on December 5] . . . was the first Garrison taken on either side; for *Farnham* Castle in *Surrey*, whither some Gentlemen who were willing to appear for the King had repair'd, and were taken with less resistance than was fit . . . some few days before, deserv'd not the name of a Garrison." [12]

Denham was sent prisoner to London, together with his men. The prisoners had arrived by Saturday the 3d, but their particular fate thereafter becomes unclear. Provision was made for release of certain of the "common" prisoners at once, but some prisoners taken at Farnham were being committed to Lambeth House on the 23d, "there to remain in safe Custody, till this House take further Order." On the 16th of January Waller was formally thanked for his action at Farnham, but no mention in the record is made of the prisoners. On March 15 the Farnham prisoners are mentioned again, but only Parson Keeley by name. How long, therefore, Denham remained a prisoner, and when exactly he was released,

---

[12] Clarendon, *History of the Rebellion*, II, 83. The fall of Farnham Castle is recounted in detail by Vicars, who says that "the Cavaleers within threw their Armes over the wall, fell downe upon their knees, crying for Quarter, (not so much as having once offered or desired to treat of any honourable conditions, to depart like Souldiers, before the castle was entred)" (*Jehovah-Jireh*, p. 223); by John Rushworth, *Historical Collections, The Third Part*, II (London, 1702), 82; as well as by H. E. Malden in the works cited in n. 6, above.

cannot be determined.[13] The publication of *Mr. Hampdens Speech* by March 23, however, at least suggests that Denham was at liberty before that date. He proceeded to Oxford to rejoin the King's forces, and there, probably during April, he brought out another edition of *Coopers Hill*.[14] The publication at Oxford of any sort of edition of *Coopers Hill* after Denham's arrival in that city should stand as prima facie evidence against the ill-founded assumption that all the pre-1655 editions of *Coopers Hill* are piracies. The war-caused difficulties faced by the Oxford printer in bringing out the book tell strongly against the notion that he published it as a venture for profit; but above all, the authoritative Oxford correction of errors in the London text of 1642 demonstrates that Denham had a hand in this edition. Quite simply, *Coopers Hill* was a distinguished piece of Royalist propaganda, and only as such found a place in 1643 among the output of Oxford printing.[15] Two lesser pieces from Denham's pen contributed to the support of Royalist morale after his coming to Oxford, although neither appears to have seen print earlier than in the *Rump Songs* of 1662. The first, "A Western Wonder," datable from internal evidence to the middle of May 1643, ridicules a grossly exaggerated Roundhead account of a victory in the west of England, which was in fact followed by a smashing defeat. "A Second Western Wonder," on a similar theme, belongs to July. Both poems are written in a fairly popular *Rump Songs* anapestic stanza (usually printed as a quatrain with alternating four-foot and three-foot lines, internal rhyme in the first and third lines, and the second and fourth lines rhyming

[13] *Commons Journal*, II, 879, 904, 933.

[14] An instance of the way in which successive biography can distort the truth of a historical incident may be seen in the progressive unconscious softenings of Denham's responsibility for the loss of Farnham in the accounts of his acts from October 1642 to April 1643 given in turn by Aubrey, Wood, Samuel Johnson, and, as merely one sample of the last reduction of the story, Manning and Bray's *Hist. Antiq. Surrey*. The progress of the account through this derivative succession is detailed in App. A, pp. 259–260, below.

[15] A full discussion of the circumstances of this publication may be found in the introduction to *Expans'd Hieroglyphicks*, my edition of *Coopers Hill*.

together, it may also be conceived of as a six-line stanza with the same rhyme scheme as *Mr. Hampdens Speech*, namely *aabccb*). What other services Denham contributed to the King during these years of the war do not appear, but he seems never to have held either military rank or further command after Farnham.

When Denham left Egham in 1642 to go to war, he left his home there for the last time. The fortunes of war determined that he would never again be master of "The Place," but the pillage of Wither's house at Farnham ensured a vigorous and vindictive campaign on Wither's part during the ensuing years to search out every piece of property Denham might anywhere hold title to. The Order of Commons of February 9, 1642/3, already noticed, specifically authorized Wither "to repair himself for his said Losses out of the Estates of the said Sheriff . . . wheresoever the said Captain *Wither* doth find any of the Goods or Estate belonging [to Denham *et al.*]." The parliamentary practice of raising money by the sequestration of the estates of "malignants" and "delinquents" had by now already been established, although without the refinements that were later to mitigate its operation. Wither was forward therefore to seize Denham's estates at Egham, as well as what he could lay hands on of the property of Denham's Royalist associates, but what he grasped failed to satisfy his sense of loss, and all kept slipping through his fingers.[16] Wither's biographers seldom show him much sympathy during these years of his life, and the impression left by the record of his activities between 1642 and 1656 is certainly that of an unceasing whine. His first cause for complaint arose on May 11, 1643, when Anne Denham, who had been left behind when John embarked on the martial adventures that brought him to Oxford, was granted permission by Commons to have "her Childbed Linen, and such other Necessaries" as should be thought fit, in view of her imminent confinement.[17] From

---

[16] See chart of Wither's petitions and grants in "Four Scarce Poems of George Wither," pp. 94–95.

[17] *Commons Journal*, III, 80.

Wither's protesting pamphlet, *Se Defendendo*, published shortly
thereafter, it appears that Parliamentary charity went as far as to
put Anne once again into possession of her house for the occasion,
even at the cost of the eviction of Wither's family.[18]

A biography of Denham at this point is conventionally expected to narrate the celebrated anecdote of Denham's witty saving
of Wither's life. Unfortunately the story has no authoritative source
other than Aubrey, and it cannot be made to fit into what is known
of the careers of the two principals. Here is the tale as Aubrey tells it:

In the time of the civill warres, George Withers, the poet, begged
Sir John Denham's estate at Egham of the Parliament, in whose
cause he was a captaine of horse. It [happened] that G. W. was
taken prisoner, and was in danger of his life, having written severely against the king, &c. Sir John Denham went to the
king, and desired his majestie not to hang him, for that whilest
G. W. lived he should not be the worst poet in England.

This makes too good a story to abandon without reluctance, and
it has often been effectively used. Wither's *DNB* biographer, for
instance, uses the poetic insult implied to account for Wither's
animosity toward Denham, and seems to suppose the capture took
place shortly after Wither's loss of Farnham, adding the unsupported
detail that Wither was "captured by a troop of royalists." It is possible that some obscure event involved in the passage of Farnham
Castle from Wither's hands to Denham's gave rise to the story,
but the occurrence cannot have been as told. One is free to speculate, for instance, that Denham's instructions for the seizure of

---

[18] As Wither bitterly complains: "And, when . . . I justly entered upon the
house of the said *Denham*, purposing to harbour my said wife and children therein,
Mistris Denham . . . (though her husband sought, and, yet, seekes the destruction
of the *Kingdome*) was, upon false suggestions, put againe, by *Order*, into possession of that house: because, as her charitable Patron alledged, shee was, forsooth, a
Gentlewoman, big with childe, and had a Fancie to the place" (*Se Defendendo*,
p. 13). Wither does not here name the "charitable Patron," but from his later virulence toward the man, a plausible guess would be that he was Sir Richard Onslow
(see below, and n. 20).

the castle from Wither might have contemplated the hanging of the latter, and Denham might have demurred in something like the terms reported. At that early stage of the war a genuine Royalist plan to hang enemy prisoners for treason seems to have been afoot, but if it was it was scotched by a retaliatory ordinance enacted by Parliament in December, and the war was thenceforth conducted on both sides with minimum atrocity. At any rate everything indicates that Wither reached Kingston safely along with his men on November 10, and he appears in Kent shortly thereafter, where he certainly also was on the 5th of January following.[19] Thereafter he appears so regularly in the records as a petitioner of Parliament and pursuivant of the estates of John Denham that he would seem to have had little opportunity for capture by the Royalists. Moreover, Wither's frequent catalogues of his sufferings and perils on behalf of Parliament never include the ordeals either of capture by the enemy or of threat of hanging. Wither's first recorded civil war imprisonment, in fact, was one he incurred from his own side, when in 1646 his second pamphlet of grievances, *Justitiarius justificatus*, was condemned by Commons to be burned as a libel on Sir Richard Onslow, chief supporter of the Parliament in Surrey, and Wither himself was clapped into jail.[20] On a subsequent occasion indeed Wither was imprisoned by Royalists for his seditious writings at a time when Denham was in some position to affect his fate, but that was not until 1661 when Wither was sent to the Tower for a satire upon the new Parliament of which Denham happened to be a member. Therefore Aubrey's oft-told tale must be regretfully set aside as apocryphal.

---

[19] *Commons Journal*, II, 920. The counterdesigns relative to putting prisoners to death as traitors are mentioned by Vicars, *Jehovah-Jireh*, p. 233.

[20] *Vic. History Surrey*, II, 604. In *Justitiarius justificatus* Wither alleges that Onslow had put him out of "some Committees, and out of my habitation," which may indicate that Onslow was Anne Denham's "charitable Patron." But in this hysterical pamphlet Wither shows marked traces of paranoia: he blames the loss of Farnham Castle on Onslow's machinations and accuses Onslow of secret "malignancy."

Denham's own whereabouts during the remainder of 1643 and the following year of 1644 cannot be certainly established, but he probably remained in attendance upon the King during the latter's almost continuous residence at Oxford. Early in June 1643, before Denham wrote his "Second Western Wonder," news of the exposure of "Waller's Plot" in London reached Oxford. Edmund Waller discreditably saved his own life while his Royalist associates went to the scaffold, but it nonetheless may be safely postulated that the news did *not* make John Denham's "ears tingle and his hair stand on end." This venture into historical fiction on the part of Edmund Gosse is based on a completely imaginary notion of the relationship between Denham and Waller, and on a very inaccurate notion not only of the textual evolution of *Coopers Hill*, but even of its printing history. There is absolutely no ground, in fact, for regarding "Waller's Plot" as in any way an episode of Denham's life, or as having had the least effect on either the composition or the revision of any of his poems, *Coopers Hill* or any other.[21]

The next certain mention of Denham's name implies more than it specifies about his activities or his presence. Qualification 4 of Article 14 of a set of proposals drawn up by Parliament on November 8, 1644, as conditions for a peace treaty with the King, required that a number of named persons, John Denham among them, "be removed from His Majesty's Counsels, and be restrained from coming within the Verge of the Court; and that they may not, without the Advice and Consent of both Kingdoms, bear any Office, or have any Employment, concerning the State or Commonwealth."[22] This blackballing indicates that the King's enemies, at least, estimated Denham's standing at court more highly

---

[21] The "plotting" lines of the "A" text of *Coopers Hill* were not dropped until about 1653, in the course of the drastic revision that produced the "B" text. The matter is canvassed thoroughly in my edition. See also my " 'Lost,' 'Authorized,' and 'Pirated' Editions of John Denham's *Coopers Hill*," *PMLA*, LXXIX (1964), 242–253.

[22] *Lords Journal*, VII, 55.

than any direct evidence can do. Wither's unremitting hue and cry after Denham's remaining property may have served to enlarge Denham in the Parliament's eye, and Wither is almost certainly the instigator of the next recorded occurrence of Denham's name, an occurrence that reveals nothing, however, about Denham's own activities. That was an order, on January 1, 1644/5, to search the house of one Mr. Sherwood in Fleet Street "for goods of John Denham, which are to be sold," an order to which the note was subsequently added, "none found." [23] Even Wither's researches fail to yield any solid news of Denham during the remainder of 1645. Yet later developments were to show that Denham, although never a principal courtier, had gained the confidence of the King to a degree inexplicably in excess of any services he is known ever to have rendered. Similarly, in crucial junctures to come, the Queen entrusted more to Denham than can readily be accounted for either by his known accomplishments or by his social standing.

To the otherwise blank period of 1644–45, nevertheless, one at least of Denham's poems may be inferentially attributed. In the letter dedicatory "To the King" prefixed by Denham to the 1668 edition of his *Poems and Translations* he asserts that in July 1647 his verses "To Sir Richard Fanshaw upon his Translation of *Pastor Fido*" had been written "two or three years since," that is, in 1644 or 1645. The poem was first printed in 1648, with Fanshawe's *Pastor Fido*.

During this time also Denham's gambling fever remained unabated, for Aubrey remarks, "I remember about 1646 he lost 200 li. one night at New-cutt." If this is indeed a personal recollection on Aubrey's part, then the night he remembers must have been a

---

[23] *Calendar of Proceedings of the Committee for Advance of Money*, ed. M. A. E. Greene (London, 1888), I, 39. A MS note by Oldys in a book in the British Museum (Langbaine's *English Dramatick Poets* [see chap. vii, p. 205 n. 41, below]) asserts that the Royalist newssheet *Mercurius Aulicus* carried notice of a sale of Denham's goods on June 19, 1644, but I have been unable to verify the reference. On January 19, 1645 (which may mean 1644/5 or 1645/6), the Committee for Compounding, at Haberdashers' Hall, ruled that "Mrs. Denham is to hold her husbands estate being sequestred for Recusancy" (S.P. Dom., ser. 23, Vol. 77, pp. 502, 503).

night at Oxford in 1644 or 1645, for Aubrey could have seen little or nothing of Denham during 1646, as will appear.[24]

The collapse of the Royalist war effort in 1646 brings Denham once more into visibility. In the middle of January 1645/6 the Royalist stronghold of Dartmouth surrendered to Sir Thomas Fairfax. For some reason Denham was in Dartmouth at the time, and not without influence. The town itself having been taken by assault, the next morning the governor, Sir Hugh Pollard, yielded the castle, himself, and all officers and soldiers, upon quarter, sending out Denham, the Earl of Newport, and a Colonel Seymour as hostages, and apparently to arrange the details.[25] Denham and the Earl of Newport were then sent to London upon parole, in the company of the famous Parliamentary preacher, Hugh Peters, to render themselves prisoners within ten days. Although Peters was a fanatic partisan in the war, and was to be the harshest of the Puritan clergymen who beset the captive Charles I, Denham somehow managed to ingratiate himself with the preacher. This sort of response to the manifest power of a foe is a recurring pattern in Denham's life, as is likewise the fact that he later took advantage of his friendship with Peters to benefit his own side. On Friday, January 23, Peters reported to the House of Commons the attendance of the two prisoners, whom he described as having been "serviceable to the General in the Gaining of the Forts which held out at Dartmouth, after the Town was taken," whereupon the House ordered an examination of Denham that afternoon by the Committee of Examinations.[26] Less than two weeks later, on

---

[24] How this memory dated to 1646 can be reconciled with Aubrey's assertion that he "had the honour to contract an acquaintance with" Denham in 1653 is not at once clear. Perhaps an explanation may lie in the fact that Aubrey was but a nineteen- or twenty-year-old student at the time of Denham's loss of £200, whereas Denham was then a thirty-year-old Cavalier. Aubrey might have become aware of the incident at the time without actually being acquainted with Denham.

[25] Bulstrode Whitelock, *Memorials of the English Affairs from the Beginnings of the Reign of Charles the first to the happy restoration of King Charles the Second* (Oxford, 1853), I, 563 [= folio p. 189].

[26] *Commons Journal*, IV, 415, 416; *Lords Journal*, VIII, 126.

Wednesday, February 4, 1645/6, Commons approved a resolution to exchange Denham for a Major Harris, "a Prisoner to the Enemy at Exceter."[27] Denham in fact very probably never reached the royal garrison at Exeter, but his misadventures following the order for his exchange illustrate some of the anomalies made possible by the waging of a civil war in a country with a juridical system still largely intact.

Exeter, the last major stronghold in the west left to the King, did not long stand firm before Fairfax's relentless pressure. On April 9 Sir John Berkeley, the commander, sued for terms, and Fairfax, moved no doubt both by the impending end of the war and by the richness of the prize (which included the King's daughter, the Princess Henrietta), was exceptionally generous, so that on Monday the 13th the garrison marched out in surrender.[28] To be covered by the Exeter surrender terms became an important asset to many an indigent Cavalier, for the terms included the privilege of compounding to free estates from sequestration at very much more favorable proportions of estimated prewar value than the usual standards enforced by the Committee for Compounding.[29] Other articles of the capitulation agreement included the choice of immediate departure overseas or retirement at home upon engagement to take no further part on the King's side in the war. Regardless of which alternative Denham might have wished to elect, for a time he appeared to be cut off from the efficacy of any terms whatsoever. An order for his immediate discharge issued on April 27 by the Committee for Prisoners reveals that Denham had been by then for some time a prisoner in London. Despite that order, he continued a prisoner until May 11.

Denham's difficulties arose not out of flaws in the surrender treaties, nor out of Parliamentary suspicion, but out of his private

---

[27] *Commons Journal,* IV, 429.

[28] Wedgwood, *The King's War,* p. 548.

[29] *C. Com. Comp.,* V, xvi–xvii. Usual compounding rates and practices are explained in the preface to this work (I, i–xix).

debts and the complication of his fiscal affairs, and from some time after his official exchange on February 4 until his ultimate release in May, he was a civil prisoner of the King's Bench rather than a prisoner of war. On Monday, May 4, 1646, the House of Lords entertained a petition from Denham for a writ of habeas corpus which, with its attendant documents, indicates pretty clearly that Denham was not personally present at the surrender of Exeter. Nothing is said about Exeter in the petition, which advances these four main points: (1) "Petitioner, a prisoner of war, has been exchanged by order of the Commons"; (2) "he is charged with divers actions and executions in the King's Bench"; (3) "the Committee for Prisoners has notwithstanding ordered him to be discharged"; (4) "Sir John Lenthall, however, will not let him go, conceiving the same to be no legal discharge." The accompanying documents include, besides the claims of Denham's creditors and various alleged precedents, a copy of the order of Commons of February 4 approving the exchange for Major Harris, and a copy of the order for Denham's discharge dated April 27.[30] A week later, on May 11, Denham himself appeared before the Lords, who ordered him released; the brief notice of the occasion in the *Lords' Journal*, however, illuminates the preceding events: "This Day Mr. Denham was brought to this Bar, by a *Habeas Corpus*; he being a Prisoner of War, and exchanged, was arrested by his Creditors before he was out of the Parliament's Quarters. And it is Ordered, That he be released from his present Imprisonment." [31]

---

[30] "House of Lords Calendar 1646," *Sixth Report*, p. 115; *Lords Journal*, VIII, 294, 295.

[31] *Lords Journal*, VIII, 313–314. This entry does not indicate that Denham "was arrested by his creditors before he left the precincts of Parliament, and on the Lords' order was at once released" (Banks, *Poetical Works*, p. 12). It is also incorrect to say that on May 4, 1646, "the Lords voted to approve the action of the Commons of February 4 in exchanging [Denham] for Major Harris" (*ibid.*). This is a misreading of the paragraph in the *Lords Journal* for May 4, beginning "Resolved, &c. That this House doth approve of the Exchange of Mr. *Denham* . . ." as a record of a current action of the Lords. It is a mere transcript of the Commons resolution of February 4, submitted along with Denham's petition as supporting documentation.

In the parlance of the English Civil War, "the Parliament's Quarters" means the territory of England controlled by the Parliament. Its correlative is "the King's Quarters."[32] Denham, therefore, although an exchanged prisoner of war, was arrested by his creditors before he could cross the lines into Royalist country. Since the Exeter surrender terms could not have required Denham to cross the lines — no place that he could legitimately call home remained under royal control by May 11, which was in fact the day that the final siege of Oxford began — and since his status as an *exchanged* prisoner depended exclusively upon the Dartmouth surrender, what clearly happened is that Denham was seized in February while on his way to Exeter. That seizure by the civil law violated the military exchange agreement, and nullification of the seizure by the Lords allowed Denham to be counted as *de jure* present at Exeter, and so eligible to benefit by the Exeter terms, even though he was not physically present at the capitulation.

After his release in May 1646 Denham disappeared into France for almost a year, presumably taking advantage of the Exeter provisions in order to avoid further harassment by his creditors. An enigmatic letter to the future Earl of Clarendon dated from Caen on July 8 (June 28 O.S.?), 1646, places Denham at that city shortly theretofore, as a party to a design to dissuade the Prince of Wales from acceding to his mother's request that he abandon Jersey and retire to her at Paris. The letter has also been construed as indicating that Denham was freshly arrived in France at the time.[33] Despite this apparent opposition to the Queen's designs,

---

[32] A petition of Anne Denham to the Committee for Sequestration on November 25, 1645, asserts that "she hath ever lived in the parliament quarters," to which in response the committee agreed she was not subject to the ordinance "for taking away ye 5th pte . . . if shee have not lived in ye Enimyes Quarters" (S.P. Dom., ser. 20, Vol. 2, p. 11). Similarly, on May 2, 1645, Stephen Soame of Kent deposed that "he receives little from his estate . . . because it is in the King's quarters" (*C. Com. Comp.*, II, 887).

[33] This construction appears in *C.Cl.S.P.*, I, 324: "1646, Caen, July 8. Mr. Godolphin to Sir E. Hyde: Sir John Berkeley, Col. Ashburnham, and Mr. Denham, arrived from Hampton the day after the Lords went towards Jersey." "Hampton"

Denham's dedication "To the King" in his 1668 *Poems and Translations* suggests that during this period of exile he chiefly attended upon Henrietta Maria in Paris. The next actual record of his whereabouts is provided by another order of the House of Lords, this one, dated March 24, 1646/7, succinctly granting that "Mr. John Denham shall have a Pass, to come out of *France*, to compound for his Delinquency." [34] If Denham took immediate advantage of his pass he must have returned forthwith to France, for in July 1647 he had but newly arrived in England on a commission from the Queen to the King. Denham says he volunteered to reach the King, who had fallen into custody of the Army, because of the acquaintance he had contracted with Hugh Peters after his capture at Dartmouth. [35] Sir John Berkeley independently corrob-

---

would be Southampton or, more generally, Hampshire (often called "Hampton-shire" in the seventeenth century), directly cross-channel from Caen. The relevant portion of the actual letter (Clarendon S. P., B.2256), is more ambiguous: "Sr John Berkeley arrived heer from Hampton, the day after the Lords went towards Jersey, was hugely disgusted at their errand, and would have overtaken them, but that a chollerique sense of a disesteeme upon his councells, stayed him in his course. There was with him Coll: Ashb. and Mr Denham. . . ." This passage fails, it will be noticed, to specify that either Denham or Ashburnham had arrived from "Hampton." The Lords going toward Jersey were Jermyn, Digby, Wentworth, Wilmot, Capel, Colepepper, and others, and their errand was, on behalf of the Queen, to persuade the Prince of Wales to come into France. The time, according to Clarendon, was about the end of June (*History of the Rebellion*, III, 24), but Clarendon likewise says that Ashburnham was then in Paris, though he later moved to Rouen (*ibid.*, pp. 24, 54), and that Berkeley did not arrive in France until six months after the surrender of Exeter (of which he had been commander) (*ibid.*, p. 53). June 28/July 8 was less than three months after the surrender.

Whatever the significance of these apparent errors in Clarendon's *History of the Rebellion*, the conjunction of Berkeley, Ashburnham, and Denham at this time and place is faintly disquieting because of the coincidental reunion of precisely this trio in the Isle of Wight (just across the water) during November and December of 1647 — eighteen months in the future — at the time of the King's escape from Hampton Court. There is also something uncanny about the persistence of the name "Hampton" throughout these adventures.

[34] *Lords Journal*, IX, 98. Denham's intention to compound may have stimulated renewed interest in his affairs on the part of the sequestrators, for on May 29, 1647, the County Committee for Buckinghamshire reported to the central committee for Compounding at Goldsmiths' Hall in London that John Denham, delinquent, had an estate at Horsenden in Bucks. to the value of £244 2s. 6d. (*C. Com. Comp.*, I, 66).

[35] "To the King," in *Poems and Translations* (1668). See p. 68, above.

orates this story exactly.[36] Because Cornet Joyce did not take the King from Holmby to the Army at Newmarket until June 4, 1647, Denham must still have been in France in June when word of the seizure reached the Queen.[37] Through Peters (whom Berkeley denominated "a powerful person in the army"), Denham achieved access to the King at "Causham" (Caversham House, near Reading), where the Army kept the King from the 3d to the 23d of July.[38] There, about the 13th, Sir John Berkeley found Denham in the company of Sir Edward Ford, who had been sent on a similar mission by the Queen, as had Berkeley himself.[39] The instructions given to all three emissaries seem to have entailed more than the communication of news to the King, and in fact to have contemplated their serving as intermediaries in negotiations between the King and the Army. Although Henrietta Maria might herself have had sufficient confidence in Denham's capability, she and the Prince of Wales sent Sir John Berkeley to supersede him because, in Berkeley's words, "they conceived it necessary to employ some to the army that might be supposed to have greater trust, both with the Queen in France, and with the King in England, than either Sir Edward Ford or Mr. Denham had." [40] Berkeley nonetheless accepted the advice of both Ford and Denham that the "Adjutators" of the army regiments were currently the real holders of power in England.[41] An instance of the confidence reposed by King Charles in Denham occurred shortly thereafter, when Denham was one of an eleven-member council called by

---

[36] "The Narrative of Sir John Berkeley (June to December, 1647)," in *Memoirs of the Martyred King*, ed. Allen Fea (London, 1905), pp. 162–166.

[37] Consequently the pass ordered for him by the House of Lords the preceding March could not have been requested merely as a cover for the mission in July, as has been suggested. Denham's motivations for requesting permission to return must have been chiefly personal, and were doubtless connected with the death of his wife (see below).

[38] The King left Caversham before July 23, not on August 24, as stated by Banks (*Poetical Works*, p. 59 n. 227).

[39] "The Narrative of Sir John Berkeley," p. 166.

[40] *Ibid.*, p. 163.

[41] *Ibid.*, p. 166.

the King at Woburn in Bedfordshire (where he stayed from July 23 until August 1), to draw up an answer "both in point of law and reason" to the proposals for a settlement put forward by the Army.[42]

When, at the beginning of August, the King was moved from Woburn to Stoke (near Guildford in Surrey), the Royalist negotiators apparently came to London. A letter of intelligence dated August 9, 1647, "Munday," conveyed, along with the news of the King's presence at Stoke, that there had arrived in town "persons of good understanding and employed betwixt the king and the armie. . . . their names are Jack Berkley and Jack Denham. I was told that Jack Ashburnham was not farr of the toune, but durst not hazard to come in."[43] These were the same three men who had appeared at Caen the preceding summer, and their names remained linked for some time to come. King Charles himself drew nearer to London on August 24, when he was established by the Army at his palace of Hampton Court. Denham was certainly in frequent attendance on the King during the remainder of that sojourn.

During a private interview at Caversham, Denham later recalled, the King had commented favorably on Denham's verses "To Sir Richard Fanshaw," but had expressed the hope both that they had not been recently written, and that Denham would no more "vent the overflowings of [his] Fancy that way," now that he was "thought fit for more serious Employments." Denham was not quite candid in his response to this priggish caution, for he had in fact dallied at least once more with his Muse since the composition of the Fanshawe verses. During that same year of 1647 Humphrey Robinson and Humphrey Moseley together brought out the first folio *Comedies and Tragedies* of Beaumont and

---

[42] *Ibid.*, pp. 174–175.

[43] Clarendon S.P., B.2572. The letter, signed "13," is addressed "for Mr John Gardiner" (a blind for Sir Edward Hyde?). The names are written in a substitution cipher, deciphered by the recipient. The name "Jack Denham" appears as "LGFM KHPODO." The letter has been calendared in *C.Cl.S.P.*, I, 387.

Fletcher, a volume that contained a prefatory poem by Denham "On Mr. John Fletchers Works." That poem was no doubt inspired more by the impending edition than by a spontaneous outburst of admiration for Fletcher, and so in all probability was written for the occasion. Nevertheless Denham merely assured the King that the Fanshawe verses had been written "two or three years since," and "stood corrected as long as [he] had the honour to wait upon him," which means in effect that Denham wrote no more poetry until after the execution of King Charles.

For the meanwhile, at least, Denham had little opportunity for idle pursuits, and when on November 11, 1647, the King fled from Hampton Court to the Isle of Wight, Denham was implicated in the conspiracy. He was suspected by the enemy of being in the plot, and revealed actually to have been so by Sir John Berkeley.[44] Denham's own statement that at the King's "departure from *Hampton* Court, he was pleased to command me to stay privately at *London*" also implies Denham's presence during the escape.[45] During the Isle of Wight fiasco Denham's name was also to acquire an undeserved bad repute in some Royalist circles, occasioned by no more than a failure of character analysis and an unlucky friendship. It was Denham's friend, John Ashburnham, who made the ill-conceived suggestion to the King that he call for help on Governor Hammond of the Isle of Wight. When Hammond responded by locking the King up in Carisbrook Castle, Ashburnham was widely, though unjustly, accused of having played Judas. Denham's closeness to Ashburnham would in any event have served to tar him with the same brush, but Ashburnham ensured that result by indicating, in justifying his own fatal advice, that "that which made him [Ashburnham] conceive the best hopes of [Hammond] was the character Mr. Denham . . . gave of him."[46]

---

[44] "The Narrative of Sir John Berkeley," p. 182; see the letter of Edward Helaw to Commons, November 11, 1647, transcribed by Banks, *Poetical Works*, p. 13.

[45] Denham's own recollections are set forth in his prefatory letter "To the King," in *Poems and Translations* (1668).

[46] "The Narrative of Sir John Berkeley," p. 182.

After the entrapment of Charles his companions of the flight from Hampton Court lingered on the Isle of Wight, holding a frigate for escape into France through weeks of diminishing hope that the King might elude his guards and come to them. Sir John Berkeley recalled that Denham joined the group, probably early in January: "I moved to Mr. Ashburnham, to Mr. Legge, and Mr. Denham (who was then come to us from London) that some one might be sent to the Queen from us all; which was consented to, and I was made choice of by the rest to go on that business."[47]

However far Denham's brief venture to the Isle of Wight took him, on the whole he obeyed the King's injunction to remain in London. On December 13, 1647, the Commissioners for Compounding with Delinquents received the humble petition of John Denham Esq. of Horsley in the County of Essex, showing that "your p^{tr} did adhere to his Matie in this Warr ag^{t} the Parliamt. for wch delinquency his Estate is under Sequestration, He is Comprized within ye Articles at the Surrender of Exceter. He humbly prayes to be admitted to his Composition for his said Estate & Delinquency according to his said Articles."[48] Attached is a certificate dated "17th day of January 1647" and signed by Fairfax, to the effect that "John Denham, Esqr was an Inhabitant in the Citie and Garrison of Exeter within the time expressed in the Articles before the Surrender thereof, and is accordingly to have the benifitt of the said Articles." Whether the date of this certificate represents January 1646/7 or 1647/8 is unclear. At the earlier date Denham had been out of the country, but if the later is correct the certificate must have been obtained and attached to the petition a month after the filing of the petition. In either event there is no reason to interpret the certificate as Fairfax's testimony out of his own memory that Denham was in fact present at the surrender of Exeter in April 1646. Denham no doubt merely

---

[47] *Ibid.*, p. 196.
[48] S.P. Dom., ser. 23, Vol. 80, pp. 169–172 (*C. Com. Comp.*, III, 1790).

76

showed the acquiescent earl the *de jure* evidence of his exchange for Major Harris.

As an adjunct to his petition Denham submitted a particular of his estate, listing only four properties as still within his claim: "little Horsley in Essex; Weston Milles in Suffolke; Horsenden, Bucks.; and Tewsbury, Gloucestershire." His property at Egham he asserted had been "sould [i.e., mortgaged, as later appears] to Thomas Knowles Esq about nine years since" (about 1638 or 1639), and that payments were £840 in arrears. Subsequent evidence was to indicate that Denham retained some other property not acknowledged in this list, but perhaps the concealment was more inadvertent than cunning amid the tangle of Denham's affairs and the complication of sales, leases, and mortgages through which he had successively alienated much of his patrimony. The present particular lists some £4,040 in debts charged against the estate (including £200 for seven years to "Collonell Tychbourne lieuetenant off yᵉ tower," presumably Denham's companion-at-arms at Farnham), "all which he prayes may be considered in the setting off his fines." Of most personal interest in these documents, however, is the note attached to the listing of the Horsenden property: "being the inheritance off his late wife." This note reveals that Anne Denham had died sometime between the grant to her of her fifth of Denham's estate in November 1645 and this December of 1647. It may have been her death that directly moved that request by Denham to return to England which was allowed in March of 1647. Perhaps from what she retained of the estates she had from time to time remitted funds for his maintenance abroad. What provision was made in the meanwhile for the care of Denham's three minor children, John, Elizabeth, and Anne, no record clearly reveals, although by 1650 the children are mentioned as already under the guardianship of a Colonel Fielder, M.P. for St. Ives in Cornwall.[49]

---

[49] Two later documentary references to Anne Denham might give an unwary re-

Denham's move to compound for his estate permitted him relatively undisturbed residence in London now that he had outlived his usefulness as a negotiator. A letter to the Earl of Lanerick, signed in cipher under date of January 4, 1647/8, places Denham in London, "a person as I conceave wholly to bee trusted." [50] A month later, on February 8, another disguised correspondent takes a contrary view, writing, "I dare not trust Denham, being Mr. Ashburnham's creature." The Isle of Wight poison was beginning to work.[51] But later Royalist legend magnified Denham's reputation and his deeds of this time. Aubrey asserts, for instance, that Denham "conveyed, or stole away, the two dukes of Yorke and Glocester from St. James's . . . and conveyed them into France to the Prince of Wales and Queen-mother." Wood correctly reduces the number of dukes in this escape to York alone, and supplies the correct year, 1648. The Duke of York slipped away from St. James's on April 21, but whatever the actual part played by Denham in the adventure, it is unlikely that he accompanied the young Duke so far as to France.

Denham later explained his business in London during this time to have been that of sending to and receiving from the King all his correspondence at home and abroad, and added that he "was furnisht with nine several Cyphers in order to it." [52] The nature of this work is reflected in a surviving exchange of letters between

---

searcher the impression that she was still alive in 1651 and 1652. The first is a legal opinion filed in S.P. Dom., ser. 23, Vol. 130, p. 218, containing the clause "if the said John Denham, and Anne his wife, doe joyntly soe long live." But accompanying documents make amply clear that she is dead, and one must simply assume that the author of this opinion was not apprised of the fact. Similarly, Vol. 80, p. 181, of the same series, in recording the sale of some of Denham's lands, notes the sale as "for the life of the said Mrs Denham." Here "Mrs Denham" is a copyist's error for Mrs. [Anne] Long, the actual purchaser. For Colonel Fielder, see p. 82, below, and n. 62.

[50] *The Hamilton Papers*, ed. S. R. Gardiner, Camden Society Publications, 2d ser., 27 (London, 1880), 147–148, no. 91. The Earl was next brother to the Duke of Hamilton, whom he succeeded in the dukedom upon the latter's execution in 1649.

[51] *Ibid.*, pp. 152–153, no. 96.

[52] "To the King."

Denham and the Marquis of Ormonde; they deal obscurely with Royalist intrigues in Ireland. Ormonde's reply to Denham's undated letter was sent from St. Germains on April 15, 1648 (probably April 5 O.S. for Denham).[53] Denham's continued presence in England as a trusted royal agent is attested for May 13/23 by no less an authority than Charles, Prince of Wales, in a letter to the Marquis of Hertford.[54] The Prince also, on June 22/July 2, 1648, instructed one Humfrey Boswell, on dispatching him to London, "to repair immediately to Mr. Denham and to acquaint him with his employment . . . and proceed in all things by his advice. He is to pay any money he receives to Mr. Denham, taking his acquittance."[55] This episode in his life Denham later recalled to have lasted about nine months. Reckoned from the King's flight from Hampton Court in November 1647, it would have ended approximately in August 1648. Then, Denham relates, "being discovered by their knowledge of Mr. *Cowleys* hand, I happily escaped both for myself, and those that held correspondence with me," and fled once more to the Continent.[56]

In retrospect, therefore, Denham's career in the civil wars from 1642 to 1649 was a succession of failures. On the military side of the war his presence is associated only with surrenders — at Farnham, at Dartmouth, and perhaps at Exeter. Aside from verse, his positive contributions to the Royalist cause, in diplomacy, counsel, or espionage, all bear the same taint. His diplomatic value depended entirely, not upon his skill, intelligence, or tact, but upon his successful ingratiation of himself with his captor, Hugh Peters.

---

[53] *A Collection of Original Letters and Papers, Concerning the Affairs of England, From the Year 1641 to 1660. Found among the Duke of Ormonde's Papers,* ed. Tho. Carte (London, 1739), II, 351, 353. Ormonde was the King's most loyal supporter in Ireland.

[54] *Pepys MSS,* p. 279.

[55] *Ibid.,* p. 211.

[56] "To the King." For Cowley's role as amanuensis for the Queen at the Paris end of the correspondence, see A. H. Nethercot, *Abraham Cowley: The Muse's Hannibal* (London, 1931), p. 116 and *passim.*

As a counselor to the King, Denham apparently must take some blame for the disastrous flight that ended in "Carisbrook's narrow case," particularly for his faulty estimate of Governor Hammond's character. Yet throughout Denham was enacting a behavioral sequence that grew out of his own character, and that he was to reenact at various levels on several later occasions of his life. The elements of it were present when Denham wrote his tract against gambling to placate his angry father only to gamble away much of his inheritance thereafter. Ready submission to superior opposing strength, and a willingness to protect himself by outward conformity to the opponent's will, can be seen as clearly in Denham's military surrenders and in his friendship with Hugh Peters as in the composition of *The Anatomy of Play*. The other aspect of Denham's response to coercion — an inward refusal to match the outward conformity, and a secret truculence seeking a safe or disguised retribution against the coercer — appears at this time in his London espionage or correspondence service. Within this behavior pattern lies the key to Denham's character, and to the nature of much of his subsequent activity, as his life unfolded.

During this final stay in England before his longest exile, Denham's compounding process had been progressing but slowly. Of the numerous estates he had inherited from his father, many had been alienated even before the war, and others were encumbered in various complicated ways. Like other Royalists, Denham also no doubt endeavored to conceal such of his holdings as he could. In March 1647/8 John Denham's name appeared on three several lists filed with the Committee for Compounding at Goldsmiths' Hall. These were, respectively, a list of persons sequestered for delinquency in Westminster (Denham noted as "goods only"); a similar list for the hundreds of Lexden, Tendring, Thurstable, Witham, and Winstree, in Essex; and a list of delinquents "still under sequestration" in Suffolk.[57] And on March 22 Wither

---

[57] *C. Com. Comp.*, I, 91, 95, 96.

vengefully reappeared. Wither, it will be recalled, in February 1642/3 had seized estates belonging to Denham, Tichborne, Hudson, Browne, Andrews, and others involved in the Farnham episode of the preceding November. Since then, on March 5, 1644/5, he had been granted the right to one-half of whatever concealed delinquents' estates he might uncover. On August 12, 1645, Andrews compounded for his estate, and Wither lost that. The following year, 1646, the war being lost, Hudson compounded on September 7, Tichborne on September 18, and Browne on December 26. Despite Wither's determined opposition, Browne's compounding, which had been held up, was confirmed on May 20, 1647.[58] After all his sacrifices for the cause, Wither had now left only some fragments of Denham's estates, and Denham's motion to compound could deprive him even of those. Therefore Wither must have felt some triumph in producing the information, on March 22, 1647/8, that "Denham, who was in arms against the Parliament, has an estate at Egham in reversion, concealed, and not yet sequestered."[59] But this proved a will-o'-the-wisp for Wither and Denham's way with an estate is recognizable in the contents of a clerk's notation of June 17, after Wither's tip had been followed up: "John Denham's estate in Surrey is worth 140 *l.* a year, and there were also goods discovered and seized. There are two mortgages on the estate, one to Thomas Knollys [obviously the Thomas Knowles to whom Denham in his petition to compound said he had "sould" the estate], whereby there seems due to him [Knollys] 120 *l.* a year for life, and many hundreds in arrear."[60] The bureaucratic machinery nevertheless continued to grind on, and kept on grinding even after Denham had become a political fugitive abroad. Within a month of Denham's flight the Committee for Compounding issued to his acquaintance, John Thynne, an influential M.P., a certificate dated August 25, 1648, that "this

---

[58] "Four Scarce Poems of George Wither," p. 94.
[59] *Calendar of Proceedings of the Committee for Advance of Money*, II, 872.
[60] *Ibid.*

Committee hath lett the land of Mr Denhamb a delinqt at Eggham at fforty shillings p Annum called Sprewell [Prunewell?] hill for one yeare and att the best time it is worth but three pounds p. Annum." This parcel of land included "The Place," and the certificate effectively preserved Thynne's interest from Wither's raiding. Actually Denham had sold "The Place" to Thynne on the 12th of June for thirty pounds, and on August 31, 1648, when Denham had just departed the country, Thynne discharged the estate from sequestration for a small fine and got clear title into his own hands.[61] On April 2, 1650, a fifth of his estate was allowed to the absent Denham, and on April 11 that fifth was ordered paid to Colonel Fielder as guardian and trustee for Denham's children.[62] It now became Fielder's task, in rivalry with Wither, to determine the true extent of Denham's estates, but his succeeding battles with mortgage foreclosers and others of Denham's creditors, and his purchase of several of Denham's properties on his own account, form no proper part of Denham's own life, except as he was their occasion.

---

[61] The certificate is page 239 in S.P. Dom., ser. 23, Vol. 206; Thynne's motion to compound, with the details of Denham's assignment to him of "a peece of Land called Prune hill and two Coppices of wood in Egham," begins page 237. *C. Com. Comp.*, III, 1790, gives the amount of the fine as £4 10s., but to my eye the entry reads, "fyn £7/10s."

[62] *C. Com. Comp.*, III, 1790.

IV: Exile

At Paris, *at* Rome,
At the Hague *they're at home;*
The good Fellow is no where a stranger.

DENHAM HIMSELF next appeared at The Hague, among the entourage of the Prince of Wales, but he was not allowed to rust there unused. Early in September 1648 he was recommended to Prince Charles as a fit man to send to Scotland to deal with the Committee of States and the Assembly of Divines.[1] On September 11/21 Secretary Long drew up a set of "Instructions for Mr. Denham," and on September 13/23 the Prince himself delivered to Denham a letter to the Committee of States, and another to William Earl of Lanerick, accompanying the letters with a written set of instructions for Denham's guidance on his mission. The letter to the committee promised a supply of arms, and the letter to the Earl was endorsed "By Mr. Denham, who is to communicate all things to encourage him to continue his endeavours notwith-

---

[1] *C.Cl.S.P.*, I, 459. From the dates of his instructions there can be no doubt that Denham was recommended to the Prince before the middle of September, but the substance of this sentence depends upon Hyde's minutes relating to a conversation among himself, Mowbray, and Mungo Murray: "W[ill] Murray advised the Prince to answer the letters from the Committee and Assembly with gentleness; to take the Covenant if pressed to do so, and to send Mr. Denham into Scotland." These minutes, however, are dated "1648, Dec. 5, 7" in the *Calendar*, a dating more difficult to understand than to accept, since the Prince had long ago written to the Committee and Assembly, and ordered Denham to Scotland. Perhaps the dating is an error for Sept. 5, 7; otherwise it must be assumed that Denham had not gone to Scotland in September after all, and perhaps never went, in spite of the surviving copies of his instructions and letters. By December the Earl of Lanerick was no longer so influential in Scotland as he had been, that kingdom for the while having come under the virtual dictatorship of the Marquis of Argyle.

standing the late misfortune of the Scotch army in England."[2] The Prince's instructions to John Denham embraced six notable points: "1. He shall repair to Edinburgh and deliver the Prince's letter; 2. He shall inform them of the despatch of arms; 3. He shall move them to assist the war in England; 4. He shall confer with the dissenters and learn why they are against, and whether they intend to sit still or move; 5. He shall inform himself of the true state of affairs; 6. He shall remain in Scotland until recalled."[3]

While Denham was in Scotland the Parliament of England considered for the last time a set of proposals for a final settlement with the defeated but recalcitrant King. Among the provisions of the so-called Treaty of Newport discussed in the House of Lords on October 17, 1648, Denham's name occurred again in a proposed act concerning delinquents which exactly duplicated the requirements of the qualification of the peace proposals of November 1644 which had similarly blacklisted him.[4] Failure of the Treaty of Newport not only guaranteed the King's eventual execution but effectively terminated the value of Denham's employment in Scotland.

When Denham was recalled does not appear, but he was back at The Hague before March 15, 1648/9, by which time Charles I had been killed and (in February) the monarchy officially abolished in England. The Prince of Wales was now, to his own followers, and since the beginning of February to the Estates of Scotland, King Charles II of Great Britain, France, and Ireland. On March 15/25 Denham was reported as having gone to France

---

[2] "Catalogue of Letters taken at Worcester," *Pepys MSS*, pp. 271–272, nos. 4 and 14. The "late misfortune of the Scotch army" was its disastrous defeat at Preston in August 1648, at which the Duke of Hamilton, Lanerick's brother, its commander, was captured, and for which he was to be beheaded early in 1649, shortly after the execution of the King.

[3] *Pepys MSS*, p. 226; notes by Secretary Long on these instructions are reproduced in *ibid.*, p. 227.

[4] *Lords Journal*, X, 548–549.

with the Duke of York.[5] He soon returned, however, and continued to act as a courier between the Queen and the new king, who set out in May to visit her at Paris. A letter from London containing political news was addressed on April 26, 1649 (May 6 N.S.), to Mr. John Denman (*sic*) at Antwerp; this otherwise unknown person may be Denham.[6] On May 26/June 5, Charles Parker wrote from Paris to Lord Hatton at Caen: "His Majesty, as Mr. Denham brings word, was to sett forward on Thursday last and wee expect him with what speede such a train can travaille and his entertainments att Breda, Antwerp and Bruxelles will permit."[7] About the middle of the following September, the relationship between the King and his mother having become strained, Charles set out from St. Germains to Jersey, to await a favorable opportunity for a possible landing in Ireland. At that time, as Denham later reminded him, he "was pleased freely (without my asking) to confer upon me that place wherein I have now the honour to serve." The place was that of surveyor general of Works, upon which Denham entered immediately after the Restoration.[8]

Although Denham in 1668, recalling this appointment, attempts to give the impression that his abstinence from poetry con-

---

[5] Historical Manuscripts Commission, *Report on the Manuscripts of F. W. Leyborne-Popham, Esq. of Littlecote, Co. Wilts* (London, 1899), p. 10: "Your friend Denham went to France with the Duke of York." Perhaps this is the basis of the story that Denham brought the Duke to France *from England*.

[6] *C.Cl.S.P.*, II, 9. But "Mr. Edward Denman" seems to have been a cover name on occasion for Sir Edward Hyde himself, as also "Madame [Elizabeth] Denman" and even (once) "Madame Elizabeth Denham."

[7] *Nicholas Papers*, I, 128–129.

[8] Denham's statement is to be found in his letter "To the King," prefixed to his *Poems and Translations* (1668). Despite Denham's explicitness, Aubrey wrote that "King Charles the first, who much valued him for his ingenuity . . . graunted him the reversion of the Surveyor of His Majestie's buildings, after the decease of Mr. Inigo Jones," an error continued through Wood down to *DNB*. Denham never made any such claim, and indeed had to contend with the plausible assertion of John Webb, Jones's nephew, that the late king had promised the reversion to him. The strength of Denham's claim was that it depended on the living king, not the dead one.

tinued, except for a few diversions in verse suggested by the young king himself, such was not really true. On June 24, 1649, the youthful Lord Hastings died of the smallpox, provoking no fewer than ninety-eight elegies upon his loss. The ensuing collection, *Lachrymae Musarum: or the Tears of the Muses* (1649), contained a genuinely noble "Elegie upon the Death of the Lord Hastings" written by John Denham. The fact that Denham did not reprint this work in 1668 presents somewhat of a puzzle, which may only be resolved on the supposition that he feared misinterpretation of some lines contained in a passage of the "Elegie" which are otherwise of particular interest as the only explicit poetic commentary by Denham on the execution of King Charles I:

> The late Great Victim that your Altars knew,
> You angry gods, might have excus'd this new
> Oblation; and have spar'd one lofty Light
> Of Vertue, to inform our steps aright:
> By whose Example good, condemned we
> Might have run on to kinder Destiny.
> But as the Leader of the Herd fell first,
> A Sacrifice to quench the raging thirst
> Of inflam'd Vengeance for past Crimes: so none
> But this white fatted Youngling could atone,
> By his untimely Fate, that impious Stroke
> That sullied Earth, and did Heaven's pity choke.
>
> (lines 21–32)

The intimation that Charles I had paid the penalty for "past Crimes" is not in fact the reflection on the probity of that King it might be interpreted to be. The notion was an obsession with the King himself, who believed he was paying the price of Henry VIII's crimes against the Church.[9] Denham in *Coopers Hill*

---

[9] On April 13, 1646, just before his escape from the beleaguered city of Oxford, Charles wrote out and entrusted to Gilbert Sheldon (later archbishop of Canterbury)

expresses exactly the same view of King Henry, a superstition that he and Charles I were not alone in sharing.[10] At the time of writing the Hastings elegy he probably felt no necessity to clarify, the adjective "past" indicating sufficiently that the crimes were not contemporary; by 1668 he might have felt it wiser to forget the poem than ostentatiously to revise it.

Regardless also of Denham's pretended abstinence from verse, his reputation as a poet had continued to grow. The first public acknowledgment of his merits came in Robert Herrick's *Hesperides* of 1648, a volume that includes "To M. Denham, on his Prospective Poem." [11] These verses offer no particularized insight into *Coopers*

---

a vow to restore to the Church all lands and lay impropriations held by the Crown if he should ever be restored to his "just kingly rights."

[10] See, for example, the pamphlet *Nuntius a Mortuis* (1657), translated and published in London as *A Messenger from the Dead, or, Conference . . . Between the Ghosts of Henry the 8. and Charles the First . . .* (1657/8). In this piece the ghost of Henry VIII almost boastfully explains that it was for Henry's sins that Charles had suffered; the fact that Charles's last days were associated with Hampton Court and with Whitehall Henry explains by his own seizure of both those palaces from the Church (i.e., Wolsey). "By the divine providence," Henry assures Charles, "you were destined to be a Sacrifice, for the expiation of the crimes of your predecessours. . . . Neither do I believe it is without the providence of God, that so direfull a revenge hath fallen on you, the most moderate, and the most innocent of them all, that so all might understand that not so much your sins, as the hereditary Evils, and the wickedness annexed to your Crown and your titles, are taken vengeance of in your person."

[11] Herrick's brief poem is reprinted in A. B. Grosart's ed. of Herrick's *Complete Poems*, II (London, 1876), 220 (I have slightly emended the punctuation of the first four lines):

> Or lookt I back unto the Times hence flown
> To praise those Muses, and dislike our own;
> Or did I walk those *Pean*-Gardens through
> To kick the Flow'rs, and scorn their odours too;
> I might (and justly) be reputed (here)
> One nicely mad, or peevishly severe.
> But by *Apollo*! as I worship wit,
> (Where I have cause to burn perfumes to it;)
> So, I confess, 'tis somewhat to do well
> In our high art, although we can't excell,
> Like thee; or dare the Buskins to unloose
> Of thy brave, bold, and sweet *Maronian* Muse.

Hill, but do recognize that it is a distinctively modern piece, rivaling the ancients, while being at the same time "Maronian." The praise of Denham himself as a poet is extravagant: " 'Tis dignity in others, if they be / Crown'd Poets; yet live Princes under thee." Likewise the request, from whatever quarter it came, for a contribution by Denham to *Lachrymae Musarum* must be interpreted as a further tribute to his fame. And despite Denham's exile, *Coopers Hill*, the object of Herrick's "Pean," remained apparently a vendable commodity. On November 3, 1649, the London bookseller Humphrey Moseley accepted transfer from Thomas Walkeley, who had brought out the 1642 edition, of the right to publish *Coopers Hill*, and on or about January 21, 1649/50, issued a new edition of the poem in a volume that included also the verses "To Fanshaw" and the Prologue and Epilogue to *The Sophy*. On February 4 Moseley also acquired from Walkeley the rights to *The Sophy*, and although he seems not to have published the play, he perhaps brought out still another edition of *Coopers Hill* the following October.[12] By way of new composition, it appears not unlikely that Denham wrote the set of polished and witty triplets first published in 1668 under the title "Natura Naturata" sometime during 1650.[13]

In May of 1650 Denham appears still to be attached to the exiled court, and favored by the King, for a letter dated from

---

But since I'm cal'd (rare *Denham*) to be gone,
Take from thy *Herrick* this conclusion:
'Tis dignity in others, if they be
Crown'd Poets; yet live Princes under thee:
The while their wreaths and Purple Robes do shine,
Lesse by their own jemms, then those beams of thine.

Herrick's line 6 perhaps echoes *Coopers Hill* ("A" text) line 64: "Both gently kind, both royally severe."

[12] The details of these publications are discussed in the introduction to *Expans'd Hieroglyphicks*, my edition of *Coopers Hill*. See also my " 'Lost,' 'Authorized,' and 'Pirated' Editions of John Denham's *Cooper Hill*," PMLA, LXXIX (1964), 242–253.

[13] See Banks, *Poetical Works*, p. 107 n. 3.

Breda on the 12th said that "Sr William Boswell is dead if S^r Ed: Nicolas refuse to succeed him, as I beleeve he will, it is thought Mr Denham shall have it 2 much different persons to be in competition (for so it is mistaken) for ye same place. Crofts shall shortlie be furnished for his Embassie." [14] Boswell had been the King's resident, or representative, to the Estates General of the United Provinces. Neither Denham nor Nicholas succeeded him. [15] Instead, Denham was joined to Crofts in his "Embassie." It was perhaps June when Denham was sent together with William Crofts on a mission to raise money for the King among his Scots subjects resident in Poland. [16] With the cooperation of the Polish Diet, which levied a capital decimation tax on the English and Scots under its control on behalf of the King, and despite the machinations of one John Molleson, Crofts and Denham managed to extract £10,000 from the reluctant merchants. Molleson seems to have produced a forged letter from Charles relieving his subjects in Poland from further exactions, but the timely arrival of William Sandys, sent in June 1651 from the King, now in Scotland, reinforced the authority of Crofts and Denham and

---

[14] Letter to "My deare Brother," signed "Ri. Watson," in Clarendon S.P., Vol. 39, f. 196 (*C.Cl.S.P.*, II, 58).

[15] Clarendon, *History of the Rebellion*, III, 242, Book XI.

[16] The appointment of Crofts as ambassador to Poland may have been formally made as early as August 1649. Banks says that it was, and cites in support *Perfect occurrences of Every Daies journall in Parliament, Aug. 3–10, 1649* (*Poetical Works*, p. 14 n. 74), a source I have been unable to consult. Despite Banks's intimation, however, I am unable readily to believe that the appointment included Denham at so early a date. Clarendon says that Crofts (he never names Denham) was sent to Poland "when the king went to *Jersey* in order to his Journey into *Ireland*" (*History of the Rebellion*, III, 442), which would have been about September 1649, and Denham by his own testimony was in St. Germains at that time. The letter of May 12, 1650, from Breda does not prove that either Denham or Crofts was actually in Breda at the time, although it suggests that they were. The letter does indicate rather strongly, despite Clarendon's assertion, that Crofts had not yet set out for Poland at the time of writing. After May 1650 seems a reasonable guess as to the time of the departure of the mission, Crofts and Denham probably journeying together.

checked Molleson.[17] The triumphant envoys returned with the money about September or October 1651.[18]

In the demoralized idleness of the expatriate court after the disaster at Worcester, Denham returned to his old vices and may also have indulged in vices that perhaps were new. The least venal

---

[17] This version of the events in Poland is deduced from Denham's poem "On My Lord Crofts and my Journey into Poland" and a letter sent from Daniel O Neill to the Marquis of Ormonde on June 20, 1651. In the poem Denham says that the Scots in Poland at first refused to respond to the warrant — "our Letter so well penn'd" (line 15) — that he and Crofts had brought from King Charles; the Diet, however, had constrained them to "pay one in ten" (line 26). But a further attempt to defeat the mission arose with John Molleson's "wicked Lye," a letter purporting to be from "our Kings Majesty" (lines 43–45). This maneuver miscarried, however, because "Fate / Brought the Letter too late, / 'Twas of too old a date" (lines 46–48), and the recalcitrants were shipwrecked: "On *Sandys* they ran aground" (line 65).

The last allusion is clarified by O Neill's letter. Writing from Stirling in Scotland to Ormonde, then in France, O Neill says: "I have moved his Majesty to allow you 1000 *l.* out of what Money Mr. *Crofts* gets in *Poland*: he with great chearfulness told me, he would send by Mr. *Sands* who goes to him to let you have that sum, if he could spare it" (Thomas Carte, *A Collection of Original Letters and Papers* [London, 1739], II, 31–32). The present tense of the verb *gets* suggests that the getting is still going on at the time of writing, and the verbs *send* and *goes* seem to me to compel the interpretation of the crucial personal pronouns in the second half of the sentence as follows: "he [Charles] . . . told me, he [Charles] would send by Mr. *Sands* who goes to him [Crofts] to let you have that sum, if he [Crofts] could spare it." Sandys then would have been on his way in June 1651 to join Crofts in Poland, and his arrival with fresh authority from the King — now *de facto* king of Scotland and at least nominally regnant in that kingdom, where he had been crowned at Scone on January 1 — perfectly explains Denham's allusion.

Although Banks cites O Neill's letter by way of annotation on the name "*Sandys*" in Denham's poem (*Poetical Works*, p. 110), he fails to see its significance for the interpretation of the allusion, and he also misreads the letter as an indication that the Polish mission had returned by the time of its writing. Therefore he imagines that Molleson's false letter was dated earlier than the letter carried by Crofts and Denham, and so unable to supersede their authority (*Poetical Works*, p. 109 n. 4). That would have been an instance not of Fate's running counter to Molleson's "quaint Invention," but of incredible incompetence on the forger's part. But Denham's line on Sandys indicates that Molleson's forgery, though no doubt dated later than Crofts and Denham's warrant, was dated too early to countermand Sandys's fresh new letters from Scotland, an advent Molleson could not have foreseen.

[18] "Mr. *Crofts* . . . returned . . . about the time that his Majesty made his escape from Worcester" (Clarendon, *History of the Rebellion*, III, 442). Worcester was lost on September 3, 1651; Charles escaped to France on October 15. According to Clarendon the ten thousand pounds from Poland and an even larger sum brought

was that of versifying—on topics, he recalled, that the King was
"pleased sometimes to give me . . . to divert and put off the evil
hours of our banishment." [19] To this period certainly belongs
"On My Lord Crofts and my Journey into Poland, from whence
we brought 10000 *l.* for His Majesty by the Decimation of his
Scottish Subjects There." [20] By August 1652 Denham had written
the satirical verses "On Mr. Tho. Killigrew's Return from his
Embassie from Venice, and Mr. William Murray's from Scotland." [21]
Also most probably written around this time were "To Sir John
Mennis Being Invited from Calice to Bologne To Eat a Pig,"
and "A Dialogue between Sir John Pooley and Mr. Thomas Killigrew." Denham also wrote a sizable but indeterminate share of the
twenty or so Latin and English poems that went to make up the
volume called *Certain Verses Written by severall of the Authors*

---

back by Lord Colepepper from "*Mosco*" fell into the hands of Queen Henrietta Maria
and her creatures, and so was of little use to the reexpatriated King.

Banks's statement that Denham's mission to Poland ended in "May or June 1651,
when he undoubtedly returned to the court of Charles" (*Poetical Works*, p. 15),
overlooks Clarendon's contrary testimony and is apparently based on a misreading
of O Neill's letter to Ormonde (see preceding note). In May or June 1651 there was,
properly speaking, no court of Charles II that Denham could have returned to. The
King was in Scotland at the time, and the Covenanting Scots did not welcome his
English courtiers (see Clarendon, *op. cit.*, III, 366–367).

[19] "To the King," in *Poems and Translations* (1668).

[20] First printed in the 1668 *Poems and Translations*, from which this title is taken.
The reference to Crofts as "My Lord" is a polite anachronism, Crofts having become in 1658 Baron Crofts of Saxham.

[21] A copy of these verses in the Clarendon S.P. (Vol. 43, f. 236) is dated August
1652 (*C.Cl.S.P.*, II, 143). Killigrew's "embassy" to Venice was a kind of confidence
trick: "The Ambassador of *Venice, Pietro Bassadonna*, a Noble *Venetian*, was a
Man, as all that Nation is, of great Civility and much Profession. He was the first
who told the Ambassadors, that the King their Master had a Resident at *Venice*;
which was Mr. *Killigrew*, which they did not at first believe, having before they
left St. *Germains*, dissuaded the King from that Purpose; but afterwards his Majesty
was prevailed upon, only to gratify him, that in that Capacity, He might borrow
Money of *English* Merchants for his own Subsistence; which He did, and nothing
to the Honour of his Master; but was at last compelled to leave the Republick for
his vicious Behaviour; of which the *Venetian* Ambassador complained to the King,
when He came afterwards to Paris" (*The Life of Edward Earl of Clarendon . . .
written by himself* [Oxford, 1759], p. 116).

Friends; to be reprinted with the Second Edition of Gondibert, of which George Thomason purchased a copy on April 30, 1653. Davenant had published his uncompleted *Gondibert* at Paris in 1651, to see it become at once the butt of all the court wits; several of the latter wrote the anonymous mock laudations that were printed as *Certain Verses,* but Aubrey says that most of the contributions are Denham's. Denham himself, by adding transcripts of six of these poems (with textual variations) to his own copy of his *Poems and Translations* (1668) which has recently come to light, effectively claims their authorship.[22] One survival from the same prank which was not included in *Certain Verses* was printed by Denham in 1668 as "An occasional Imitation of a modern Author upon the Game of Chess," and in his own copy he transcribed two other never published poems also on *Gondibert.*

---

[22] The authors of *Certain Verses* identify themselves as Clinias, Dametas, Sancho, and Jack-Pudding, and frequently refer to their number as four. At least one poem, however (no. 13), mentions Denham by name (*"Denham* come help me to laugh"), and I. D'Israeli identifies the four as Denham, Jack Donne, Crofts, and Alan Brodrick (*Miscellanies* [Paris, 1840], p. 159). Brodrick was to be a coconspirator with Denham toward the end of the interregnum. Despite D'Israeli's identifications, the Duke of Buckingham is generally allowed to have had a hand in the game.

The six poems from the collection which Denham added in holograph to his own copy of the 1668 *Poems and Translations* (recently come to light upon its acquisition by Mr. James M. Osborn of Yale University) are: "Upon the Preface" ("Room for the best of Poets heroick"); "Upon the Preface of Gondibert" ("As *Martials* life was grave and sad"); "To Sir W. Davenant" ("After so many sad mis-haps"); "The Author upon himself" ("I am old *Davenant* with my fustian quill"); "A Letter sent to the good Knight" ("Thou hadst not been thus long neglected"); "Canto 2" ("Rais'd by a Prince of *Lombard* blood"). Banks in his edition of Denham's *Poetical Works* gave only two of these poems to Denham ("To Sir W. Davenant" and "A Letter sent to the good Knight"), but assigned him three others not confirmed by the 1668 holograph. Of the unpublished poems, one begins "Sr William's no more a Poet / Hee cares not who doth know it," and the other "As I came from Lombardy / Wth my fustian Style." A third satire on Davenant postdates Sir William's death on April 7, 1668, and so must have been newly written when Denham transcribed it into the 1668 volume.

Mr. Osborn describes Denham's copy of *Poems and Translations* thoroughly in an article in the *Times Literary Supplement* for September 1, 1966.

Thomason's copy of *Certain Verses* (British Museum shelf mark E.1484) is dated "April 30." By that date Denham himself had been back in England for about a month.

A more serious relapse on Denham's part was into his old addiction to gambling, if he had ever been free of it. On May 13/23, 1652, Secretary of State Sir Edward Nicholas wrote from The Hague to his friend Lord Hatton, then residing at Paris: "Mr. Denham hath here lately had very ill luck at play, which hath made him (I am told) in great want at present. He talks of going for England, but it is thought intends not to adventure it, more for fear what his creditors than the rebels there will do against him."[23] For the moment fear of creditors seems to have overcome the pangs of want, for Denham did not venture to England for almost another year.

Yet a third vice may have afflicted Denham during these evil hours of banishment, the besetting vice of Charles's court: venery. Denham's "Dialogue between Pooley and Killigrew" is in fact a discussion of venereal diseases, their causes, symptoms, and cures; among the latter one specific mentioned is "Mongo Murry's Black Elixir." Mongo Murray had been one of those who had recommended sending Denham to Scotland in 1648; he was not a physician but a courtier, and this reference reveals the prevalence of the amateur practice of venereal medicine among those who had most need of it. Another amateur practitioner was the Sir John Mennis addressed in Denham's verses on "Being Invited To Eat a Pig"; by profession Mennis was a naval officer, out of employment through the King's want of a navy. After the Restoration he became chief comptroller of the Navy, and one night in his cups boasted to Samuel Pepys "of his cures abroad . . . and above all men the pox. And among others, Sir J. Denham he told me he had cured, after it was come to an ulcer all over his face, to a miracle."[24] This incident, if it embodies the truth, must also belong to these dissipated years; other later stories were also to

---

[23] *Nicholas Papers*, I, 300. Ironically, this evidence of Denham's continued thralldom to gambling occurs just about a year after the publication in London of his *Anatomy of Play*, of which Thomason dated his copy April 28, 1651.

[24] Pepys, *Diary*, IV, 217–218, Aug. 15, 1664.

recall Denham's being subjected to some sort of "cure" in Holland, and it may well have been for the pox.[25]

From his own occasional verses written in exile, from contemporary letters and other documents, from remarks of various writers made at later dates during the interregnum, and from various post-Restoration reminiscences, a catalogue of Denham's

---

[25] The self-reference to Denham's pox which has been seen in "On Mr. Tho. Killigrew's Return from his Embassie from Venice, and Mr. William Murray's from Scotland," proves, however, to be illusory. The fourth stanza of that poem reads as follows:

These Statesmen you believe
Send straight for the Sheriffe,
For he is one too, or would be;
But he drinks no Wine,
Which is a shrewd sign
That all's not so well as it should be.

This stanza Banks explicates by saying "The 'sheriffe' is Denham himself, who was appointed High Sheriff of Surrey in 1642 by Charles I. The third line of the stanza refers to his mission to Poland with Lord Crofts . . . from which he had recently returned; and the last three lines probably refer to the venereal disease from which he suffered when abroad" (*Poetical Works*, p. 112 n. 15). The 1653 Clarendon S.P. MS version of this stanza, however, while retaining the venereal overtones, suggests a somewhat different interpretation:

These Statesmen you'll beleive sent straight for ye Shreefe,
(for he is one too, or would be)
but he drinkes noe Wyne, wch is a fowle signe
that all's not soe sound as it should be.

In a review of Banks's edition G. C. Moore Smith commented: "It is strange if Denham speaks of himself in 1652 as 'the Sheriffe' ('the shreefe' is the better reading) on the ground that he had been sheriff of Surrey ten years before. It is not clear to me that Denham is here in question" (*RES*, V [1929], 234). Smith's position is well taken and his preference of the MS reading "shreefe" (the significance of which will emerge) is supported by rhyme and meter. That the reference is not directly to Denham is confirmed by a passage in Killigrew's autobiographical play, *Thomaso, or, The Wanderer*, written a few years subsequently in Madrid, and published in Killigrew's *Comedies and Tragedies* of 1664 (Wing K450; the two parts of *Thomaso* each have a separate title page dated 1663). In Part Two, Act V, scene vii (p. 456), three Cavalier exiles in Madrid reminisce about Holland in the period 1651–1652, in terms that echo Denham's poems from that time. Their recollections include eating a "Sowes-baby" (cp. "To Sir John Mennis," line 46: "To a goodly fat Sow's Baby") along with "old Satan of the *Disser*," i.e., Will Murray, Lord Dysart (cp. "On Killigrew's Return," line 14: "How *Satan* the old"); meeting "Embassadour *Will* [Crofts]"

friends, associates, and acquaintances during this period may be drawn up. These included, among men of his own or the older generation, Admiral Sir John Mennis, Sir John Pooley, Thomas Killigrew, William Crofts, and William and Mongo Murray. One of his three collaborators in *Certain Verses to be reprinted with Gondibert* was reputed to be Jack Donne, scapegrace son of the

---

(cp. "On My Lord Croft's and My Journey into Poland"), and "Resident *Tom*" (cp. "On Killigrew's Return," line 1: "Our Resident Tom"); as well as the lampooning of *Gondibert*; and the mission to Poland. The persons alluded to are identified in marginal notes, and the last mentioned is "M. Sheriffs Secretary, *John* the Poet with the Nose," identified in the margin as "Jack Denham." The reference to *Gondibert* immediately following suggests "with the Nose" was intended to contrast Denham with the noseless Davenant. (For calling to my attention this allusion by Killigrew to Denham I wish to thank my student, Mrs. Julia Bolton Holloway.)

Although the "M. Sheriff" whose secretary Denham is said to be remains unindentified (the margin carries no note on him, and I have not found any likely contemporary *named* Sheriff), it is virtually certain that he is the "Sheriffe" or "Shreefe" of Denham's poem, and quite certain that he is not Denham himself. I think the word is not the familiar designation of a county official, but rather represents the word listed by the *OED* in such variants as *sheriffe, sheriff, shreefe, sherife, shreeve, seriph, seriff, ceriffe, shirreef* as a title of certain Arab princes. The topical reference of Denham's stanza remains obscure, but the general drift of it implies a parallel between the religion of Islam (with its sexual license but prohibition of wine) and the disease of the pox. Perhaps "Sherife" was somebody's nickname, as "Old Satan" was Will Murray's.

Why Denham should be considered the "Sheriffe's" secretary is equally mysterious. He may have served Crofts in the capacity of secretary during the mission to Poland, but the records offer no confirmation for the conjecture. He may have served effectively as secretary to the group that lampooned *Gondibert*. In neither instance is it clear why his principal should have been designated "M. Sheriff." As a purely conjectural identification, admittedly worth very little, I would suggest Sir John Pooley, one of the two speakers in Denham's "A Dialogue between Sir John Pooley and Mr. Thomas Killigrew," of approximately the same date as the other poems under discussion. Because Denham in that poem recorded Pooley's confession to Killigrew, Denham might justly if facetiously be dubbed Pooley's secretary. Pooley's confession is that he has contracted a very bad case of a "Venereal . . . nuysance," which not alone would keep him from imbibing alcohol but might as well, from the connotations noted above, have earned him the temporary nickname of "The Sherife."

Whatever the truth of the matter, the beginning of the next stanza as printed in 1668 is a thoughtless miscorrection of the MS version. It reads, "These three when they drink," apparently referring to Killigrew, Murray, and the "Sheriffe," but the poem states specifically that the "Sheriffe" does *not* drink. The poem is a celebration of Killigrew and Murray only, and the MS version, "These Lads when they drinke," avoids the anomaly, compelling recognition only of the poem's two heroes as the "Lads."

eminent dean and poet. Denham appears also to have been intimate at this time with Aubrey de Vere, the sulky twentieth Earl of Oxford, and with George Villiers, second Duke of Buckingham, hero of the civil wars and future Restoration debauchee (and another of Denham's collaborators in *Certain Verses*). Both these erratic noblemen were considerably younger than Denham, but in Royalist belief at least, throughout the interregnum, Denham had special access to the confidence of each. It is noteworthy that all these men were members of Charles's court, at The Hague or elsewhere, rather than of Henrietta Maria's coterie at Paris. Denham seems not to have been much in touch with the Paris group, and to have held little intercourse during this period with his former companions Sir John Berkeley and the Ashburnhams, or with his fellow poets Waller, Davenant, and Cowley, all of whom spent longer or shorter spells of exile at Paris. Waller, Davenant, and Cowley all returned to England before Denham did, and conformed more openly and wholeheartedly to the Commonwealth and Protectorate regimes. Surprising therefore is the fact that, despite his evident dissociation from the Louvre, Denham seems always to have been coldly regarded by Chancellor Hyde, the Queen's implacable opponent, and that he continued throughout the interregnum to bear the imputation of membership in the Queen's party.

During Denham's long absence from England his name was kept alive at home by more than the reputation of his poetry. From the time in April 1650 that Denham's petition to compound was granted, and one-fifth of his estates allowed to Colonel Fielder as trustee for his children, until August 2, 1654, when Gupshill Manor, Tewkesbury Parish, County Gloucester, was bought by Robert Tokeley, the *Calendar of the Committee for Compounding* and the *Calendar of the Committee for Advance of Money: Domestic* between them contain no fewer than forty-four entries pertaining to John Denham's fiscal affairs. Fielder and Wither continued to compete in the recovery of Denham's assets, the one presumably from altruistic motives, the other in pursuit of his grievances. Aside from two debtors (*mirabile dictu*), they uncovered estates attributed to Denham, in addition to those at Egham and Horseley Parva, at "Barfol Hall and Wormingford" (this pair of names disappears, to be replaced by "Barholt and Woodhall Manors," perhaps the same places) in Essex; Wissington Mills, Suffolk; Horsenden Manor, Buckinghamshire; Gupshill Farm and Manor, Whittington Manor, and another unnamed property, all in Gloucestershire; and Cottonsland, Carmarthenshire. In general, however, they reckoned without Denham's precocious talent for indigence, and the various county sequestrators for the most part fell upon indignant holders who insisted they had purchased the lands from Denham, free and clear, "before the wars."

Thanks also largely to the care of George Wither, Denham's name came to the attention of the House of Commons three times during his exile. On Thursday, January 2, 1650/1, while Denham was in Poland, the House of Commons agreed that despite all the seizures Wither had undertaken since 1643, his original loss of £2,000 had now grown to £3,958 15s. 8d. plus interest. The committee reporting this matter to the House added that "they humbly conceive it reasonable, that the Manor of *Little Horksly* . . . in *Essex*, with *Wiston-Mills* [Wissington Mills], near adjoining thereunto, in *Suffolk* . . . being Two hundred and Forty Pounds *per Annum*, be settled upon the Petitioner . . . being Part of the Inheritance of *John Denham* Esquire, the said Petitioners chief Plunderer, a Delinquent excepted from Pardon." On what basis the final allegation was made does not appear. The House reacted less specifically by ordering the payment of a lump sum to Wither, and in addition, "that, in full Satisfaction and Discharge of all other Demands of the said Major *George Wither*, One hundred and Fifty Pounds *per Annum*, of the Lands of *John Denham* Esquire, be settled upon the said Major *George Wither*." [26]

---

[26] *Commons Journal*, VI, 518–519.

On Tuesday, the first of July 1651, Denham's name was especially added to a bill under debate for the sale of delinquent's lands, and the bill became an act on July 16, 1651.[27] The act, "for the sale of several Lands and Estates forfeited to the Commonwealth for Treason" directed the sale to George Wither Esq., of "Lands . . . of the clear yearly value . . . of One hundred and fifty pounds out of the Estate of John Denham in this Act named." [28] Inconsistently, however, a seven years' lease of Horseley Parva to Colonel Fielder was confirmed on October 17 of the same year, and the estate was not purchased by Wither until March 23, 1651/2.[29] Only the following year, 1653, Wither for some reason was ejected from Little Horksley.[30]

Such was the tangle Denham returned to when early in 1653 he ventured once more into England after an absence of four and a half years.[31] On March 1, 1652/3, the Council of State appointed a committee of four, including Colonel Fielder, "to examine Mr. Denham, lately come from France, and to report his examination." [32] What they learned from Denham is nowhere on record, but he appears to have encountered no further trouble, even from his creditors. Denham had returned to a comparatively tranquil England, under the Protectorate of Oliver Cromwell, and for the time, at least, Royalists were relatively free from molestation.[33]

---

[27] *Ibid.*, p. 594; *Acts and Ordinances of the Interregnum 1642–1660*, ed. C. H. Firth and R. S. Rait (London, 1911), II, 521.

[28] *Acts and Ordinances of the Interregnum*, II, 545.

[29] *C. Com. Comp.*, III, 1790, 1791.

[30] "Four Scarce Poems of George Wither," pp. 94–95.

[31] Denham had been away since August 1648. Now he apparently dropped out of Royalist view some little time before he reappeared in England. At least in a letter written from Paris on December 7, 1652, Sir Edward Hyde informed Secretary Nicholas that "I know nothinge of Mr Denham, he is not heare, and I thinke he was not at Antwerp, when my last letters were dated thence" (Clarendon S.P., Vol. 44, ff. 128–129; *C.Cl.S.P.*, II, 160). One gathers that Denham's whereabouts were as little known to Nicholas (at The Hague?).

[32] *C.S.P.D.: 1652–1653*, p. 193.

[33] Actually Cromwell's expulsion of the Rump did not take place until April 1653, the month following Denham's questioning on behalf of the Council of State. Crom-

Additionally, Aubrey tells us, Denham had a highly placed protector of his own: "being in some straights [he] was kindly entertayned by the earle of Pembroke at Wilton. . . . He was, as I remember, a yeare with my lord of Pembroke at Wilton and London." The fifth Earl of Pembroke, Philip Herbert, a man some four years younger than Denham, had succeeded his father to the title in 1650. Like his father, he had been a Parliamentarian throughout the wars, and had been a member of the Long Parliament from the beginning. The Lords' House having been abolished, he continued to sit in Commons as his father had before him, even after inheriting his title. In 1651 he had been elected to the Council of State, and during 1652 had been briefly its president; now he continued in that body, which functioned in effect as Cromwell's cabinet. What previous acquaintance he had had with Denham is not apparent. Denham during this period seems to have occupied himself chiefly with literature, and his stay at Wilton was possibly one of the most fruitful periods of his career. Yet, although no evidence exists to convict him of treason, and his loyalty was never called in question by his important contemporaries, a reader of the documents surviving from this time cannot escape the suspicion that Denham, like many another impoverished or dispirited Royalist, at least "cooperated" with the Cromwellian authorities during the next several years.

The exact length or the precise dates of Denham's stay with the Earl of Pembroke cannot be established, nor are his movements otherwise easy to trace during this interlude. On September 10/20, 1653, his name occurs in an unusual context, but one that offers no clue to his actual whereabouts. On that date a Cromwellian spy among the Royalists in Paris sent to his master, John Thurloe,

---

well, however, had been virtual ruler of England at least since his victory at Worcester, and his initial policy of conciliation toward the Royalists had been in effect since shortly thereafter. As early as May 1652 Royalists returning to England were reported as having been "very well received and kindly used" (see David Underdown, *Royalist Conspiracy in England 1649–1660* [New Haven, 1960]), p. 59 and nn.)

in London, what must be one of the least informative intelligence letters in the history of espionage. The writer complains of a hangover incurred in the course of establishing his authenticity as a Cavalier, and, so that the Commonwealth should not lack some fruit of his self-sacrifice, encloses a mildly ribald French drinking song, which, he adds, "if Englished by one Denham, I hear to be the state's poet, truly it will be much to the instruction of the youth of our country." [34] This, one may guess, is less an indication that Denham's "poetical reputation was high" than a tribute to his facility at bawdy rhymes, and Thurloe's agent probably heard of Denham from his Cavalier drinking companions of the night before. No doubt it was also the suggestion of the revelers that Denham had gone back to England to become "the state's poet," that is, poet laureate of the Commonwealth, *the state* being the term that since 1649 had replaced in antimonarchist circles *the realm* or *the kingdom*.

Not until more than a year after his return does Denham materialize in the records on a certain date at a certain place. On April 6, 1654, at his home at Deptford, John Evelyn recorded, "Came my *Lord Herbert*, Sir *Kenhelme Digbie*, Mr. *Denham* and other Friends to Visite me." [35] Which Lord Herbert this was cannot be established, but despite the coincidence with Denham it is unlikely to have been William, son and heir of the Earl of Pembroke, at that time only fourteen years old. Sir Kenelm Digby is well known, and Denham was later to be associated with George Digby, second Earl of Bristol, Sir Kenelm's cousin. This visit to Evelyn is not very enlightening, but the next record of Denham is slightly more so. The following month, on Friday, May 12, 1654,

---

[34] *S.P. Thurloe*, I, 470–471. Since this song never came to Denham's hands there would be little point in reproducing it here, even if it did not present a stiff editorial challenge in itself. As Birch prints it, it has been sadly garbled: the first line, for instance, "Avons les plus francs desbauchez," obviously should read "À vous, les plus francs desbauchés," and so with the rest.

[35] *The Diary of John Evelyn*, ed. E. S. de Beer, Vol. III, *Kalendarium 1650–1672* (Oxford, 1955), p. 94.

the Council of State referred to committee a petition of John
Denham, the purport of which, however, is not noted. That it
had to do with his finances may nonetheless be inferred from the
further order of the council that "meanwhile the Trustees for forfeited lands . . . are not to sell his estate of 50 *l.* a year in Co.
Carmarthen, for which he compounded on the Act of grace for
South Wales."[36] How the Carmarthenshire property had remained
untouched since it was uncovered by Colonel Fielder in March
1650/1 continues to be a mystery, but Denham's continued possession of this small property may well explain the journey into
Wales he undertook sometime the following year, if it did not
provide cover for another motive. For Denham in a shadowy way
was becoming involved in the wispy Royalist underground in England.

Before we attempt to chart Denham's path through the murky
wilderness of conspiracy, however, his literary respite at Wilton
should be considered. It was at Wilton, Aubrey recalls, that he
himself "had the honour to contract an acquaintance" with
Denham.[37] Sharing Pembroke's hospitality at the same time was
Aubrey's friend, Christopher Wase, who was then tutor to the
young William, Lord Herbert. On the generous-minded Wase Denham made, during their association at Wilton, a deep and last-
ingly favorable impression. Denham became something of an idol
to Wase, and upon at least two subsequent occasions of seeming
slighting of Denham's reputation Wase was moved to aggrieved
and passionate verses in his defense. From his own memory
Aubrey recalls that at Wilton Denham translated a "booke of
Vergil's *Aeneis*, and also burlesqu't it," and with the augmentation
of Wase's memory he adds: "He burlesqued Virgil, and burnt

---

[36] *C.S.P.D.: 1650*, p. 174; see also *C. Com. Comp.*, III, 1790. This estate was "Cottonsland," which Denham doubtless acquired through his marriage to Anne Cotton.

[37] This statement by Aubrey offers an apparent conflict with his earlier statement,
"I remember about 1646 he lost 200 *li.* one night at New-cutt," but see above, chap. iii,
p. 68 n. 24.

it, sayeing that 'twas not fitt that the best poet should be so abused."
The burlesque of Vergil appears irretrievable, but probable fruit
of the serious translation survives. Not until early in 1656 did
Humphrey Moseley issue *The Destruction of Troy: an Essay
upon the Second Book of Virgils Aeneis: Written in the year,
1636*.[38] Despite the ascribed date of composition, this work probably represents the translation mentioned by Aubrey. Since the
Hutchinson manuscript version of *Aeneid* II–VI clearly shows a
less finished version of Book II than that published in 1656, the
process of translation that went on at Wilton can perhaps best
be described as a revision of a previous translation that could very
well have been made as early as 1636.[39] The partial translation
of *Aeneid* IV which Denham first published in the *Poems and
Translations* of 1668 under the title "The Passion of Dido for
Aeneas" may also be a product of Wilton, since it too is a variant of
the Hutchinson manuscript version, although one that offers special
problems.[40]

---

[38] Entered by Moseley in the Stationers' Register on February 5, 1655/6, as *"The
Destruction of Troye, being a translation of the second booke of Virgills Eniods* by
John Denham, Esqr"; announced in *Mercurius Publicus*, no. 306 (April 17–24, 1656),
as "recently published." Thomason's copy in the British Museum is dated May 19, 1656.

[39] An edition I have prepared of Denham's two published fragments of *Aeneid*
translation collated with their comparable passages in the Hutchinson MS makes
clear the nature of the revisions effected (see chap. i, pp. 12–13n. 17, above).

[40] Banks cites "The Passion of Dido" as evidence of a connection between Denham
and Waller during the period after Denham's return to England in 1653. He may be
correct as to the connection, but it cannot be demonstrated in the way he attempts.
In 1658 Humphrey Moseley published a joint translation of *Aeneid* IV by Sidney
Godolphin and Waller under precisely the title Denham was to use for his partial
translation of that book: *The Passion of Dido for Aeneas*. Waller's share in this work
can be identified, because of later separate publication, as a passage of 134 lines covering 147 lines of Vergil (*Aeneid* IV, 437–583). Denham's "Passion" omits from translation a passage that corresponds roughly to the lines translated by Waller, but Banks
overstates the case in saying that Denham "omits altogether a passage of about 130
lines, save for a few scattered lines to bridge the gap. These lines omitted by Denham
are precisely the lines translated by Waller" (*Poetical Works*, p. 39). The only adequate
way to compare the two translations is on the basis of the Latin lines involved in each,
since the number of English lines required by either is unpredictably variable. Of the
147 lines translated by Waller, Denham translates 25 and omits 122. The 25 translated

The Destruction of Troy is a work of considerable significance in the history of English Augustan poetics. Although Tom May's translation of Vergil's *Georgics* into English decasyllabic couplets had appeared in 1628, as late as 1647 Fanshawe could still reproduce the fourth *Aeneid* (the matter of Denham's "Passion of Dido") in Spenserian stanzas. The immensely successful couplet translation by John Ogilby of the complete *Works of Publius Virgilius Maro* had, it is true, gone into at least two editions prior to the publication of Denham's *Destruction* in 1656, but later Augustan translators and practitioners of the couplet, such as John Dryden, made a point always of sneering at Ogilby and praising Denham. Denham himself makes no reference to Ogilby, unless by implication, but the insistence of the title page of *The Destruction of Troy* that the translation was made in 1636 may have been intended as a claim of precedence over Ogilby, whose work dated from 1649 or 1650. Denham prefixed to *The Destruction of Troy* a prose preface in which he declares his purpose in presenting this

---

fall into three groups: (*a*) 13 lines (437–449), for which Denham requires about the same number in English; (*b*) 2 lines (476–477), for which he requires only 1; (*c*) 10 lines (494–503), which he translates in 8. Denham therefore breaks off 13 lines after Waller begins, bridges a 44-line gap by translating 2 lines occurring approximately in its middle, then translates 10 consecutive lines, after which he leaves an 80-line gap, and resumes once more at line 584, the line directly following the last line translated by Waller.

Although the only clear match between Waller's translation and Denham's omissions occurs at lines 583–584, the general contention must be granted that Denham avoids translating that part of *Aeneid* IV which Waller translates. But the coincidence is less striking than Banks thinks it is, and, while not quite accidental, is susceptible of explanation upon other grounds than a share-the-work compact among poets or, as Banks puts it, Denham's wish not "to compete with his friend." What motivated Waller to translate just this portion of *Aeneid* IV and not the rest? The answer begins to appear as soon as Banks's emphasis is reversed: why did Godolphin (like Denham) omit these lines?

Godolphin had fallen in battle in 1643, leaving behind, among a small body of unpublished verses, a partial translation of *Aeneid* IV. This version contained at least 568 lines, rendering 558 lines of the Latin (1–436, 554–705), and at some indeterminable date Waller completed the translation of the entire book by translating the missing sequence in 134 lines. The actual fragment left by Godolphin may not impossibly have contained some representation of the lines in the omitted sequence, analo-

fragmentary translation of the *Aeneid* to the world. It is to "do *Virgil* less injury than others have done . . . and indeed, the hope of doing him more right, is the only scope of this Essay, by opening this new way of translating this Author, to those whom youth, leisure, and better fortune makes fitter for such undertakings."

The "new way of translating" which Denham essayed to exemplify was a sympathetic and poetical freedom from the slavishness of literal translation, a doctrine that was to do much to mold the theory and practice of translation in the Augustan age, and to be especially adopted and proclaimed by Dryden. In the "Dedica-

gous to Denham's transitional bridges. The preface to the 1658 Godolphin-Waller edition states that the translation "was done (all but a very little) by . . . Mr. Sidney Godolphin," leaving unresolved the question whether that "very little" was less than Waller's contribution; and a variant version of the entire translation (including a variant version of Waller's 134 lines) survives in Lucy Hutchinson's commonplace book (in common with Denham's early *Aeneid* translation), but is attributed solely to Godolphin. Waller may therefore have adapted some of Godolphin's lines, or deleted and replaced them, either because he could not assimilate them to his own work or because they were poetically defective (the printed preface adds that Godolphin's effort was "only for his own diversion, and with lesse care, then so exact a judgment as his would have used, if he had intended it should have ever been made publick"). In any event, Godolphin and Denham appear to have approached *Aeneid* IV along parallel paths.

   The joint work of Godolphin and Waller was published under the restrictive title of *The Passion of Dido for Aeneas as it is Incomparably exprest in the Fourth Book of Virgil*, although Waller's addition converted Godolphin's work into a complete translation of the full fourth book. A permissible assumption from this is that the descriptive title belongs primarily to Godolphin's unaugmented translation. Denham's venture, though lacking most of what Waller contributed to the joint publication, was given the same title. But Waller's translation was printed separately as merely "Part of the fourth Book of Virgil's *Aeneis* translated." The difference in titles is instructive, for the passage translated by Waller is largely unconcerned with Dido's "Passion," and that fact sufficiently accounts for Denham's (and Godolphin's) omission of it. The division between Godolphin and Waller (i.e., Godolphin's omission) actually makes somewhat better sense than that between Denham and Waller (i.e., Denham's omission), for the first 13 of Waller's lines which Denham also translates (and Godolphin presumably omits) describe, not Dido, but Anna's interview with Aeneas. Perhaps Denham felt this representation of Aeneas' obduracy was necessary to motivate Dido's subsequent actions. The remaining 12 lines that Denham translates within the interval involve Dido's deception of Anna and the erection of the funeral

tion of the *Aeneis*" Dryden asserts that in his own translation " 'tis the utmost of my ambition to be thought [the] equal" of Sir John Denham, "or not to be much inferior," and in the same work he shows ample evidence of familiarity with Denham's preface to *The Destruction of Troy*. "I conceive it a vulgar error in translating Poets," Denham writes, "to affect being *Fidus Interpres* . . . whosoever aims at it in Poetry, as he attempts what is not required, so shall he never perform what he attempts . . . Poesie is of so subtile a spirit, that in pouring out of one Language into another, it will all evaporate." Dryden more prosaically echoes this sentiment with the statement, "I had long since consider'd that the way to please the best judges is not to translate a poet literally, and Vir-

---

pile, both indispensable to the story. Omitted are (1) the series of supernatural omens, lines 450–475; (2) Dido's story to Anna to account for the sacrifice, lines 478–493; (3) the account of the priestess and the sacrificial rites, lines 504–521; (4) the description of peaceful night, lines 522–528; (5) Dido's sleeplessness and self-reproaches, lines 529–553; and (6) Aeneas' vision of Mercury, his arousing of his men, and his departure, lines 554–583. Of these episodes, only the 25-line description of Dido's nocturnal torment surprises by its absence from Denham's "Passion of Dido" (and would equally were it actually absent from Godolphin's); the others simply do not describe Dido's passion. Denham follows the same principle in omitting more than 50 other lines from translation in portions of the poem which can in no way be connected with Waller, e.g., 19 lines describing Aeneas and his men (393–408, 416–418), 15 lines in which Dido hoodwinks her officious nurse (630–644), and 14 lines on Anna's discovery of the dying Dido and resultant speech (672–685). Denham's omission of irrelevancies even goes down to the fine detail of omitting Vergil's 2-line description of Iris' pinions at Dido's final moment (700–701).

Denham's resumption of his translation at line 584 following Waller's cessation at line 583 (and, of course, coincident with Godolphin's resumption at the same place) is remarkably easy to explain. Line 583 is the last line of a paragraph that describes Aeneas' departure; line 584 is the first line of a new paragraph that describes Dido's waking to find him gone:

> Et iam prima novo spargebat lumine terras
> Tithoni croceum linquens Aurora cubile . . .

which Denham translates:

> *Aurora* now had left *Tithonus* bed,
> And o're the world her blushing Raies did spread.

It is not at all unlikely that Denham knew Waller during the 1650's, but no connection between the two poets can be established through their translations from the fourth book of the *Aeneid*.

gil least of any other. For, his peculiar beauty lying in his choice of words, I am excluded from it by the narrow compass of our heroic verse . . . [and] monosyllables . . . clogg'd with consonants, which are the dead weight of our mother tongue."

Later in his preface Denham states a principle of his own translation which was to have considerable influence upon the development of the later genre of Imitation: "if *Virgil* must needs speak English, it were fit he should speak not only as a man of this Nation, but as a man of this age." Dryden adopts the same principle exactly for his *Virgil*, and in the Dedication all but paraphrases Denham: "I have endeavor'd to make Virgil speak such English as he would himself have spoken, if he had been born in England, and in this present age."

In one other regard at least Dryden followed Denham's proffered example in the translating of Vergil. While Vergil was to be made to write such English verse as an Englishman of the second half of the seventeenth century would write, which meant, prosodically, in decasyllabic couplets showing a marked tendency to closure, the translator was to be allowed the occasional freedom of a triplet. In the "Dedication of the *Aeneis*" Dryden declares the triplet with "Pindaric" (alexandrine) to be "the *Magna Charta* of heroic poetry," and frequently avails himself of the larger scope of that unit to accommodate the sweep of a figure that would be cramped within a couplet. Denham has nothing specific to say about the triplet, but offered the silent encouragement to Dryden of including six triplets within the 549 lines of *The Destruction of Troy*. Had Dryden had the opportunity of comparing *The Destruction of Troy* with the 406 lines available in the Hutchinson manuscript of Denham's earlier version of approximately the same portion of *Aeneid* II, he would no doubt have felt justified. In that original Denham had employed only one triplet, so that Dryden might have concluded that during the period of revision at Wilton Denham discovered for himself the Magna Charta of verse.

One further mark of *The Destruction of Troy* on Dryden's

translation of the *Aeneid*, however, reveals a characteristic in which Denham and Dryden as translators drastically differ. Perhaps in all some 86 lines of Dryden's translation of the first 558 lines of *Aeneid* II owe something of their English shape to *The Destruction of Troy*. Most specifically, line 763 of Dryden's version is an acknowledged verbatim reproduction of the last line of Denham's "Essay." The equivalent passages may be compared, Denham's first:

Thus fell the King, who yet surviv'd the State,
With such a signal and peculiar Fate.
Under so vast a ruine not a Grave,
Nor in such flames a funeral fire to have:
He, whom such Titles swell'd, such Power made proud
To whom the Scepters of all *Asia* bow'd,
On the cold earth lies th'unregarded King,
A headless Carkass, and a nameless Thing.
                    (*Destruction of Troy*, lines 542–549)

Dryden's version is, untypically, more succinct:

Thus Priam fell, and shar'd one common fate
With Troy in ashes, and his ruin'd state:
He, who the scepter of all Asia sway'd,
Whom monarchs like domestic slaves obey'd.
On the bleak shore now lies th'abandon'd king,
A headless carcass, and a nameless thing.
                    (*Second Aeneis*, 758–763)

The last line in each passage translates line 558 of Vergil's *Aeneid* II. Denham has managed to condense the original into 549 shorter English lines, despite his indulgence in triplets; Dryden has required 763 English lines to cover the same material. Although Denham never says so, perhaps he felt that Vergil writing in English would have written approximately as many lines of verse as he had written in Latin, for in all stages of his translations Denham always comes quite close — at some cost, no doubt — to equaling exactly the number of lines of his original.

If Denham's "Passion of Dido for Aeneas" is also a product of the period of Vergilian revision at Wilton, it shows several characteristics that oddly clash with those of *The Destruction of Troy*. Of the 558 lines of Vergil which went into Denham's *Destruction of Troy*, only some 420 are represented in the Hutchinson manuscript. In the manuscript these 420 lines are translated by 406 lines, whereas in *The Destruction of Troy* their translation requires 407 lines. The revision at Wilton which produced *The Destruction of Troy* therefore involved not only Denham's allowing himself the liberty of triplets, but also a very slightly increased expansiveness over his earlier effort. The situation with regard to the "Passion of Dido" is just the reverse. Allowing for the fact that the "Passion" is a deliberately restricted translation of excerpts only from the fourth *Aeneid*, not an attempt at the whole book nor even at a single continuous sequence of lines (see n. 39, above), it still represents about 255 of Vergil's original hexameters. The "Passion of Dido" uses 258 English lines to render the 255 of the Latin: numerical approximation is close, but the ratio is contrary to that of *The Destruction of Troy*, wherein the English lines were fewer than the Latin. Another marked difference of the "Passion" from the *Destruction* is that the "Passion" contains no triplets, against the six of the *Destruction*. But most peculiar of all are the results of comparing the "Passion of Dido" with the equivalent parts of Denham's *Aeneid* translation preserved in the Hutchinson manuscript. In the latter version the 255 Latin hexameters are represented by about 286 English lines (exact equation is impossible) among which occur *five triplets*. Revision of the Hutchinson *Aeneid* IV, then, required Denham to compress, and to eliminate triplets, in order to achieve "The Passion of Dido for Aeneas," whereas revision of the Hutchinson *Aeneid* II to produce *The Destruction of Troy* involved the reverse procedure: expansion, and the addition of triplets.

A far more important work of poetic revision that Denham almost certainly carried out during his leisure at Wilton was the major overhauling to which he subjected *Coopers Hill*. The "A" text published in 1642, 1643, and 1650 was broken to bits, melted down, and largely recast, so that it was only by coincidence that the new version, the first recension of the "B" text, should have exactly the same number of lines (354) as the original. Hardly a line remained unaffected, and the internal proportions of the poem were drastically altered; the political allusions of the 1642 poem had now become pathetically outmoded, and many of the changes were attempts, if not to bring the references up to date, to make them more universal, less susceptible to loss of meaning with the vicissitudes of time. Among the additions that went to constitute the "B" text were the famous "Thames couplets" which were to carry the fame of *Coopers Hill* well into the eighteenth century, if not even to our own time, but they were not needed to guarantee the poem's high reputation among Denham's contemporaries. The new text of *Coopers Hill* was brought out by Humphrey Moseley (who already had brought out the "A" text editions of 1650) under a title-page date of 1655. The volume carried an ambivalent and somewhat mendacious statement "To the Reader," signed only with the initials J. B., the net purpose of which was (understandably) to have the "B" text supplant the "A." Unfortunately, George Thomason did not rise to J. B.'s bait, and neglected to add this edition of *Coopers Hill* to the two (1642 and 1650) already in his collection.[41] Since

---

[41] Thomason appears not to have been alone in failing to respond to J. B.'s contention. Although the 1655 first edition of the "B" text of *Coopers Hill* (Wing D996) is not a very rare book, it seems to have had no discernible effect on the growth of appreciation of the poem. No allusion to or quotation from *Coopers Hill* prior to 1668 (date of the second edition of the "B" text, in *Poems and Translations*) can or need be exclusively identified with the "B" text. Imitation of the famous "Thames couplets," unique to the "B" text, which might be crucial in dating the reception of the "B" text, in fact proves not to be. Except for a rather flaccid "strong and easy, deep and clear," in Charles Montague's *On the Death of Charles II* (1685), the couplets appear hardly to have struck the poetic imagination until after Dryden's comment on them in his "Dedication of the *Aeneis*" (1697). The imitation that Banks finds in Fage's *St.*

Moseley did not need to reregister the poem, no direct clue survives as to the time of year *Coopers Hill* appeared in its new text. Denham's *Destruction of Troy,* however, *was* new, and Moseley entered his right to that in the Stationers' Register on February 5, 1655/6. Although the latter poem was issued under date of 1656, it seems permissible to infer that Denham or his agent conveyed manuscripts of both poems to Moseley at more or less the same time. The proximity of publication of the two poems, both revisions of earlier work, and certain indications of interinfluence between their texts permit virtual certainty that the revision of *Coopers Hill* belongs to the same Wilton period as the revision of the *Aeneid* translation.[42]

Leonard's Hill (1666) (*Poetical Works*, p. 343) — "To taste of Hellicons inspiring streams, / Although perhaps not half as clear as Thames" — cannot be specified as imitating the "Thames couplets." The lines lack the characteristic antithesis that fascinated the imitators, and the ideas are all to be found in the "A" text of *Coopers Hill*, apart from the "Thames couplets" context. The first line corresponds to *Coopers Hill*, lines 2–3 (both "A" and "B" texts): "did taste the streame / Of Helicon"; the second to a line on the Thames in the Narcissus passage ("A," 239; "B," 213): "The streame is so transparent, pure, and cleare."

Surprisingly, only two utilizations of the 1655 "B" text edition of *Coopers Hill* can be established: (1) a copy of that edition, corrected, served as copy text for the compositor who set the 1668 edition in type; (2)more surprisingly, it was this edition that served as the basis of Moses Pengry's Latin translation of *Coopers Hill*, published at Oxford in 1676, when the fuller version of 1668 had already been twice published (1668, 1671).

Most surprising of all, however, is the fact that in an advertisement in which Moseley lists Denham's *Destruction of Troy* as "printed this Terme" (therefore presumably dating the advertisement to the spring of 1656), he lists among his other stock "Coopers Hill, a Poem written by Mr *John Denham* Esq, the 2d Edition with Additions, 4º" — that is to say the "A" text edition of 1650 — and fails entirely to mention J. B.'s edition, which nonetheless he must have published prior to *The Destruction of Troy*. (Moseley's continuing to list the "Second Edition" as late as this casts considerable doubt on my argument [*PMLA*, LXXIX (1964), 242–253] that the "Third Edition" listed by White Kennet for 1660 must, if real, have belonged to late 1650; most likely, it would now appear, that edition never existed.)

[42] Compare *Coopers Hill*, line 132: "But Princes swords are sharper than their stiles" with *Destruction of Troy*, line 48: "Their swords less danger carry than their gifts"; and *Coopers Hill*, line 176: "nor mock the plowmans toyl" with *Destruction of Troy*, line 295: "And mocks the Ploughmans toil." These resemblances did not exist between the respective earlier versions of the works (see my "Vergil's First Georgic and Denham's *Coopers Hill*," *PQ*, XLII [1963], 542–547). The "A" text of *Coopers Hill*, however, already contained several explicit echoes of Denham's un-

By way of original composition, perhaps the poem "The Progress of Learning" may also be assigned to this same period. It is a long essay (224 lines) in the meditational style of parts of *Coopers Hill*, and on a theme stated in the better-known poem: "Can knowledge have no bound, but must advance / So far, to make us wish for ignorance?" (*Coopers Hill*, "A," 179–180; "B," 145–146). In 1668, when it was first published, this poem was prefaced by eight lines (beginning "My early Mistress, now my Antient Muse") in the valedictory style Denham affected in his last years. That fact may indicate that "The Progress of Learning" is also late, but the poem may still very well have been written in the Wilton period, with only the preface being late. It is certainly a poem composed within the penumbra of *Coopers Hill*.

Even without benefit of the revision that produced the "B" text and the "Thames couplets," *Coopers Hill* was increasing in reputation. Herrick's tribute of 1648 to Denham's "Prospective Poem" has already been noticed, and in 1652 Henry Vaughan, in *The Mount of Olives*, passingly alluded to Cooper's Hill as echoing yet the pipe and wit of its "learned swain." The year 1654 produced an example of what is said to be the sincerest form of flattery: in celebration of the conclusion of a peace with Holland, Oxford University issued, under the title of *Musarum Oxoniensum* Ἐλαιοφορία, a collection of verses in Latin, Greek, Hebrew, French, Welsh, Anglo-Saxon, and English, addressed to the Lord Protector. Among the English contributions was one fifty-line effort by William Godolphin, student of Christ Church, which was almost entirely a shameless pastiche of lines plagiarized from *Coopers Hill*.[43] In 1657 *Coopers Hill* was again associated with plagiarism

---

published translation of the *Aeneid*, and Herrick, as has been seen, had already discerned the Vergilian quality of *Coopers Hill* (see n. 11, above). All these matters are more thoroughly canvassed in *Expans'd Hieroglyphicks*, my edition of *Coopers Hill*. See also my " 'Lost,' 'Authorized,' and 'Pirated' Editions of John Denham's *Coopers Hill*," *PMLA*, LXXIX (1964), 242–253.

[43] See *Expans'd Hieroglyphicks*, App. C.

of a more benign sort, when at least twenty-nine lines of the "A" text found their way into twelve of the choice "Epithets . . . Phrases [and] . . . General Forms upon all Occasions, Subjects, and Theams" compiled by Joshua Poole in his poetasters' and plagiarists' handbook, *The English Parnassus: or, a Helpe to English Poesie.*[44] Robert Fage's derivative *St. Leonard's Hill*, among the earliest of many imitations, although not printed until 1666, may nonetheless also be ascribed to the early fame of *Coopers Hill*, for analysis reveals its distinct affinity with the "A" rather than the "B" text of Denham's poem.[45]

---

[44] See my "Denham's *Coopers Hill* and Poole's *English Parnassus*," *MP*, LXI (1964), 253–260, and *Expans'd Hieroglyphicks*, App. D.

[45] See *Expans'd Hieroglyphicks*, App. E.

v: Conspiracy

Some study plots, and some those plots t'undoe,
Others to make'em, and undoe'em too.

MEANWHILE POSSIBLY the first intimation of Denham's participation in Royalist conspiracy comes to us from March 1654/5. In that month the traitor Henry Manning, a tool of Thurloe the chief of Cromwell's intelligence system, handed to the King a paper pretending to prove the Earl of Pembroke's readiness to countenance and sustain a Royalist rebellion. The paper, bearing the Earl's seal, gives details of men, arms, and supplies allegedly assembled at Wilton, which presumably still was Denham's refuge.[1] What Pembroke's real role in the affair was remains impenetrable, but early in the same March Penruddock's rebellion in the west of England had come to grief, accompanied both before and after by a wave of arrests of Royalists by an alert government.[2] Thur-

---

[1] "My Lord of Pembroke will have (& hath att present near 40 horse att Wilton in his Stables & Parke Some very good) on notice though he do not shewe himselfe. Also of one Sort of Armes & other altogether neare 500. In Mr Jeffery Betts hands living in his house there & Mr Arthur Saunders att Salisbury neare 5000ʰ in money, etc. All these things my Lord would willingly have seized for the advance of his Maties Service on any occasion" (Clarendon S.P., Vol. 50, ff. 292–293 [*C.Cl.S.P.*, III, 219]).

[2] A general uprising had been planned throughout England for February. The date was first set for February 6, then successively postponed to February 13 and March 8. Government vigilance, however, was already in evidence before the end of 1654; arrests began as early as January. The general rising was effectively disrupted before it began, and only at Salisbury (but without any noteworthy support from Pembroke) and westward into Dorset and Somerset did it break out in the least according to plan, only to be quickly crushed. The succeeding arrests occurred in two stages. The first, which occupied March and April, was an attempted roundup of those directly implicated in the rising. The second, in May and June, was stimulated by Manning's report from Cologne on May 14 of a plot to assassinate the Protector, and was aimed at

loe's intelligence apparatus increased its activity, and in May Manning wrote to Thurloe from the court of Charles II to inform him that John Denham was one of a number of Royalist agents in England who sent weekly reports to the King.[3] Early in the next month, apparently on the evening of Friday, June 8, Denham was one of a batch of ten Royalists seized by the authorities "in and about London." The following day the Council of State committed five of the group to the Tower, four to the sergeant at arms, and ordered that "Mr John Denham be confined to some place which himselfe shall make Choice of being not less then twenty Miles from London."[4] This favoritism is hard to understand, especially in view of Manning's incrimination of Denham in May. On June 21/July 1 Manning wrote again: "Remember the Colonells Francis Lovelace, Edward Villars, & one Mr John Denham. . . . I am confident you have hindered the Protector's murder by your diligence."[5] The very next day he wrote, "speaking of Devonshire's emprisonment, I told [Gerrard] I could not im-

---

breaking up the entire Royalist subversive network. It was when this second purge spread back from the provinces to London in June that Denham was caught in the dragnet. For a full and enlightening discussion of this entire series of episodes, see David Underdown, *Royalist Conspiracy in England 1649–1660* (New Haven, 1960), esp. chaps. 7, 8.

[3] "I am glad to heare you lay about you, remember Denham, the Lady Isabella Humphrey, Painter the Chirurgeon, Mr Symon Potter that remayneth at the Lady Stanhops & Sir Luis Kirke who are weekely Intelligencers here" (S.P. Dom., ser. 18, Vol. 97, no. 109 [f. 225] [*C.S.P.D.: 1655*, p. 193]). A copy of this enciphered letter, partly deciphered, is in Clarendon S.P., Vol. 50, f. 81.

[4] Order Book, Protector's Council (S.P. Dom., ser. 25, Vol. 76, pp. 128–130): "Saturday 9 June 1655 . . . The Lord Lambert Reports the names of some persons that were apprehended the last night in and about London. Ordered by his Highness with the advise of his Counsell That the Lord Newport, Andrew Newport his brother, Jeffrey Palmer, ffrancis Lord Willoughby of Parham and Henry Seymor Esqr be committed to the Tower of London. That S^r ffrederick Cornwallis, Mr Edward Prodgers, Mr Thomas Panton and Maior Generall Ayers be Committed to the Custody of the Serjeant at Armes attending the Counsell. That Mr John Denham be confined to some place which himself shall make Choice of being not less then twenty Miles from London till further order."

[5] S.P. Dom., ser. 18, Vol. 98, no. 43 (f. 127v) (*C.S.P.D.: 1655*, p. 212; a similar letter is in Clarendon S.P. (see *C.Cl.S.P.*, III, 43).

agine for what, unlesse it should be for lending Charles Stuart money, hee replyed to me againe hee did know of the summe he lent, & so doth Denham." [6] On June 29/July 9 Manning mentioned Denham again, but no further move was made against him, although arrests and rearrests of other Royalists went on. [7] The Royalists abroad seem to have had a confused picture of the episode too, for on July 30[?]/August 9 Joseph Jane wrote from The Hague to Secretary Nicholas: "Capt. John Moore . . . reports yr Mr. Denham is not taken vpp, which was confidently reported and beleeved here." [8] Denham's rustication cannot be considered even a mild punishment, for according to a diary entry by Henry Townshend on June 20, the ban on coming within twenty miles of London extended to *all* Cavaliers, whether arrested or not. [9] A proclamation to that effect was soon issued by the Protector, and its enforcement was not relaxed until the following February. [10] Also, despite Denham's seeming confinement to one place, he visited Wales sometime between the "last design" and September 14[?]/24, for on that date another of Thurloe's agents wrote from Cologne that "when Denham went to the Earle of Carbery from London into Wales" it was to continue activity against Cromwell in collusion with the Earl and Sir Francis Cobb of Yorkshire. [11] Whatever the truth in this,

---

[6] S.P. Dom., ser. 18, Vol. 98, no. 65 (f. 185); a deciphered copy. *C.S.P.D.: 1655*, p. 220, erroneously reports this letter as saying that Denham does *not* know.

[7] *C.S.P.D.: 1655*, p. 220; and see Underdown, *Royalist Conspiracy*, chaps. 7, 8.

[8] *Nicholas Papers*, III, 28.

[9] *Diary of Henry Townshend of Elmley Lovett, 1640–1663*, ed. J. W. Willis Bund (London, 1915), p. 29.

[10] Underdown, *Royalist Conspiracy*, p. 167; see also notes to copies of proclamations listed in *Catalogue of the Pamphlets . . . Collected by George Thomason* (London, 1908).

[11] Clarendon S.P., Vol. 50, ff. 142–143 (*C.Cl.S.P.*, III, 58): "Mr Thomas Alsop, from Cullen the 24 Sept 55. . . . There is one Sr Francis Cobb, that I knew not of before, a Yorkshire man who hath been a chief agent in the last designe & is still acting against you. I know this by discourse with Morgan & Curtis here who tell me that when Denham went to the Earle of Carbery from London into Wales hee ordered them to produce their dispatches from this Sr Francis. . . ."

it failed to cost Denham his freedom, and on January 5, 1655/6, at a time when the ban against Royalists entering London was still in effect, Denham visited Evelyn at the latter's home at Sayes Court, Deptford, well within the twenty-mile limit, and in rather mystifying company: "Came to visite me, my Lord *Lisle* sonn to the Earle of Leycester, with Sir Charles *Ouseley*, tw[o] of the Usurpers Council; Mr. Jo: *Hervey*, & Jo: *Denham* the Poet &c." [12] It is gratifying to see Denham identified as "the Poet," although one wonders what Evelyn intended by "&c." Nonetheless Denham is thus revealed to be on social terms with no fewer than three members of the Protector's Council, counting also the Earl of Pembroke. Perhaps the fact in itself is enough to account for his immunity from imprisonment; perhaps Thurloe's more reliable informants indicated to him that Denham was really harmless; perhaps there is a less creditable reason. What lies behind an anonymous letter of news sent from England to the royal court on February 19, 1655/6, one may only guess. After a recital of daily arrests and committals to the Tower and other prisons, the writer adds another message in invisible ink:

. . . I have wrote several [letters] to Mr C: but have never heard from him, he is in towne, I have beene at his lodging and sent thither; but he conceales himselfe from mee, upon what reason I canot imagine; and therefore am ye less troubled, but I believe Mr Rainsford and Mr Denham whoe were allwayes great enemys of your kindnesse to mee disswade him from it; to my certayne knowledge they have in past transactions done mee severe preiudice with you, and will doe agayne if within [their] power; but I will bee soe vayne as to say I have been generally in ye right and they in ye wronge; and I thinke I am like to be soe still. I have noe defence agaynest calumny, but y^r knowledge. . . . [13]

In the absence of identification of the parties involved it cannot

---

[12] *The Diary of John Evelyn*, ed. E. S. de Beer, Vol. III, *Kalendarium* (Oxford, 1955), p. 165.

[13] Clarendon S.P., Vol. 49, ff. 384, 386 (*C.Cl.S.P.*, III, 21). The letter consists of a

be determined if this reveals merely a petty Royalist backbiting intrigue, or an obstructionism more reprehensible. Whatever the truth, the seeming ambiguity of Denham's role in the events of 1655 appears to have done no damage to his good name among his Royalist friends, nor ever to have been cast up against him. Nonetheless, it is hard to believe that Denham would wish to commemorate in verse his role in the arrests of 1655.

Banks has advanced to Denham's canon a set of Royalist "Verses on the Cavaliers Imprisoned in 1655," but there is practically no reason to believe that Denham really wrote this poem. He did not include it in his *Poems and Translations* of 1668, nor was it ever ascribed to him by any contemporary; the suggestion that it is Denham's was in fact put forward by nobody prior to the late C. H. Firth, who did so on the basis of the wispiest of arguments.[14] The speaker in the poem reviews the cases of some four-

---

folded sheet with the cover letter on the right-hand openings, the invisible-ink message on the blanks.

[14] Firth's argument, which consists of four main points, was put forward in *N & Q*, 7th ser., X (1890), 41–42. Although elaborately argued, the reasoning is quite void of substance. The four points are as follows:

"1) John Denham was arrested with the persons mentioned [in the poem] early in June 1655. [Firth then quotes the order-in-council of June 9, naming those arrested on the 8th.]

2) In the second place, it is exactly in the style of those occasional poems which Denham was fond of writing — full of the personal references in which he was accustomed to indulge. Compare the poems on 'Lord Croft's Journey to Poland,' on 'Killigrew's Return . . .' and on 'Sir John Mennis going from Calais. . . .' . . . The metre of this poem — not a very common metre — is the same as that of the poem on Killigrew. . . .

"3) This poem is from a copy in the Clarendon MSS. in the Bodleian . . . Mr. Macray [editor of *C.Cl.S.P.*, I–III] . . . thinks the poem to be a copy, and not an original. It is remarkable that a copy of Denham's poem on Killigrew is also to be found amongst Clarendon's papers. . . .

"4) If it was not written by Denham the absence of any allusion to so prominent a Cavalier as Denham is difficult to understand."

Since there is no logic binding these arguments, they may as well be dealt with in order as they occur:

1) Fourteen Cavaliers are named in the poem; ten are named in the order-in-council as having been arrested on June 8. Of those named in the order-in-council only three are also named in the poem: Sir Frederick Cornwallis, Ed. Progers ("Ned

teen imprisoned Royalists, and pretends ignorance of what they are in prison for (most were, in fact, held without specific charge).[15] He also represents himself as one of the prisoners — "Wee prisoners all pray" (line 45) — a claim Denham could not honestly have made. Only a self-defeating and perverse argument for Denham's authorship would entail on itself the explanation that Denham failed to print the poem in 1668 because it contains the

---

Progers" in the poem), and Thos. Panton ("Tom Panton"). Of the five prisoners important enough to be sent to the Tower on June 9, not one is mentioned in the poem, although the poem does mention several other Tower prisoners. Therefore it is not true to say that Denham "was arrested with the persons mentioned." Eleven of the persons mentioned in the poem were arrested on quite different occasions. The only immediate connection between Denham and those prisoners is that all were arrested, with many others, during the same year.

2) The general style of occasional poem to which "Verses on the Cavaliers" belongs is widespread in the period; yet distinctive differences might be pointed to between that poem, with its catalogue of names, and the three Denham poems with which it has been compared. Two of the latter involve Denham himself directly; that on Killigrew's and Murray's returns from their embassies deals exclusively with the debauchery of that pair of *soi-disant* statesmen. Nor is the meter shared by the "Killigrew" and "Cavaliers" poems so uncommon as Firth wishes to imply. Quite separately from any endeavors that can be attributed to Denham, no fewer than sixteen of the *Rump Songs* are written in the same meter. As might be expected, the meter seems to derive from an air to which the verses were expected to be sung: one of the *Rump Songs* in this meter ("A City Ballad," *Rump*, II, 37) identifies its tune as that of *Down in a Bottom*, another ("A Psalm sung by the People," *Rump*, II, 86) as that of *Up tails all*; two others ("Rump Rampant," *Rump*, II, 19, and "The History of the Second Death of the Rump," *Rump*, II, 128) less facetiously identify the air as the same as that for "Last [or, The] Parliament sat as snug as a Cat." None of the printed *Rump Songs* begins with this line, but the line occurs (*Rump*, I, 317) as the opening of the fourteenth stanza of the poem entitled "The Rebells Reign" (*Rump*, I, 315–318), datable by internal references to 1653. The last half of the poem, beginning with this stanza, may well have circulated as a separate poem, and become connected with the first half, on roughly the same subject — the establishment of the Protectorate — through identity of metrical and rhyme pattern.

At best, "meter" and superficial subjective judgments about "style" stand as fairly flimsy evidence for authorship, but here, unless all poems of the period in this "style" and meter are to be attributed to Denham, they would seem to constitute no evidence at all.

3) Perhaps this point has some cogency that escapes me. I am prepared to grant that Denham's poem on Killigrew is to be found in the Clarendon MSS. I am equally willing to agree that the poem on the Cavaliers is to be found in the Clarendon MSS. Is it suggested that Denham had an exclusive purveyorship of verses to Sir Edward Hyde's State Papers? (The two poems are copied in different handwritings.)

false implication (if he was the author) that he had suffered more severely in 1655 than he actually had. Denham could presumably have rectified the prevaricating lines had they been his; otherwise the poem is one that he, or any Royalist who could warrantably claim it without embarrassment, should have been quite happy to own in the Restoration. The most sensible conclusion to reach is that Denham had nothing to do with this poem.[16]

---

4) It is hard to know at which end to pick up this argument. Three statements may be made, however, perhaps pertinent to its implications:

a) Denham was *not* a very prominent Cavalier.

b) The poem fails to allude to very many quite prominent Cavaliers imprisoned in 1655. Especially worthy of note is the absence of any allusion to such prominent Cavaliers as Lord Newport of High Ercall and his brother Andrew Newport, or to Henry Seymour, chief Royalist financial agent in England, close personal associate of the King, and brother of the powerful Marquis of Hertford (see Underdown, *Royalist Conspiracy*, pp. 64–66, 165), or even to the Presbyterian "New Cavalier" convert to the King, Lord Willoughby of Parham, all of whom were named in the same order-in-council with Denham. If the poem *was* written by Denham the absence of such allusion is difficult to understand.

c) Denham was not one of the Cavaliers imprisoned in 1655. He was ordered released after only a single night in custody.

Firth's reasoning seems to me wholly without merit. I can see no more reason for accepting the "Verses on the Cavaliers Imprisoned in 1655" as Denham's than I can for any other unattributed anonymous seventeenth-century political satire.

[15] One surprising piece of inside information seems to have been possessed by the author of the "Verses on the Cavaliers" which, as far as I know, has not been noticed. In May 1655 a certain Richard Hannam informed Thurloe that a group of Royalists was planning to kill Cromwell with a "stone-bowe made after a very extraordinary manner, & would shoot a bullet of Carbine bignesse about 40 yards with an incredible strength" (quoted by Underdown, *Royalist Conspiracy*, p. 163, from *S.P. Thurloe*). Following this report there was a roundup of Royalists in the Covent Garden district on May 21 which brought in, among others, Richard, Lord Byron (Underdown, p. 163). Although Underdown doubts the truth of the stonebow story, the author of "Verses on the Cavaliers" shows himself perfectly aware of the basis of Lord Byron's arrest:

> Lord Biron wee know was accus'd of a Bow
> Or of some other dangerous Plott
> But hee's noe such foole, for then (by the rule)
> His Bolt had bynne sooner shott.
>
> (lines 21–24)

[16] Because I continue to find unconvincing the case for a friendship between Denham and Waller at this time, I cannot use the manifestly unfriendly reference

After the visit to Evelyn in January 1655/6, Denham drops out of sight for a year and a half.[17] During the interval *The Destruction of Troy* was published, and *Coopers Hill*, if it had not previously come out. When next he comes to light, in June 1657, he is on the Continent again, in Brussels; he is named to Thurloe in a letter of intelligence as having knowledge of a Royalist "desperate designe" to be carried out in England by his young companion the Duke of Buckingham.[18] In December he is referred

to Waller in "Verses on the Cavaliers" as evidence against Denham's authorship. On the contrary, the reference almost moves me to accept Denham as the author. Waller by 1655 had separated himself completely from Royalist politics, and in that year two editions appeared of his "Panegyrick to my Lord Protectour" (entered on the Stationers' Register May 20). The author of "Verses on the Cavaliers" excuses himself from continuing his catalogue of names by explaining that "Waller intends to use them as ends / To patch up his next Panegyrick." Despite Denham's compliment to Waller in *Coopers Hill*, and despite the habit of other writers of linking their names together, occasional evidence hints that mutual ill will may have subsisted between Waller and Denham.

[17] What may be another faint echo of Denham's affairs is heard on February 21, 1656/7, a Saturday, when a harassed House of Commons postponed until the following Monday the reading of a petition from the indefatigable George Wither (*Commons Journal*, VII, 495). Its subject matter is not revealed, nor does it appear in the records for Monday, nor ever again.

[18] The letter, sent on June 7/17, from Col. Bamfield, states: "[I] am told for Certayne the Duke of Buckingham is in England which I doe very much believe & that (if he be there) 'tis about some desperate designe, either for some rysing in ye Citty, or some attempt upon ye protector person . . . I am told positively he is there & that his designe (what ever it is) is knowne by one Mr Denham who is here . . ." (intercepted copy in Clarendon S.P., Vol. 55, ff. 47–48 [*C.S.P.D.: 1657–1658*, p. 6; *S.P. Thurloe*, VI, 364; *C.Cl.S.P.*, III, 307]). The letter goes on to implicate in the plot Sir Frederick Cornwallis, the Countess of Newport, Major Anscot, and Col. Rogers. The erratic Duke's presence in England was also reported in a letter dated June 2/12, but perhaps of the preceding year: "It is believed that Bux is privately in England . . . treating for a marriage with Ld Fairfax's dgtr. This seems a little romantic" (Clarendon S.P., Vol. 93, f. 164). In the latter judgment Bamfield was wrong; Buckingham's marriage to Mary Fairfax was a political act that Cromwell recognized as subversive (see p. 125, below, and n. 24).

Bamfield was acquainted with Denham, for it was Bamfield who accompanied the Duke of York to France in the escape to which Denham was an accomplice. In the demoralizing poverty of exile Bamfield had been seduced into informing for Thurloe. His predecessor, Manning, had been "executed" by Royalists outside Cologne in December 1655.

to again in another letter in a somewhat puzzling context. Sir Allen Apsley writes to Hyde on the 12th, using code names, that he finds it hard to choose suitable books for him, but has given directions to have sent, among others, a "small piece lately translated out of French, they say by Mr. Denham, and much commended by the wits."[19] What this "small piece" might be no clue reveals; among Denham's known translations of poems none is from the French, nor did he publish any known translation during the 1650's except for *The Destruction of Troy*. Apsley's informants of course might have been wrong in their ascription of this piece, whatever it was, and the possibility should not be overlooked that the "piece" had no literary existence at all. The Royalist correspondence of the interregnum is couched in various sorts of ciphers, including codes based on the jargon of commerce: place-

---

[19] Clarendon S.P., Vol. 56, f. 335 (*C.Cl.S.P.*, III, 401): "Rob Townsend [Apsley] to my goode friende Mr Towser [Hyde]: Decemb. ye 12 . . . you have imposed a harde taske on mee to chuse a booke ffor you. Those kynde of bookes I reade are such as you have neyther leaysure or patience to endure. I have given my kynsman dyrections to sende you a small booke called Tylenus agnst the tryers, which is a smarte peice. I have also desyred hym to sende you another smale peice lately translated out of frenche they say by Mr Denham, and very much commended by our witts, but I prefer Tylenus before it." "Nal" Apsley, brother of Lucy Hutchinson, matriculated at Trinity College, Oxford, on the same day as Denham, November 18, 1631 (Foster, *Alumni Oxonienses*, I, 393). The two appear to have grown increasingly involved in the same Royalist underground groups toward the end of the interregnum. The suggestion has already been made that Apsley may have been the avenue through which his sister acquired her copy of Denham's *Aeneid* translation (see chap. i, p. 12 n. 17, above). His uncertainty as to Denham's part in the French translation is therefore surprising, if the reference is to a genuine literary production. In a quite separate letter of November 26, 1658, the word "books" served as code word for "money," and in a letter written by Hyde on July 9/19, 1659, "books" meant "letters of intelligence."

"Tylenus," however, was at least a real piece: *The Examination of [Daniel] Tilenus before the Triers; in order to his intended settlement in the office of a Publick Preacher in the Commonwealth of Utopia*, entered in the Stationers' Register by R. Royston on October 31, 1657, and published under date of 1658 (Wing W3343). This piece was a militant High Church tract by Laurence Womock (1612–1686), later bishop of St. David's.

Daniel Tilenus was a sixteenth-century reformer.

names are interchanged, names of commodities substituted for arms, ships, military units, and so forth. Perhaps the books discussed by Apsley are of a similar nature, and Denham's "translation" means a different kind of transaction entirely lost now to discovery. Whether Denham was then in or out of England, Apsley's letter in no way indicates.

When three months later, in March 1657/8, Denham comes into evidence again, he is once more certainly in England. On the 3d of the month, because of a resurgence of subversive activity, a new proclamation ordered all Papists and Royalists to leave London and to stay within five miles of their usual residences. Denham probably no longer had a "usual residence" outside London, and on March 11 he was granted a license, under the signature of the Protector, to live in "Bury, co. Suffolk," that is, Bury St. Edmunds.[20] Why he chose this spot is not immediately clear, although a few motives may be suggested. It was for one thing central to East Anglia, near various of his like-minded Royalist friends, such as Sir Allen Apsley and the Earl of Oxford. Other motives may be suggested by another reference to Denham in the same month, but this reference involves Denham in a complicated background of Royalist intrigue that requires some preliminary elucidation before Denham's place in it can be made moderately clear.

The Royalist party in England, like that abroad, was split into several quarrelsome factions. Through the years from 1648 to 1660 these factions dissolved, coalesced, and changed coloration, but throughout the period two dominant factions remained at all times prominent, perhaps because they alone had the self-awareness, at least within their leaderships, to recognize that they were factions. These two were the "Louvre" or "Queen's Party" and the "Old Cavaliers." [21]

---

[20] *C.S.P.D.: 1657–1658*, p. 552.

[21] The following discussion of the Royalist factions is heavily indebted to Underdown's study, *Royalist Conspiracy*.

The division between these parties had its formal origin in the middle of 1646, when Queen Henrietta Maria had urged the removal to Paris from Jersey of the sisteen-year-old Prince of Wales; it was to bring him to her that she sent that deputation of Lords who crossed Denham's path at Caen.[22] The Prince's advisers, led by Sir Edward Hyde, strenuously objected that the youth's abandonment of British Crown soil would jeopardize his father's negotiations with the Army and with the Scots and would create public distrust in England. Thereafter Hyde's long-range policy was one of waiting for the English republic to collapse of its inner inconsistencies, and above all he opposed alliances with the Scots to restore the King at the cost of his sovereignty, or with the English Presbyterians desirous of restoring a king shackled by the provisions of the Treaty of Newport. In this Hyde was at one with the solid core of Anglican Old Cavaliers in England, who loathed both the Scots and the Presbyterians. After the defeat at Worcester Hyde's influence became dominant over Charles II, who made him High Chancellor.

Henrietta Maria's policies varied, but were constantly opposed to those of Hyde. Her only principle was to regain the throne, and afterward to break as opportunity afforded whatever compacts or treaties expediency dictated. She showed her Bourbon heritage also in her failure to learn from her husband's mistakes (which she may have stage-managed) or from the defeat of the Scots at Worcester. The dislike and distrust she inspired in the true-blue protestant enemies of the throne was matched by the suspicion with which many of the loyal Anglican Cavaliers came to regard her.

Denham's first period of political exile, in 1646, had been spent in attendance on the Queen. It was from the Queen he had been sent with messages to Charles I at Caversham; it was chiefly with Jermyn, the Queen's secretary and one of the leaders of the Louvre faction, that he had conducted his correspondence in

---

[22] See chap. iii, p. 71 n. 33, above.

the months after the King's flight from Hampton Court; and he was later considered a fit man to send as an emissary to Scotland. He perhaps never thought of himself as a member of the Louvre faction, but it is clear why Hyde and his friends did. Hyde in his correspondence is always chilly and distant on the subject of Denham, and it is worth remarking that although Denham's name occurs frequently in the Clarendon State Papers, he is not mentioned once in the *History of the Rebellion*, even when Hyde is narrating incidents in which Denham took a prominent part.[23]

As an instrument to control and coordinate all the Royalist activity in England, Hyde had brought into existence in 1653 a secret directory under the portentous title of the Sealed Knot. The Knot, however, carried Hyde's policy of patient waiting to such an extreme of pusillanimity that Penruddock's rising of 1655 was carried out almost despite the Knot, although Hyde had had the King order the Knot at least to cooperate. The rebellion's failure somewhat restored the prestige of the Knot, and for the next two years it was able to carry on efficiently its policy of doing nothing.

---

[23] Denham's name does not occur in the index to Clarendon's *History of the Rebellion*, and I have been unable to find it in the text. Clarendon describes the mission sent by Henrietta Maria to the King at Caversham in 1647, but names only Sir John Berkeley and John Ashburnham as present; he records the flight from Hampton Court, and names only Berkeley, Ashburnham, and William Legg; as instrumental in the escape of the Duke of York he mentions only Col. Bamfield. From Clarendon's report of the mission sent by Charles II to collect money in Poland can be gathered only that it was conducted by Mr. Crofts. Perhaps the most flagrant example of what seems a deliberate suppression of Denham's name on Clarendon's part — there can be no question that the Chancellor was well aware of Denham's existence and of his part in all these transactions — is in that report of Denham's occupancy and loss of Farnham Castle earlier noted (p. 61, above), where Denham is effaced by reduction with his followers to "some Gentlemen who were willing to appear for the King."

The Chancellor's real motives for dislike of Denham may never be known, but the dislike at least seems to have been reciprocated. In 1667, the year of Clarendon's downfall, Denham dedicated a poem to the Earl of Bristol, who had initiated the attacks on Clarendon as early as 1663. Denham's second wife was reputed to be of Bristol's party, and was distantly related to the Earl. Other reasons, of course, one of which has been earlier suggested (see p. 31, above), might have motivated Denham's dedication.

By March of 1658, however, action appeared once again imminent: a long-standing Spanish promise of an invasion force to aid the King seemed almost about to materialize. A group chiefly of "new sprung up Cavaliers, such as young gentlemen lately come into their lands and estates," was preparing to support the Spanish landing by a new Royalist rebellion planned for March 1658. But the Sealed Knot's inertia had now become complete impotence by virtue of the treason of one of its members, so Hyde, regardless of the King's direct commission to the Knot, had to accord separate recognition to the New Cavaliers. Between the Knot and the New Cavaliers lay therefore an open space ideally suited for the breeding and chasing of private chimeras. One of the huntsmen on this plain was the Duke of Buckingham, and for a time at least John Denham seems to have ridden as one of his attendants.

Buckingham's vast estates in Yorkshire had been seized by the Parliamentary victors and bestowed upon the Lord General Fairfax. A rapprochement between Fairfax and Buckingham had obvious attractions for both men, providing mutual insurance against further revolutions of the wheel of state, and as early as 1653 hints began to appear of some such possibility. Buckingham's hopes of marrying Fairfax's daughter began to be bruited, and Buckingham seems also to have entertained hopes of converting Fairfax, unenthusiastic about Cromwellian monarchy, to support of the legitimist alternative. Official royal circles entertained similar hopes, but remained unwilling to trust Buckingham. When, therefore, Thurloe's agent at Brussels in June 1657 informed his employer that the Duke of Buckingham was in England "upon some desperate design" known to Denham, Denham was being credited with more knowledge of the Duke's idiosyncratic plans than was available even to the Royalist high command. In September 1657 Buckingham succeeded finally in marrying Mary Fairfax, but that achievement did not apparently complete his plans. In October 1657 he was arrested by the Council of State, and by the following March he was once more engaged in scheming.[24]

As the time for the Spanish invasion drew near, Hyde sent Daniel O Neill to England, as a personal emissary from the King to the underground. In carrying out this commission O Neill came upon Denham, and on March 3, 1657/8, he wrote to ask Hyde how far Denham might be trusted. The relevance of the question becomes clear in O Neill's report that Denham "denyes to have any correspondence in France," obviously a rejection by Denham of allegations of his partisanship with the Louvre. Further information conveyed to Hyde by O Neill about Denham was that "hee converses much [with the Duke of Buckingham] and has much interest with Lord Oxford." Finally O Neill implicated Denham in the private plotting of this confused time by adding that "hee is now going [to Lord Oxford] . . . with some foolish design from [Buckingham]."[25] What this foolish design was never appears,

---

[24] Buckingham's cousin Katherine Villiers was married to Denham's old patron, the Earl of Pembroke. In September, the month of Buckingham's marriage to Mary Fairfax, he was reported to Hyde at Brussels to have been arrested in Kent, whither he had allegedly gone to reconcile the Earl with his Countess (*C.Cl.S.P.*, IV, 82). In November, after his arrest, Buckingham was again reported to Hyde as being at York House, free on the Earl of Pembroke's bail of £10,000 or £20,000 (*ibid.*, p. 111). He was finally released in the new year, upon security of £20,000 given by his father-in-law Fairfax. Buckingham's arrest, ostensibly for violating an order to stay away from London, was really a response to his temerity in allying himself to the Lord General of whom Cromwell was growing suspicious. An anonymous letter sent to Fairfax at the time of the arrest reveals this aspect of the affair in a curious light. Members of the Protector's council had said, according to the letter, "that the Protector had all the king's priviledges of a king; and that no nobleman was to marry their children, or themselves, without the king's consent (*S.P. Thurloe*, VI, 617). (The occurrence of a copy of this letter in Thurloe's papers testifies to the surveillance kept by the secret service over Fairfax's correspondence.) The design, therefore, to which Denham was alleged to be privy, to some extent actually was a design against the Protector, however Bamfield misinterpreted its gravity or details.

[25] Clarendon S.P., Vol. 57, ff. 260–261: " 'Subtle' [O Neill] to Hyde: I pray lett [MS, 'tell'] mee know how far I may trust d.e.n.h.a.m. hee denyes to have any correspondence in f.r.a.n.c.e. hee converses much b.u.k.d.u.k.e. and has much interest with Lord ox.f.o.r.d. with whom hee is now going I feare with some foolish design from the other. . . ." The punctuated names are in (deciphered) cipher in the original: "Denham" is written "23.48.49.10.8.4"; the name rendered "b.u.k.d.u.k.e" signifies

but O Neill's notice of its existence reveals Denham in 1658 as an intimate of both Oxford and Buckingham, and as much more actively engaged in Royalist schemes than the evidence indicates he had been in 1655. Denham's familiarity with Buckingham went back at least to their collaboration in the ridicule of *Gondibert*, and that with Oxford also at least to Denham's period of exile. Oxford is mentioned in Denham's verses "To Sir John Mennis Being Invited from Calice to Bologne To Eat a Pig" as having upon one occasion shared a cart ride from Dunkirk to Calais with Mennis, Denham, and "a fat Dutch Woman."[26]

Hyde's reply to O Neill, however, shows that Denham's efforts for the King still lacked the Chancellor's esteem: "Wee know nothinge of Mr Denham, nor hath he any authority from hence."[27] Denham's next appearance in the records no doubt came about from his desire to remedy this professed ignorance on the part of the Royalist headquarters of his loyalty or his nature.

Before O Neill received his recall notice to the continent the Spanish invasion was called off, and the Royalist rebellion was effectively canceled without the damage of local uncoordinated outbreaks. The government was, as always, on the alert, and widespread arrests were made, but the absence of any actual insurrec-

---

of course, the Duke of Buckingham (*C.Cl.S.P.*, IV, 21; portions quoted by Underdown, *Royalist Conspiracy*, p. 225).

[26] The second stanza of the verse to Mennis begins with the lines, "Hadst thou not thy fill of Carting / *Will. Aubrey* Count of Oxon!" and the stanza in 1668 carried Denham's marginal note: "We three riding in a Cart from *Dunkirk* to *Calice* with a fat *Dutch* Woman who broke wind all along." Denham's modern editor glosses the second line with the note: "Perhaps this is William Aubrey, younger brother of John Aubrey, the author of *Brief Lives*. The title here given to him is, of course, jocular" (*Poetical Works*, p. 100 n. 3). But the entire poem is addressed to John Mennis and the apparent direction of this stanza to "Will. Aubrey" makes no sense — Mennis, too, was in that cart. G. C. Moore Smith provided what must surely be the answer to this problem in his review of the edition (*RES*, V [1929], 234) by proposing the irresistible emendation of "*Will.*" to "With," and so reading, "Hadst thou [Mennis] not thy fill of Carting / With *Aubrey* Count of Oxon!" Aubrey de Vere (1626–1703), the man to whom Denham went from the Duke of Buckingham in March 1657/8, was the 20th Earl of Oxford.

[27] Letter dated March 12/22, 1657/8, in Clarendon S.P., Vol. 57, f. 217.

tion meant that most of the prisoners were free again by autumn. Denham was not arrested, and his name appears once again in the records on September 14, less than a fortnight after the death of Cromwell, as the recipient of an official pass, for "William, Lord Herbert, John Denham, and five servants to go beyond seas." [28] William Herbert, called Lord Herbert by courtesy, was the eighteen-year-old son of Denham's patron, the Earl of Pembroke, and this journey may have been presented as a projected Grand Tour on which Denham would act as conductor to the young nobleman. But if Denham really did go beyond seas that September, it is evident that his real purpose was to establish himself more firmly with the exiled court as an authorized agent in England, and it is equally possible that Lord Herbert may have gone chiefly as an intermediary between his father and the King.

By November 20, at latest, Denham was already back in England, and evidently on a much firmer footing with the court. For on that date Henry Pryce wrote to Hyde from London a letter full of speculation about the vicissitudes in government to be anticipated from Oliver's death, and citing Denham as an authority on affairs: "Mr Denham inclines to their opinion who beleeve they [will] owne [Richard] Cromwell he complying with them in all their desires, rather then joyne with the Army who call into them all the Sects wch they abhor. The trueth is their distraction is great, but noe judgement can yet be made what the issue will be. Mr Denham wisht that the King in his letter to him had mentioned something of grace to Cromwell and the family; if fitt hasten it by a safe hand to some one for me; Mr Denham is very shy & hath reason." [29] From this it is evident that Denham

---

[28] *C.S.P.D.: 1658*, p. 580.
[29] Clarendon S.P., Vol. 59, ff. 220–223 (*C.Cl.S.P.*, IV, 111): " . . . It is now beleeved that extreme necessity of Money will inforce a Parliament wch will at least keepe of[f] a breach till it be called and for some time after though it be impossible to guesse what it will produce, though most thinke a Common-wealth, because it is like to consist of old Members & Presbiterians; yet Mr Denham inclines . . . [as in text]."

had had some kind of empowering letter from the King, and also that Denham believed himself to have some kind of access to Richard Cromwell. A further indication of Denham's enhanced standing is that his name is not spelled out in the cipher, but is represented by the single code designation "180," showing at the least that he had become an established topic of correspondence. The nature of Denham's "shyness" is unclear; either he was shy of revealing himself too openly to Richard Cromwell as a Royalist agent, or he was shy of approaching the court for an enlargement of his powers, possibly because of Hyde's implacability toward him. Further correspondence suggests, however, that it was on the former rather than on the latter score that Denham chiefly suffered trepidation.

In Pryce's next letter, at any rate, written to Hyde on December 2, 1658, he indicates that it was distrust of the new Protector's discretion that made Denham nervous: "Mr Denham is gone into the Countrey, beleeving that he is not capable of doing good in this Conjuncture. Whether Cromwell or Ld: Falconbridge were too open in their discourses I know not but the Councell came to the knowledge of it, from whence the disorders amongst themselves at Whitehall, I presume, first grew, & since Cromwell hath been persuaded to other wayes. Mr Denham will returne shortly, & what information he can collect amongst them for you or what other service he can doe you, he will. But Mr Rawlins . . . hath taken the manage of that affaire."[30] The matter is carried some way further in a subsequent letter, written to Hyde on January 17, 1658/9, by Denham's cousin Morley, one of the King's chaplains: "Mr Rawlins since his returne hither came to me with as much familiarity as if he had never injured me, & remembred my Cousin Denham to me, who as he sayth, bid him excuse him for not writing to mee, as being at this tyme suspected & observd, wch makes

---

[30] Clarendon S.P., Vol. 59, ff. 253–255. The letter begins with speculations on events to come, now that Oliver's funeral is over. "Falconbridge" was Thomas Belasyse, Earl Fauconberg.

him more wary then he would be otherwise, as being so advised by some great ones amongst them in whom he hath a great Interest."[31] Difficult as it is to read between the lines of these letters, it is evident from 1655 onward that Denham enjoyed some sort of countenance by certain of the Cromwellian grandees, including especially the Earl of Pembroke, and that now he was trying, in the more auspicious atmosphere following Oliver's death, to engage the less republican of these on behalf of a restoration of the King. His Cromwellian acquaintances had presumably saved Denham from imprisonment in 1655, and now they were advising him of the danger he stood in from Thurloe's still active intelligence service. In return, it was doubtless the communication with the King facilitated by Denham which allowed such a leader as Pembroke to glide gracefully with the tide and ultimately be honored at the coronation of Charles II.

When Denham's name next appears in the correspondence, on May 23, 1659, it is in a new constellation of conspiracy. On that day Alan Brodrick wrote to Hyde that "Mr Denham expresseth a desire of going to my Ld Oxford," and that Brodrick may have to send him, "it being very unfitt to leave that gentleman [Oxford] alone," although Brodrick "had much rather he were councelled by a faithful subject of the Kings, then any who is accounted a Partisan of the Queenes."[32] Little seems altered: Denham is still carrying messages to Lord Oxford, and is still suspected of belonging to the Louvre despite his protestation to O Neill of more than a year before, and despite his flirtation with Richard Cromwell reported by Pryce. Only the person writing to

---

[31] *Ibid.*, ff. 406–407.

[32] *Ibid.*, Vol. 61, ff. 9–12 (*C.Cl.S.P.*, IV, 209; also published in *State Papers collected by Edward, Earl of Clarendon* [Oxford, 1786], III, 477–478): " 'Hancock' [Brodrick] to Hyde: Mr Denham expresseth a desire of going to my Ld Oxford; if my dearest Cousin [Nal Apsley] doe not undertake that peice of freindship, after my advice, wch I suspend till my Cousin have absolutely resolved, as much more fitt then the other [Denham], but if my Cousin decline it, I will send downe Denham, it being very unfitt . . . [as in text]."

Hyde is different, and the emergence of Alan Brodrick is an index of the changes that had taken place in the Royalist underground — and in the government of England — since the cancellation of the proposed rebellion of March 1657/8. Among the New Cavaliers planning that uprising none had been more vigorous than John Mordaunt, younger brother of the Earl of Peterborough. Upon release from his consequent imprisonment he had at once signified to the King his willingness to resume active conspiracy without delay. Hyde at last decided to undo the Sealed Knot, and Mordaunt was granted at the very beginning of March 1658/9, together with the title of Viscount Mordaunt, a document called the "Great Trust and Commission." [33] Mordaunt gathered into the Great Trust representatives of a much wider spectrum of Royalist plotting than had been comprised under the Sealed Knot, including numerous Presbyterians and various activists. Although this new course was sanctioned by Hyde he may not have been entirely happy with it, and the strength the Trust derived from its broader base was partially offset by resentment against it on the part of older Royalists of all persuasions. Some resentment was no doubt that of Old Cavaliers toward the Presbyterians under Mordaunt's wing, but even Louvrists resented the Trust, and the strongest single factor in all the resentment seems to have been personal dislike of Mordaunt's youthful brashness and arrogance.

Alan Brodrick had been employed as secretary to the Sealed Knot, and upon dissolution of that group instead of submitting to Mordaunt and the Trust had begun correspondence with Hyde, in April 1659, on behalf of a small group of his own friends. On May 4, 1659, Brodrick had asked the King for formal recognition of his group, and a qualified recognition had followed, although Hyde instructed the group to take orders from the Trust.[34] Meanwhile, as we have seen, Denham had also embarked on inde-

---

[33] Underdown, *Royalist Conspiracy*, p. 235 (amply documented).
[34] *Ibid.*, p. 244.

pendent courses, using his influence with the Earl of Oxford at first as an instrument against Mordaunt, then as the basis of a separate Royalist faction led by himself. It was this sequence of events that led to the conjunction of Denham and Brodrick reported by the latter to Hyde in his letter of May 23. Whose influence upon Oxford was immediately responsible cannot be said, but the Earl refused an invitation from Mordaunt to join the Trust. Brodrick himself had some degree of friendship with Oxford, as did also Brodrick's first cousin and Denham's friend, Sir Allen Apsley, and all three shared a strong dislike for Mordaunt.[35]

Another Royalist who equally disliked Mordaunt had a much more flattering opinion of Denham than that implicit in Brodrick's letter. This was Philip Froude of Kent, who suggested to Hyde that a rival committee be set up to negotiate with the more responsible Royalist nobility who had no confidence in the Trust. Writing to Daniel O Neill on June 8, Froude named as men "of more years and knowlege in the world," fit for negotiations with "the more wary sort," William Ashburnham, Colonel John Russell (a member of the Sealed Knot), Sir Thomas Fanshawe, and Denham. The letter strongly supports Denham, and clears him not only of Louvre associations but also from imputation of the latest heresy: desire for a "compromise" restoration setting up the Duke of York as king. Froude conveys assurances from Ned Russell (Edward Russell, younger brother of Colonel "Jack" Russell), Denham, and others that much can be done "if the King or the Duke of York come over," and adds that Denham "by solemne protestation" denied correspondence with Lord Jermyn, and that "noe man alive doth more definitely and more earnestly rebuke those whoe owne or express a disafection to the King and preferring the Duke of York; his credit is great with the Lords of Hartford, Dorchester, Southamton, Carbery and divers others of great concernment whoe will concert with him and noe other;

---

[35] *Ibid.*, p. 236.

hee is now uppon contriving to rayse a good sum of monny for the King. . . ." The letter concludes with reference to Sir Henry Jones, "a person of good esteem with [Richard] Cromwell, with a promise from the latter of serving the King with the remainder of his power and his brother's [Henry Cromwell, governor in Ireland], and that then if the King would go to the fleet he doubted not to prevail; the persons interested durst not trust Cromwell, and so the matter was laid aside." [36] This last reference seems, then, to be to a continuation of the approaches to Richard Cromwell initiated by Denham.

On June 26 Allen Apsley wrote an obliquely worded letter to Hyde, revealing that he had been down to see the Earl of Oxford (presumably in response to Alan Brodrick's desire, alluded to in Brodrick's letter of May 23) whom he had found passionately loyal to the King, eager for an occasion to serve him, unwilling to take orders from Mordaunt, and fiercely defensive of Denham "whom hee has most desyre to trust having a greate oppinion of hys wisdome." Oxford had hotly insisted that Denham was not duped by a certain "most bitter enemy" to the King (perhaps Richard Cromwell) and that Hyde's communications with the Earl should

---

[36] Clarendon S.P., Vol. 61, ff. 131–132 (C.Cl.S.P., IV, 225, with some misreadings): "Much can be done if the King or 'Yorkduke' come. . . . Mr Denham doth assure me that if any such thing happens as that the King come that way [of] collchester in wch are manny foot Army wth other preparations . . . I might now say a word or two of your plenipotentiarys [Mordaunt?], I hope I shall have your pardon if not your thanks for it, for to say the truth many of the kings frinds and of great quality find themselves overlooked and are not well pleased att it; and least I should bee thought to speake beyond my knowlege, I shall instance you some particulars, Mr Denham sayes My Ld of Oxford is very ignorant of the kings designes, so is Ld Capell. . . . There is another sort of the kings frinds whoe take themselves to bee above the direction of Mr Mordent and Mr Newport, and they think the confidence to great for thir years and experience. The expedient for it, is that some of more years and knowlege in the world, have order to negotiate with the more wary sort of men; fit for this are Will: Ashburnham, Jack Russell, Sr Thomas Fanshaw and Mr Denham. Now because formerly when I pressed that Mr Denham might negotiate wth such persons as hee had interest wth, out of the beleefe hee did correspond wth My Ld Jermin, you did not think it fitt though he did by solemne protestation deny it. I am sure noe man alive . . .[as in text]."

be directed through Denham.[37] Less than a fortnight later, on July 8, Brodrick wrote that Oxford, who was expected in town, "resignes Himself very much to ye advice of Mr J. D."[38] A week later Brodrick wrote to Hyde, on the 16th, expressing friendliness toward Denham but still reflecting the imputation of Louvrism, although moderately, and suggesting its irrelevance: "Mr Denham lately offered me to goe to the King with full Instructions from all Partys, wch I had as frankly embraced, as he offered (being very kindly my freind, and finding it impossible to waite on you my selfe) had I not beleeved him too much of the Queene's faction. But there is now no roome for debate. . . ."[39]

Hyde delayed responding to Apsley's letter until July 29/August 8

---

[37] Clarendon S.P., Vol. 61, ff. 333–334 (C.Cl.S.P., IV, 251): "For Mr Towser [Hyde]: Most deare Sir, . . . in my last I tould you I would make a visit to that friend of myne [Earl of Oxford], least those reports which I tould you I had receyved from others, should bee arrived to hym; I fynde hym as passionate a lover of Mr Marshe [the King] hys person and interestes as I am of hys or yours. . . . Hee desyred mee to say as much to you and yr loving friend Mr Marshe as you would desyre to heare from one that truly loves you . . . hee desyres that when you write to him you will dyrect yrs to Mr D[enham] whom I mentioned in my last, and of whom hee has a very greate oppinion. my cosen [Brodrick] will convey them to hym. I tould hym what I mentioned to you of Mr D[enham] hys greatness with .445. [Richard Cromwell?] which uppon all occasions does continue to expresse hymselfe a most bitter enemy to Mr Marshe, hee [Oxford] replyed to mee that the other [Denham] knew hym [".455."] to bee the meanest wretche of men, and had no beter an oppinion of hym then wee had — hee [Oxford] would bee very glad of a goode occasion to serve you, of which hee is as impatient as a mettled hauke, styll bayting to begonne. Pray satisfye hym in thys particular in dyrecting yrs to hym to Mr D whom hee has most desyre to trust having a greate oppinion of hys wisdome. But if you know any reason to ye contrary, If you give mee private notice of it I can put hym of from that desyre otherwise pray let hym know as soone as you canne that I have performed hys commaundes in that particular." Apsley's prior letter reached Hyde later than this one, and it could not be found among the Clarendon State Papers in the Bodleian. Hyde was unable to supply any concrete evidence against Denham, as his response indicates (see below).

[38] Clarendon S.P., Vol. 58, ff. 119–120 (C.Cl.S.P., IV, 263; portions published in State Papers of Clarendon, III, 406): . . . My dearest Cosens [Apsley] neighbour [Oxford] will bee in Towne toomorrow who resignes Himself very much to ye advice of Mr J. D. where in you need not doubt my Care."

[39] Clarendon S.P., Vol. 62, ff. 138–139 (C.Cl.S.P., IV, 281–282; also published in State Papers of Clarendon, III, 526–528).

because a prior letter of Apsley's, referred to in the letter of June 26, had been delayed. Hyde assured Apsley of the King's great esteem for Oxford "and therefore it is not possible that hee should subiect him to ye directions of any man [i.e., Mordaunt]." Then followed an acknowledgment of Mordaunt's defects, offset by an estimate of his great merits. Hyde still refused to accede to Oxford's demands that correspondence with the Earl should pass only through Denham, but the official tone toward Denham had become markedly warmer: "We have all a very good opinion of Mr Denham, and as much confidence in him as any man, though we cannot draw him into an immediate correspondence. I hope all our friends will unite together and pardon each others infirmities. . . ."[40] The last sentence sounds like a response to Brodrick's desire to end factional squabbling.

Neither Brodrick nor Denham, however, was allowed to supersede Mordaunt, and the latter continued to develop plans for a new general Royalist rising. The time no doubt seemed ripe to some, for Richard Cromwell's peaceful accession to the Protectorate of his father had been followed by an inglorious downfall in April 1659 when the generals deposed him and restored the Rump expelled in 1653. Both Cromwellian politicians and Cromwellian army officers purged from their commands during the summer of 1659 could now be expected to have soured on the "Good Old Cause" and to have become potential Royalist recruits. Unsuccessful attempts were even made to win over Richard himself, although some Royalists (like Brodrick, for instance, in his letter to Hyde of July 8) found him fatuous.[41] The rising was scheduled for

---

[40] Clarendon S.P., Vol. 63, ff. 36–37 (C.Cl.S.P., IV, 298; also published in *State Papers of Clarendon*, III, 539–540): draft by Bulteale, endorsed by Hyde: "to N. Ap: August the 8, 1659: . . . I do in ye first place assure you upon my credit, that there is not a Person in the three Kingdomes, of whom the King hath a greater value and esteeme then my Lord of Oxford, or for whom hee hath a greater kindnesse and therefore it is not possible that hee should subiect him to ye directions of any man. . . . We have all a very good opinion of Mr Denham . . . [as in text]."

[41] In an earlier paragraph of that letter Brodrick had reported: "B. Throgmorton

August 1, but for all Mordaunt's energy it failed in the same manner as the rising of 1655. Just as that earlier rebellion has since carried the name of its only leader to come out effectively in arms, and is now known as Penruddock's Rising, so that of August 1659 has become Sir George Booth's Rising. Booth was a Presbyterian member of the Trust, and his momentary success in Lancashire and Cheshire was largely a Presbyterian affair, a fact that may partially account for the more prevalent Royalist apathy. The usual arrests followed its collapse, but the Rump could not exert Cromwell's iron grip, and Booth survived to be honored at the Restoration.

Denham's obstructionist plotting was not of the sort to get him arrested in consequence of Booth's Rising, and very little connection can be traced between him and the events of August. Just two weeks before the outbreak of the rebellion the Rump's Council of State considered a petition from John Denham for leave to come to London for the cure of his lameness.[42] The ban against Royalists in the capital still officially persisted, and Denham may have used his medical business as a cover for other dealings, but there can be no doubt of the reality of his lameness. In later years almost every characterization of Denham makes some mention of his limp, and this first reference to the affliction is of value in helping to illuminate certain events of 1666.

Another of Denham's activities that may bear some distant relationship to Booth's Rising is his composition in 1659 of the unseemly poetical exercise called in 1668 "News from Colchester

---

being yesterday at Whitehall R: Cr: fell into great commendation of Himself and ye governm^t of ye 3 Nations under Him in a Golden Mediocrity between A Topping Head [his father Oliver? or Charles I?] & a Filthy Tayle [the Rump] a Dialect peculiar to Himself not without Some pleasant dreams of being reinvested w[he]n ye Commonwealthmen and Optimates had sufficiently vexed each other and grown weary of y^t vexation . . ." (see n. 38, above). Richard had remained in Whitehall Palace after his deposition in order to avoid his creditors.

[42] Godfrey Davies, *The Restoration of Charles II 1658–1660* (San Marino, Calif., 1955), p. 104.

or, A Proper New Ballad of Certain Carnal Passages betwixt a Quaker and a Colt, at Horsly near Colchester in Essex." [43] George Thomason acquired on May 20, 1659, a broadsheet copy of this report of what others also considered a newsworthy event.[44] Although Denham's interest in the Quaker's misbehavior may have been stimulated by his own associations with the suggestively named locale of the episode — Horsely Parva had after all been his own estate — the August rising in England had been preceded throughout the country by a concerted Royalist propaganda campaign against the Quakers. The Quakers in 1659 had not yet become the gentle and pacific sect they have since been throughout most of their history; then they were a violent and fanatic set of zealots who terrorized more conservative Christians by deliberately anarchistic outrages. The Royalists in 1659 took advantage of the Quakers' universal disrepute and industriously circulated rumors of an impending Quaker insurrection. Consternation was widespread, and many a Royalist gentleman was enabled to arm himself and his household on the pretext to the local authorites of protecting his family from being murdered in bed by the Quakers. Denham's narrative of the Colchester Quaker's offense seems not very likely to have increased fear of the Quakers, however, if that was the Royalist aim, but rather to have subjected them to the contrary sentiments of ridicule and contempt. Nonetheless the fact remains that his anti-Quaker poem appeared during the midst of an assiduous anti-Quaker campaign being deliberately conducted by the Royalists.

The failure of the August rebellion somewhat dimmed Mor-

---

[43] The offending Quaker was not really accused of inversion; the "Colt" of the title is the product of a strained wordplay on *Colchester*. Within the verses the incriminated animal is called a "Filly Foal." The broadsheet pamphlet as published in 1659 bore only the blunter title, *A Relation of a Quaker, that to the shame of his profession, attempted to bugger a mare near Colchester.*

[44] Another set of verses on the same incident was printed in the *Rump Songs*, I, 358–362, under the title, "The Four-legg'd Quaker."

daunt's luster, and although he continued to be charged with the official responsibility for all Royalist activity in England his opponents increased their efforts to undermine the solidarity of the Trust. By January 1659/60 Monk had commenced his march southward from Scotland, and although many crosswinds were blowing in the chaotic Commonwealth the scent of Restoration was distinct enough to cause an unprecedented burgeoning of Royalist plots. Men who had been quiescent for twelve years or more found themselves filled with zeal for the Stuart cause and eager to participate in the underground conspiracies to restore the King to his own again while time yet remained. Denham had been extending the ramifications of his little faction, and by January Alan Brodrick had decided to strengthen his own position, especially against Mordaunt, by uniting his own group more wholeheartedly with Denham's. On January 13 Brodrick accordingly wrote to Hyde, after an opening assertion that Mordaunt could never succeed in uniting all factions "be the commands never so peremptory":

Of Mr. Denham there is at this time an universal good opinion, and if your Lordship would engage him by a letter, or induce his Majesty to write, I know not anything absolutely in your own power so advantageous. The man I know full well, his former intrigues, dependencies, expectations, his present condition, temper and reputation; and though I have ever wished [the King's restoration] might be achieved by your own dependents, I must now propose his adoption into that number as the last remedy (if I were to speak my last) I could upon the most sober thought I am capable of deliver to you. This I confess, my Lord, is high presumption, but remember I beseech you, it is high duty that transports me to the boldness. Many objections I have made to myself, his familiarity with the Duke of Bucks., George Porter &c. but sure I am, they will be as much strangers to his business as acquainted with his diversions. The advantages are manifold in the uniting those, whom the late unhappy, and many former, accidents have divided, nor is he so obnoxious to the present Governors as we who remain tenants at will to our lodgings, and every hour expect removal; which I humbly submit to your Lordships consideration.[45]

Here, of course, is further evidence of the mysterious lenience with which the various interregnum authorites always treated Denham. But Hyde remained somewhat less than enthusiastic. On January 28/February 7 he wrote to inform Brodrick that

I know Mr Denham very well and am without any suspition of his want of kindnesse to mee, since I am sure hee hath no reason to be without it; and I believe I shall enclose in this a letter from ye King to him, and I will write to my Lord Mordaunt to conferr very freely with him, and I hope hee will be a good instrument to begett a good understanding betweene many of our ffriends. I have writt to my Ld Mordaunt that you will be a meanes to bring him and Mr Denham together. It is above a yeare since that the King writ to him upon a particular affaire, and I sent him a cypher at ye same time, of which hee hath never taken ye least notice, you will remember my services to him, and upon any occasion advertise mee from him, if hee declines writing himselfe. . . .[46]

Denham, it will be recalled, received a letter of some kind from the King before November 20, 1658, but he continued to maintain that he had never received the cipher mentioned by Hyde; yet Denham at that time had gone down into the country, fearful of suspicion and arrest, refusing to write, and it is not impossible that in fact he had destroyed the cipher. Hyde enclosed no letter from the King to Denham in this, but a week later he wrote to Denham directly and sent the promised enclosure.

---

[45] This letter is printed in *State Papers of Clarendon*, III, 644–646, where it was found by Banks, who reprints it partially (*Poetical Works*, pp. 17–18).

[46] Clarendon S.P., Vol. 69, ff. 11–13 (*C.Cl.S.P.*, IV, 536; extract in *State Papers of Clarendon*, III, 672–673).

Meanwhile, on February 3/13, Hyde took a somewhat more positive attitude toward Denham in writing to one Rumbold, another Royalist conspirator in England:

. . . the kinge cannot thinke of a better expedient to informe and rightly to dispose the Earle of Oxford (whose zeal to his service is unquestionable) then by Mr Denham, and to this purpose his Ma^t hath writt to Mr Denham, and if he shall desyre to speak with Ld. Mordt or you, the kinge desyres both he and you would use all freedom with him, that the Earle may be the better informed, and I have writt to my Cosen Brodricke to bringe Ld Mordant and Mr Denham togither; ther can be no reasonable scruple of trusting Mr Denham, of whom the King is well assured, and ther is as little doubt of his being intirely trusted by many persons of the 1st quality.[47]

Nevertheless on the following day, February 4/14, there returns a somewhat querulous tone in Hyde's remarks about Denham in a letter to Brodrick: "I did not forgett any thing you writt to me the last summer, yet I did not remember that you had informed me of such a particular Interest in your Cozen's neighbour [Oxford] as that there would need no other Interposition, besides I did not know him to be in the towne, and I doe not yet understand why you did in a former letter presse the conveniency of imploying Mr Dennam — whilest you have the same freedome of communication. . . ."[48] Hyde's question is not unreasonable in view of the fact that despite protestations that the Earl would receive correspondence only if delivered through Denham, Brodrick had evidently been able to communicate with him well enough.

Despite his querulousness Hyde on the same day wrote a long

---

[47] Clarendon S.P., Vol. 69, f. 49 (*C.Cl.S.P.*, IV, 540–541; two brief extracts, wrongly dated, in *State Papers of Clarendon*, III, 680–682). William Rumbold was the royal financial agent charged with transmitting funds to officially approved conspiratorial groups.

[48] Clarendon S.P., Vol. 69, f. 70 (*C.Cl.S.P.*, IV, 546).

letter to Denham, enclosing the message from the King he had
alluded to earlier:

I have no reason to believe that a cypher which I sent to you some
months above a yeare since, was ever putt into your hands, and
therefore I know not how to say that to you, which I have in
charge, but by using a cypher, which the person who finds a way
to deliver this to you, will exhybyt for you: The enclosed is
from the kinge to you, and the service he expects from you, is,
that you will informe my Ld Oxford of his Mat^s extraordinary kindness for him, and confidence in his affection, and assure
him that his maty. was never without that full kindnesse for him,
which the kinge fynds at this tyme, because he hath hearde that
my Ld. hath had some apprehension of the contrary, and it would
be no small service you would do the kinge, if you would dispose
my Ld (of whose safety his Maty. hath all imaginable tendernesse)
to such a communication with those who are intrusted by the
Kinge [the Great Trust], that he may iudge of what they
propose, & see if ther had been this last summer such a communication, greate matters would have been done, at least if trech-
ery had been out of the way: and if my Ld had rather receave
the account by you, I have writt to my Ld Mordt to confer freely
with you upon all occasyons, and to imparte all designes to you,
and the gentleman who gives this to you, will bringe you togither:
I know well ther is greate preiudice to my Ld Mordt, upon an
imagination that he hath some extravagant trust from the kinge,
to which he is not equall, which is so farr from beinge true, that I
do not know that ever he desyred any Commission for himselfe.
I am sure he hath no single power vested in himselfe alone; his
zeale and affection to the kinges service hath been very great, and
he hath prevayled with sevrall persons of honour to consulte togither and upon all occasyons to send the king ther advice, and
it was a principle instruction to them to use some proper means
to advertise my Ld Oxford of all, which was more then wee could
gett done before in above a yeares tyme. If you will returne your
advice to the kinge, it will be very well now:

Ther is a particular I must informe you of, that concernes my selfe, in which I much desyre your favour, it is some months since Mr John Harberte [Herbert] caused 200 *l.* to be returned hither to me, for which I sent my acquittance for so much receaved from Mr J. H. not thinking it fitt to inserte his name at large, least it might miscarry, and now I am put to to returne a more ample acquittance, for the satisfaction of my Ld Pembroke & his brother which I declyne out of the former consideration, not knowinge of how ill consequence it may be, if it fall into ill handes, which I am not sure it may not do. Therefore, I pray, know my Lds minde in it, and I will send such an acquittance as he shall desyre (it being you know all one to me) and I am sure he will not take this warynesse in ill part.[49]

The enclosure from the King has not survived, but its tenor may be guessed from Hyde's letter, as well as from Denham's reply. This letter is interesting also in showing the Herberts of Wilton House contributing to the exiled king's finances, as well as Denham's continued closeness to the Earl of Pembroke.

Brodrick next wrote to Hyde on February 13, but not apparently in answer to either of the Chancellor's letters. He begins, "I writ with great haste & rudeness this morning under Ned Villiers cover, and am now with Mr Denham, of whom I gave you a liberal account . . . ," and in the remainder of the letter, relating news of the turmoil of government in London, uses the first person plural pronoun consistently, apparently associating Denham with himself in the writing.[50]

Denham himself wrote to both Hyde and the King before the end of February, and both letters deal with his charge to the Earl of Oxford. The letter to the King ran to two pages, in cipher, and, as Denham's own statement, deserves reproduction in full:

---

[49] Clarendon S.P., Vol. 69, f. 66 (*C.Cl.S.P.*, IV, 545). Endorsed "myne to Mr Denham, 14 ffebr. 1660." This letter is a holograph draft, marked by cancellations and interlineations, from which the text has been derived.

[50] Clarendon S.P., Vol. 69, f. 151 (*C.Cl.S.P.*, IV, 561). This letter is an eighteenth-century copy.

Your Maty could not have commanded me, a more easy service then to satisfy Ld. Oxford of your Matys kindnesse to him who never had the least apprehension of ye contrary, having as little reason to doubt of your Matys goodnesse and Justice to him as your Maty hath of his affection to your service of which I will only give one instance to your Maty that at his last being in London I being desired to propose to him one of the best matches in England hee answerd that though ye advantage would be very great yet he could not be so much commanded for his owne Interest as to think of setling his particular family and fortune till he saw your Maty restored and y^t hee could not appeare an honest man to himselfe if he gave himself any occasion of being slack in the performance of his duty to wch the care of a family and ye Indulgence to a young wife give him some temptation.

Your Maty will shortly hear from himself out of a hope y^t ye frequent changes here might produce something for your Matys advantage and there being no body then commissioned from your Maty to consult of your Affaires, Ld. Oxford, Ld. Bellasis, C. Russell, the Ashburnhams, Sr W. Compton, S^r Th: Ingram, S^r Fr. Co: and my selfe thought it might be no unacceptable service to confer together and give our Judgements concerning ye present state of things and if any thing occurred worthy your knowledge either by one of our selves or some whom we trust to acquaint your Maty with it. To this end we have had divers meetings and upon ye discourse of your Matys preparations abroad the first particular we took into consideration was that to attend your landing with as many horse as we and our friends could possibly make beleiving y^t would bee ye greatest want your Maty would find at your arrivall but the sudden change of affayrs has for ye present made y^t a more remote consideration. What ye state of things now is, and what Judgment is to bee made of what they may produce this bearer cann better tell, then I can write. But we have consulted whither it may not bee fitt to make an offer of the service of your party to Monke not upon your Matys Interest for y^t hee will not hear of but to cooperate wth all others for ye good of the Nation and conceiving it a fitt means to put them in to a more ready posture for your service we have found a very proper person

143

to propose it if he refuse it we must sitt still and attend ye event if he accept and your Maty approve it you may please to give your allowance for ye better encouragement of such as will bee scrupulous to act with out it.

For ye musunderstanding among your freinds wch your Maty most iustly complaines of as we have not contributed any thing towards it, so nothing shall bee wanting in us to the taking it away as being a most essentiall part of your service but if your Maty approove so well of our meeting as to command us to continue it we hope it will nether appeare derogatory nor repugnant to any other trust if we desire it may still bee locked up among ourselves.

Ld: Bellasis desires me to acquaint your Maty y^t hee hath prevailed wth Ld Bruce and Mr ———— Sonne to S^r Th: to send your Maty two horses wch Ld Bellasis hath put into ye hands of Mr Cooper to convey.[51]

This letter shows Denham, in opposition to the Trust ("any other trust"), recruiting his own group from among the former members of the Sealed Knot and others, and attempting to gain formal recognition. Denham's associates were three of the six former members of the Knot (Belasyse, Russell, and Compton), and Belasyse's brother-in-law, Ingram, who, like Cobb, came from Yorkshire. The others were his old acquaintances: he had been reported in collusion with Cobb in 1655, John and William Ashburnham he had known since the civil wars, and Oxford at least since their time of common exile. But the Ashburnhams and Ingram were known to be connected with the Louvre party, and their presence in Denham's group was not likely to elicit great warmth from Hyde. Therefore Denham's hopes to reduce Hyde's animosity toward himself were essentially in vain. To Hyde Denham attempted to be placatory:

---

[51] Clarendon S.P., Vol. 69, ff. 193–194 (*C.Cl.S.P.*, IV, 579). Deciphered numerical cipher.

You may bee assured y^t ye cypher y^u mention to have sent so long since should have been made use of if it had ever come to my hands. Y^t I never received any commands from y^u I looke upon rather as Charity then a neglect by reason of my many and continueall Infirmities wch though I never shall never make a pretense to doe the King no service yet I hope it will serve for a iust excuse that I have done no better. I need not say more to y^u then I have sayd allready to the king concerning Ld. Oxford only y^t ye necessity of his being in the Country makes it not possible for him to have frequent Communication with those whom y^u mention to bee intrusted [the Trust] but whatsoever Commands they shall have from the King for him I am ready to receive and impart to him. What y^e Grounds of y^t preiudice wch is upon $+$ I know not being a meere stranger both to him and his present transactions, but finding y^e valew wch the King and your Lordsp have for him I hope it is unjust but whither it is just or unjust if the prejudice bee a [as? so?] spread that it cannot bee taken off, y^e evill consequence to the Kings affaires will be the same. I intended to have written much more at large, but ye hast of ye messenger and my wearines and long discontinuance of this way of writing [in cipher] makes me ask y^r pardon till ye next occasion y^u may be pleased to present the enclosed to the King wth such super and subscription as is necessary your cypher wanting both. For what y^u write concerning Pembrook hee not being now ye man hee was, I shall not trust his new conscience wth ye knowledge y^t I hold correspondence wth y^u, but shall find some other expedient to do ye business. Jo: Ashb: is yr most faithfull servant and so is 863, as much as any man alive.[52]

Hyde endorsed receipt of this letter on March 9 (February 27 O.S.). The King's letter would have been received in the same

---

[52] Clarendon S.P., Vol. 69, f. 196 (*C.Cl.S.P.*, IV, 579–580). Partly deciphered numerical cipher; the name "863" is undeciphered and Hyde's reply of March 6/16 suggests that he could not make out its sense. The symbol "$+$" presumably stands for Mordaunt. By his "infirmities" Denham doubtless means his lameness and attendant ills.

packet. Neither letter is dated, but both must have been written before February 21, for on that day (indeterminably O.S. or N.S.) the courier Cooper wrote to Hyde that he had no money to transport Lord Belasyse's gift of horses for the King.[53]

On March 6/16 replies were dispatched from both the King and Hyde to Denham. The King's letter conveyed little that was not in Hyde's, except to offer personal thanks for Belasyse's gift of horses and such matters:

I am gladd you finde my Ld of Oxforde so well satisfyed in my kindnesse to him, which he hath greate reason to be, but if he had never apprehension of the contrary, some who have pretended to be trusted by him, have bene much mistaken: I am so confident of his affection and zeale to promote my interest, that nothinge shall lessen or decrease it, and therefore I would not have him declyne any such good advantage as you mention when it shall be offered to him. I am gladd so many of my frends as you name have so much confidence in each other as to meete and consulte togither upon the advancement of my service, which may produce good effects, and nothinge is more to be wished then that a body of my frends could gett themselves into armes under what pretence soever, but whether it can be done the way you propose, or what other way it may be done better, cannot be so well resolved as by communication with those who have my immediate Commissyon to consider and order my affayres of that nature, in which number some of those named by you, are, and therefore I must still desyre, that you will do all that is in your power to remove all iealosyes and mistakes betweene them, which I thought had bene done, and that if they do not thinke fitt to meete togither (which I shall not presse against ther inclinations) that you will communicate ther sense and opinion to Ld Mordt, or to some other of my Commissyoners, whome I have directed to conferr with all freedom wth you, and this will prevente any rash undertakinges or other mistakes, which can hardly be prevented without such

---

[53] Clarendon S.P., Vol. 70, f. 12 (C.Cl.S.P., IV, 569–570; extract in State Papers of Clarendon, III, 688).

communication, and all accidents and opportunityes which fall out will be rightly made use of, which by consultinge and resolvinge aparte can never be done; Commende me to your frends, and thanke my Ld Bellasis for my horses, which Mr Cooper I know will send by the first conveience.

I am

your affectionate frende.[54]

Hyde wrote a diplomatically worded answer quite lacking in cordiality:

I have yours without a date by this bearer, and do wounder you never had my cypher, it was sent by Harbert Price who at that tyme pretended to be sent hither by you, as you founde by what the kinge then writt to you, the which it may be he never delivered either, for the kinge never hearde from your selfe upon this subiect, and therefore the gentleman at his last being heare found not the same countenance: I shall not inlarge upon any thinge the kinge hath sayde to you but do hope by what you say, of my Ld Oxfords never having doubted the kinges kindnesse, that what Mr Nicolls sayd as from him, was without his authority. I conceave my Lds beinge in the country (if Essex, Norfolke & Suffolke could be handsomely united in an association) may bee no hindraunce to the kinges service, but rather advance it, if you take the paynes to transmitt his opinion and advice to the Commissyoners at London, and to returne thrs, and you may upon all occasyons call to them for such blanke Commissyons signed by the Kinge as are necessary for the carrying on the service. It were indeede a thinge rather to be wished then hoped for, that the kinge could finde such persons to be imployed in his service, against whom no preiudice would be had, but since that is almost impossible, and that the preiudice very frequently proceedes from the extraordinary zeale to the service, it would be great pitty that we should suffer for ther preiudice, at least that the kinge should not do the best he can to supporte them against it, how spreadinge

---

[54] Clarendon S.P., Vol. 70, f. 97 (*C.Cl.S.P.*, IV, 587–588). A draft by Hyde.

147

soevr it is. I will not excuse those infirmityes which possibly Ld Mordt may be lyable to, but you will finde them recompensed, by greate virtues, and that he is trusted by persons of the greatest interest. You will therefore do the kinge a very greate service, if you can so dispose all persons, that mischievous preiudice and iealosyes may be removed, and that by and through you ther may be such an understanding, and communication, as may carry on the worke though they do not meete togither: I am heartily sorry that my Ld Pembroke hath not yett disintangled himselfe from those perplexityes, and shall not desyre you to do any thinge which may bringe an inconvenience upon you. I hope you will finde another way to dispatch the businesse as well as by speaking with him yourselfe, & you will shortly see a good frend whom you love well, who will inlarge from us to you upon many particulars, and will assure you that I have never been without a greate confidence in and iust esteeme of your frendshipp, and do heartily desyre to lyve to do you some service. Remember me very kindly to Jo: Ashburnham; and to all your other frends, and continue to love

your E.[55]

Thus Denham's complaint of the universal prejudice against Mordaunt is turned around into a reprimand on the prejudice and jealousy of Denham and his friends against the zeal of Mordaunt. Denham apparently made no reply to either of these letters, for none survives in Clarendon's papers, and in a letter to Brodrick of March 31/April 10 Hyde observed that he had "not received a word from Mr Denham." [56] Earlier, on March 17/27, Hyde had repeated, though a bit more amiably, the instructions he had sent to Denham:

If Mr Denham hath showed you the answer he receaved from the king by Halsy, you will by that see, how the king desyres his

---

[55] Clarendon S.P., Vol. 70, f. 96 (C.Cl.S.P., IV, 587). A holograph draft. Herbert Price may be the Henry Pryce who wrote to Hyde on November 20 and December 2, 1658; see pp. 128–129, and nn. 29 and 30, above.

[56] Clarendon S.P., Vol. 71, f. 117 (C.Cl.S.P., IV, 631).

busynesse should be carryed on, and that though his frends may consulte aparte, that he doth not wish any resolutions should be taken and prosequted without the privity of those who are more immediately trusted and commissyoned by his maty. . . . and I hope that Ld Mordt, who knowes the kinges greate esteeme of my Ld Oxforde, will carry himselfe so discreetely towards him, and show him all the kinges instructions, that my Ld will not only be satisfyed in what relates to himselfe, but in the whole businesse. . . .[57]

The true nature of Denham's faction is surrounded by ambiguity and confusion, but despite his protestations he seems to have been attempting to create a united front against Mordaunt of elements drawn from the former extremes of the Sealed Knot and the Louvre party. His group was not very cohesive, however, and Halsey, the messenger who carried the letters between Denham and Hyde and the King, has left a memorandum indicating that at the same time he had carried separate letters for Oxford and Belasyse.[58] On April 14, moreover, Hyde received a letter from Belasyse asserting that his service to the King was not confined to Denham's group, of which he nonetheless admitted membership:

. . . my constant correspondence with Sr John Greenvill & many other persons who have acted heare for his Maty doth I am confident conferme his Maty that I have nott confined my selfe singly to ye councells of those gentlemen who desired my company wth them, wheroff Mr Denham gave you accoumpt, nor indeed in any Caball have I found my self so Usefull as I am in my particular correspondences wth persons heare, & intrests in promoting ye choyse off good men to serve in the Militia & Parliament both which I am confident will strengthen the reso-

---

[57] Clarendon S.P., Vol. 70, ff. 192–193 (C.Cl.S.P., IV, 608; extract in *State Papers of Clarendon*, III, 710; printed in *S.P. Thurloe*, VII, 857–858). Holograph draft endorsed "myne to Mr Hancocke [Brodrick's cover name] 27 March 1660."

[58] Clarendon S.P., Vol. 70, f. 59 (C.Cl.S.P., IV, 580). Memoranda by J. Halsey; third item is "a letter: to my Ld: of Oxford, Bellassis, Mr Denham etc., in answer of theirs wch I brought."

lutions off Monkes Army, London & the whole Nations to that happy peace & settlement off his maty. . . .[59]

There is no reason to suppose that Hyde's disposition toward Denham was much improved by his receipt from Lady Mordaunt, under date of March 30, of the news that the "two Ashburnhams, Sir Thomas Ingram, and others are employed by the Queen here. They are sending Sir William Davenant to the King today." [60] The first part of what Lady Mordaunt had to say would not be news to Hyde; she would not be inclined to charity, and she and Hyde probably shared the conviction rather than the absolute knowledge that the persons named were employed by the Queen. Hyde no doubt would also have had little hesitation at including Denham among the "others." On April 6/16 Hyde correctly replied, "The persons mentioned have not sent over hither; if Sir Will. Davenant be the ambassador he is more likely to be sent to France." [61] Davenant had in fact gone to Paris, whether sent by Denham's group or not, and Hyde had apparently set on foot inquiries as to the purpose of his mission. On April 21/May 1, 1660, in any event, Lord Jermyn wrote from Paris to inform the King directly that "Davenant's journey was rather a visit to [me] from some old friends than a public matter." Yet either the royal admonition or the press of affairs drew Denham and Mordaunt finally together, for on April 19, 1660, Mordaunt informed Hyde by letter that "Mr Wren & Mr Denham have writ a Declaration wch we conceaved necessary & they iust now perfected it by me, and I am sending it to the Presse." [62] Unfortunately there is no way of telling which of the innumerable proclamations of the spring of 1660 was the one composed by Denham and Mr. (Matthew, or perhaps Christopher; see pp. 156, 253 below) Wren.

Even while the death rattle of the Commonwealth and of the

---

[59] Clarendon S.P., Vol. 71, ff. 256–257 (*C.Cl.S.P.*, IV, 659).

[60] *C.Cl.S.P.*, IV, 625.

[61] *Ibid.*, p. 637.

[62] Clarendon S.P., Vol. 71, ff. 305–306 (*C.Cl.S.P.*, IV, 655–656).

Good Old Cause were audible to the deafest Denham did not cease from officious scurrying on the King's behalf. On May 7 Brodrick, writing to Hyde for the first time without the use of cipher, and subscribing his own name, provided two pieces of news about Denham's activities. The first had to do with a suggestion that opposition to Hyde himself as Chancellor might hinder the King's restoration: "Mr Denham came the last night from the Speakers with whom hee had some Debate concerning Your Lp, and signifying to Him your Lps willingness to resign your office, rather y^n in the least obstruct his Mtys immediate admission, was pleased to press my opinion to ye conveniencye, leaving It to me to desire your Lp so to withdraw, if it were prest: To whom I answered what was ffitt; and humbly beseech your Lps entrance ye Same instant with his Mty, whom I doubt not in few Dayes to See enthrond. . . ." Denham's attempt to dispose of Hyde's career in conference with Sir Harbottle Grimstone (speaker of the Convention Parliament that convened on April 25) was not his sole communion with the eminent, however. Two hours after writing the above Brodrick took up his quill again to inform Hyde that "Mr Denham tells me if Lambert may be saved the King may firmly engage that whole party to Him, who have refused all overtures made by ye Rigid Presbiterians, not out of kindness to his Mty (for duty they understand not) but out of an established opinion y^t the Presbiterians are greater Rogues y^n y^mselves in their designes and contracts. This Mr Denham calls ye Greatest Secret of ye Nation, & intends (accompanying Sr J. Greenvill) to present ye particulars to his Mty with ye Names of Coll Birch his Caball, and purposes: wch I thought fitt to intimate & but to intimate lest I should usurpe upon his Province. . . ." [63]

---

[63] Clarendon S.P., Vol. 72, ff. 239*–242* (*C.Cl.S.P.*, V, 20–21; extracts in *State Papers of Clarendon*, III, 739–740, 744–745). It is notable that Denham is here working conjointly with Sir John Grenville, with whom Belasyse had claimed correspondence in his letter to Hyde of April 14.

Denham was here negotiating with two contrary wings of the old Parliamentarians. Grimstone was one of the Presbyterian members secluded from the Long Parliament; Lambert represented Independent and Army factions. Lambert had been imprisoned in the Tower and had escaped, but on April 21 was recaptured, and at the time of Brodrick's writing was once more safely confined. Denham's efforts in both quarters were redundant in the event. Although the Presbyterians had elected the Speaker, they were less than a majority in the parliament, and Restoration swept irresistibly nearer on a wave of national Royalist hysteria. As for Lambert, he remained a prisoner, but his last-minute approaches to the King may have saved his neck; whereas the other leading regicides were executed, he was allowed to end his days in modified confinement on the Island of Guernsey. So, in May of 1660 ended, along with the interregnum, Denham's career as a Royalist conspirator. In June he commenced an entirely new career.

In the period preceding the Restoration Denham may once more have indulged his Muses. Modern editors and bibliographers at least concur in accepting an attribution first advanced by Anthony Wood: "Panegyrick on his excellency the Lord General George Monk, Commander in Chief, &c. — Printed at *Lond.* in one sh. in qu. in the month of Mar. 1659/60. Tho the name of *John Denham* is not set to it, yet the frequent report was then among the Academians that he was the author of it." This description matches, of the half dozen or so panegyrics to Monk published at the beginning of 1660, only that of *A Panegyrick on His Excellency the Lord General George Monck: Commander in Chief of all the Forces in England, Scotland, and Ireland*, a single-sheet quarto of five numbered pages issued under an imprint date of 1659 by the London stationer Richard Marriot.[64] Unfortunately George Thomason did not add this pamphlet to the three other Monk panegyrics in his collection, and so the exact month of pub-

---

[64] Copies of this quarto (Wing D1004) are to be found in several collections. Denham's modern editor erroneously calls it a "broadside."

lication cannot be determined. The imprint date of course indicates that it came out no later than March 24, and it is not likely to have been published very much earlier, so Wood's dating in March may be quite correct. But although no rival claimant for this poem has appeared, Denham himself did not own it in his 1668 *Poems,* and the value of Wood's ascription has never been tested. The poem bears only the slightest resemblance to Denham's authentic work.[65]

---

[65] The poem is written in decasyllabic couplets, chiefly closed, a fact that in itself points at no specific author. Although Banks allows this poem to Denham, jealousy for Denham's reputation makes me desire to free him from responsibility for such lines as:

> Thence did their mutual Protections start;
> Together both, neither were safe apart.
> So Thou without Us safe canst hardly be,
> And we despise all safety without Thee.
> Return, Return! Enshrine Thy Glories here;
> Thou, whom both Seas and Shore do love and fear.
>
> (lines 51–56)

VI: Restoration

Return, Return! Enshrine Thy Glories here;
Thou, whom both Seas and Shore do love and fear.

CHARLES II IS SAID to have suffered shocked disgust at the swarms of clamoring place-seekers who surrounded him upon his restoration; there were in any event far more applicants than spoils at the King's disposal, and may suitors went away embittered and disappointed. More sober critics deplored the King's casual disposition of offices without adequate regard either for the fitness of the beneficiary or for prior claims of others. Yet what many missed John Denham attained without difficulty, and in June 1660 he was confirmed in the post of surveyor of the Works, through which, John Aubrey asserts, in the remaining nine years of his life he amassed some seven thousand pounds.[1] Denham owed his position ultimately to that gratuitous promise of the King in September of 1649 which Denham later recalled, but immediately to the intervention of his cousin, George Morley. This intervention took the form of two letters from Morley to Hyde. The first, written on May 1, 1660, makes its point in large and general terms:

. . . some persons of quality . . . do seem much troubled to hear the King doth give places to every one almost that is recom-

---

[1] Aubrey's figure is probably too modest and may derive from a subsequent attempt by Denham to purchase an annuity capitalized at £7,000. Denham's patent of his office is preserved in S.P. Dom., ser. 38, Vol. 19, a docket book of "Letters-Pattents Grants, 12th & 13th of King Charles the 2, Anno 1660–1661"; it is the last item on page 1 (headed "Junij 1660 Anno Regni Regis Caroli Secund. Duodecimo"): "The like Office to John Denham Esqr for his life of ye office of Surveyor of his Maties works" (*C.S.P.D.: 1660–1661*, p. 72 with an error in the page reference).

mended to him, whether they deserve it or no, some of which places they say were given to others before, namely ye Kings drawers place wch ye Dr Smith was promised to his nephew, and ye Surveyors place given before to Mr Denham under the Kings hand at Paris. . . . Dr [Sheldon] desires you to consider y^t what is done there now will be much more looked upon & lookd into as ye measure off what is to be expected from you then what may perhaps be done in ye same kind hereafter and therefore as well for y^t as for other reasons it is his humble advice y^t extraordinary care may be taken That such men may be made choice of for places both in Church and State as may answere mens expectations. . . .[2]

The second letter from Morley, dated May 4, contains less of Sheldon's golden advice and comes much more to the point of specific places:

One thing wch I told you . . . was much complaynd of is still more and more talkd of, and y^t is ye kings giving of places, and some say selling of them — without sufficient consideration whether ye persons be fit, or whether ye places have bin formerly promised or noe. Of the later I gave you . . . y^t of my Cousin Denham . . . Mr Denham tells me he hath had ye place of Surveyor under ye kings hand & seale above these 10 yeares, & he hopes y^t he hath done nothing since to deserve it should be taken away from him; And truly I think he hath done, & is able & willing to doe ye king as much service as any private Gentleman of ye whole Nation having as you know very great ability, an universall acquaintance & a very good reputation both for honesty & sufficiency with all y^t know him. . . .[3]

To assume, as some have done, that Denham was less than competent in the performance of his duties is unfair. An unbiased

---

[2] Clarendon S.P., Vol. 72, ff. 117–118, 449 (*C.Cl.S.P.*, V, 3). Dr. Sheldon is almost certainly Gilbert Sheldon, future archbishop of Canterbury and benefactor of Oxford University. Morley himself became bishop of Winchester.

[3] Clarendon S.P., Vol. 72, ff. 199–200 (*C.Cl.S.P.*, V, 13). Morley still signs his cover name, "Jeremie Baker."

scrutiny of the records of his tenure of office reveals just the contrary. But Denham's historical misfortune as surveyor of the Works was to have been a valley overshadowed by two mountain peaks: his predecessor had been Inigo Jones, and his successor was to be Christopher Wren. Nevertheless it was Denham who appointed Wren as his deputy, and arranged for Wren to succeed him despite considerable opposition; and Wren's plans both for the new customhouse and the new St. Paul's were initially drawn up as part of his work under Denham, and issued from Denham's office. Actually, under the circumstances of his appointment, the contemporary attacks on Denham's qualifications for his post were comparatively few, and not entirely disinterested.

One attack came within the same month of June as the announcement of Denham's appointment, in a petition from "John Webb Architect," a nephew of Inigo Jones. It is ironic that Webb's claim was based on a superior version of the two chief arguments Morley had employed in ensuring Denham's appointment: priority of the grant and competence for the duties. Webb complained that he had been "trained by Inigo Jones and made his deputy, and designed by Charles I to succeed" to the post, until he was thrust out in 1643 for loyalty to the Crown. More recently, he had prepared the royal houses for the King's reception, and "the Lords & Commons in parliamt & Councell of State have conceiv'd none more able then ye petr (as he hopes your Royall Maty shall find) to discharge ye trust of being Surveyor of your Maties works," and if his petition is not granted, after his many sufferings and imprisonment, he may together with his whole family be ruined at last forever. This was followed by "A Breife of Mr Webbs case," containing a direct attack on Denham:

That Mr Denham may possibly, as most gentry in England at this day have some knowledge in the Theory of Architecture; but nothing of ye practique soe that he must of necessity have another at his Maties charge to doe his businesse, whereas Mr

156

Webb himselfe designes, orders, and directs, what ever given in command, wthout any other mans assistance.

His Matie may please to grant some other place more proper for Mr Denhams abilityes, and confirm unto Mr Webb the Surveyors place wherein he hath consumed 30 yeares study. . . .[4]

All that Webb derived from this was an empty grant, in reversion after John Denham, of the office of surveyor of Works, although he was also taken into employment as Denham's active assistant. Whether this last was an official appointment or a conciliatory gesture from Denham himself does not appear from the records. The grant of reversion proved empty because Webb, although surviving Denham, did not succeed him, the position going instead to Denham's choice, Christopher Wren. According to Webb's later testimony this was because Denham had successfully opposed the reversion's passing the Great Seal.[5]

Two others to attack Denham's qualifications were John Evelyn and Samuel Butler. Evelyn's animadversions are recorded in his *Diary* for October 19, 1661, and so were not made publicly. Even so they are not free of self-interest, at least of *amour-propre*:

I went to London to visite my Lord of Bristoll, having been with Sir John Denham (his Maties surveyor) to consult with him about the placing of his palace at Greenwich, which I would have had built between the river and the Queene's house, so as a large square cutt should have let in ye Thames like a bay; but Sir John was for setting it on piles at the very brink of the water, which I did not assent to, and so came away, knowing Sir John to be a better poet than architect, tho' he had Mr. Webb (Inigo Jones's man) to assist him.

For this private aspersion, however, Evelyn was soon to make handsome public amends. In 1664 he published his translation from

---

[4] S.P. Dom., ser. 29, Vol. 5, item 74, pp. 118–119 (*C.S.P.D.: 1660–1661*, p. 76).
[5] *C.S.P.D.: 1668–1669*, p. 132.

157

the French of Roland Freart's *A Parallel of the Antient Archi-tecture with the Modern*, accompanied by two dedications. The first, dated August 20, 1664, was addressed "To the Most Serene Majesty of Charles II," and contained a commendation of "the Conduct of Your most Industrious and Worthy *Surveyor*." The second was addressed directly "To Sir John Denham, Knight of the Honour-able Order of the Bath, Superintendant and Surveyor of his Majesty's Buildings and Works," and consisted of the highest praise for Denham's accomplishments, particularly

for the reformation of a thousand deformities in the streets, as by your introducing that incomparable form of paving, to an incredible advantage of the publick, when that which is begun in Holburn shall become universal, for the saving of wheels and car-riages, the cure of noysom gutters, the deobstruction of encounters, the dispatch of business, the cleanness of the way, the beauty of the object, the ease of the infirme, and the preserving of both the mother and the babe; so many of the fair sex and their offspring having perished by mischances (as I am credibly inform'd) from the ruggedness of the unequal streets.

This description of the condition of London paving prior to Den-ham's reforms may seem somewhat comical, but is not far from the truth. Projects for paving the streets of London and Westmin-ster were of frequent concern to the House of Commons during these years, and Denham sat on several House committees to con-sider appropriate legislation to bring about such improvements as Evelyn praised and desired.[6]

Samuel Butler's attack on Denham's execution of his office is of another order entirely. In a set of verses of singular virulence he attacks not only Denham's competence as surveyor, but his honesty as well, accusing him of bilking the King both in accounts and materials. Butler's verses also, however, accuse Denham of

---

[6] See *Commons Journal* for July 25, 26, 27, 1661; March 22, 1661/2; March 24, April 5, 8, 9, 10, 11, 14, 16, 24, May 2, 1662; March 12, 1662/3; March 30, May 13, 21, June 30, 1663; May 7, Nov. 26, 1664; Jan. 24, Feb. 15, 24, 1664/5.

plagiarizing his two best-known works, *Coopers Hill* and *The Sophy,* of poetical as well as architectural incompetence, of pride, immorality, lewdness, insolence, and of disloyalty during the interregnum.[7] As factual testimony, therefore, Butler's charges must be discounted. For Denham's biography, however, the insoluble problem is raised of the motivation of Butler's exceptionally vicious attack. The paths of the two men do not cross so far as the records reveal, but Butler's own disappointment of reward for his interregnum royalism and possible consequent envy of Denham seem hardly enough to engender the spite shown in this poem.

During the remainder of 1660 Denham's name is recorded a few times, chiefly in connection with his work as surveyor. He is named once, inconsequentially, in September, as "Mr. Denham, the King's surveyor," and Samuel Pepys saw him on December 7, and attempted to see him on December 9. On the latter date Pepys went at night to see Denham about some alterations Montague desired to make to his house — a tribute of some sort to Denham's competence — but Denham being unavailable Pepys was solaced by Denham's "chief man (Mr. Cooper)" with "a cup of good sack."[8] In December also occurs one of the first signs of Denham's recuperating fortune, with the recording of the lease to him and several others (including William Ashburnham) of several "Messauges &c." at Tottenham Court, Middlesex.[9]

December 1660 also has one faint trace of Denham's literary career.[10] On the 12th Davenant was granted the privilege "of

---

[7] *A Panegyric upon Sir John Denham's Recovery from his Madness* (ca. 1666). See p. 189, below.

[8] *C.S.P.D.: 1660–1661,* p. 285; Pepys, *Diary,* I, 301.

[9] *C.S.P.D.: 1660–1661,* p. 432. Other entries for Denham in the *Calendar* for 1660 are patently misdated: three entries refer to him as Sir John, which dates them after his knighthood, April 23, 1661 (entries on pp. 452 [undated], 457 [undated], 528 [dated "March 8? 1661," should probably be 1661/2]); a fourth entry refers to Sir John Denham *and his lady* and therefore must postdate his remarriage on May 25, 1665 (p. 458 [undated]).

[10] A still fainter trace appears for October, in which month White Kennet places a "Third Edition" of *Coopers Hill* (*A Register and Chronicle Ecclesiasticall and Civil* [1728], p. 299). This entry, however, may be an error for October 1650; the

reformeing some of the most ancient Playes that were playd at Blackfriers and of makeinge them, fitt, for the Company of Actors appointed vnder his direction." Among the plays listed was "the Sophy." Davenant does not, however, appear to have thought it worth his while to make *The Sophy* fit for his company, and it was probably not performed.[11]

Another less clear literary event took place on November 19, when General Monk, become the Duke of Albemarle, presented a dramatic entertainment to King Charles at the Cockpit, the private theater at Whitehall.[12] The entertainment was conducted by Davenant, and is thus reported at secondhand by Pepys on November 20: "This morning I found my Lord in bed late, he having been with the King, Queen, and Princess, at the Cockpit all night, where General Monk treated them; and after supper a play." A special *Prologue to his Majesty* was written for the play, and afterward published by itself as a broadsheet.[13] About this Wood writes in his notice of Denham: "Among [the *Poems and Translations* of 1668] also, as I remember, is *The Prologue to his Majesty at the first play presented at the Cock pit in Whitehall, being part of that noble entertainment which their Majesties received Nov. 19, an. 1660, from his Grace the D. of Albemarle.* Which *Prologue* was printed by it self at *Lond.* 1660. on one side of a broad sheet of paper."[14] Banks accepts Wood's attribution

---

matter is discussed in the introduction to *Expans'd Hieroglyphicks*; and see my " 'Lost,' 'Authorized,' and 'Pirated' Editions of John Denham's *Coopers Hill*," *PMLA*, LXXIX (1964), 242–253.

[11] Bentley, *Jacobean and Caroline Stage*, III, 276.

[12] This was a private royal theater, and should not be confused with the Cockpit in Covent Garden.

[13] THE / PROLOGUE / TO HIS / MAJESTY / At the first PLAY presented at the Cock-pit in / WHITEHALL, / Being part of that Noble Entertainment which their MAIESTIES received Novemb. 19. / from his Grace the Duke of ALBEMARLE. / (Text) / *LONDON*, Printed for *G. Bedell* and *T. Collins*, at the / *Middle-Temple Gate* in *Fleet-street*. 1660. Broadsheet. Wing D335. Thomason's copy is dated Nov. 23 (*Catalogue of the Pamphlets . . . collected by George Thomason* [London, 1908]).

[14] Wood, *Athenae Oxonienses*, II, col. 303.

on his usual grounds of "evidence of style," but the question is complicated by the demonstrated fallibility of Wood's memory. The *Prologue to his Majesty* did not appear in Denham's *Poems and Translations* of 1668, and no amount of reasoning can sufficiently explain its omission if it really was by Denham. The poem contains nothing but conventional compliments to the King, and the fact that Denham dedicated his 1668 volume to the King completely eliminates the possible theory that in 1668 he was in no mood to flatter Charles, and so quietly dropped this poem. Wood's attribution seems to depend upon his false memory of seeing the poem in *Poems and Translations*, and when he is shown to be wrong in that memory why should the attribution nevertheless be retained? Wing's *Short-Title Catalogue* assigns this *Prologue* to Davenant, and perhaps it should be left with that poet, who did conduct the evening's entertainment, rather than shifted to Denham on the basis of a garbled story in Wood.[15]

The Restoration year, then, ended well for Denham. He who in January had been a fruitless Royalist conspirator, still an object of Hyde's chilly suspicion, in December had become His Majesty's

---

[15] Wing's attribution of the *Prologue* to Davenant is probably based upon Davenant's conduct of the evening's entertainment; the *Prologue* is not included in Davenant's collected *Works* of 1673. The British Museum catalogue and the *Thomason Catalogue*, probably on Wood's authority, agree in giving the *Prologue* to Denham. The *Cambridge Bibliography of English Literature* (New York and Cambridge, England, 1941) does likewise, but inasmuch as the article on Denham in that work is by T. H. Banks, as is apparently also that on Davenant, it cannot be considered a separate authority. A very puzzling association of Denham with the *Prologue* occurs, however, in Wheatley's edition of *Pepys's Diary*. Pepys himself does not mention either the *Prologue* or its authorship, but the index to the 1894 edition of the *Diary* refers to a footnote ("i. 303n") on "Denham (Sir John), the surveyor, his prologue to a play." This reference is repeated with appropriate page adjustment (to "i. 205n") in the two-volume edition of 1946. Yet neither edition contains any trace of the topic on the indicated page, and a diligent search of both notes and text has failed to find in either edition anything corresponding to this reference. One may only surmise that Wheatley withdrew just before publication a note already indexed, and that the 1946 index was mechanically adjusted to the new pagination without scrutiny of context. The tenor of that note and Wheatley's motive for its cancellation are equally mysterious.

surveyor of Works, just beginning to amass worldly goods to replace those earlier gambled and sequestered away. The following coronation year of 1661 was to be equally propitious.

Charles II was crowned in Westminster Abbey on April 23, 1661. Denham, in his official capacity, was in charge of physical arrangements for the event. On April 3 a warrant was issued from the Treasurer for payment of £1,000 "to John Denham, Surveyor General of Works, for an intended building of a throne and other necessary works against the coronation." [16] On the great day itself Samuel Pepys rose from bed at four in the morning "and got to the Abbey, where I followed Sir J. Denham, the Surveyor, with some company that he was leading in. And with much ado, by the favour of Mr. Cooper, his man, did get up into a great scaffold across the North end of the Abbey." This entry in Pepys's *Diary* not only records Denham's functioning at the coronation, but it also notices for the first time, albeit without comment, Denham's newest distinction. To celebrate his coronation Charles II conferred numerous honors and awards on his most notably deserving subjects. Among the subjects so dignified, John Denham was created a knight of the Honourable Order of the Bath. The signal honor implied by membership in this order need not be stressed, nor its superiority to the dignity of a mere knight bachelor. The Order of the Bath ranked subordinate only to that of the Garter (a dignity attainable solely by the highest nobility and supereminent officers of state, or by foreign potentates). Prior to the occasion of Denham's creation no knights of the Bath had been made since the coronation of Charles I in 1626, except for a special creation of five knights, including Charles, then Prince of Wales, preparatory to the Prince's elevation to the Garter in 1638. After the coronation of Charles II no further knighthoods of the Bath were conferred until George I made new creations in

---

[16] *C. Treas. Bks.: 1660–1667*, p. 232; *C.S.P.D.: 1663–1664*, p. 238. The other "necessary works" included the paving of Westminster Hall, not, as Banks says (*Poetical Works*, p. 20), of Westminster — a much larger order.

1725. Altogether, sixty-eight knights were added to the order on April 23, 1661; of these, fifteen were the sons or grandsons of noblemen. Of the fifteen, five eventually became themselves earls, and two barons. Another six of the new knights were already baronets, and the remaining forty-seven commoners bore for the most part names prominent in the history of the period.[17]

Another accolade of a different sort was conferred on Denham in the same April of 1661, although it is not easy to determine who conferred it. The Convention Parliament, having accomplished its principal business of restoring the King, had been dissolved by Charles in December 1660. Around the time of the coronation, writs were issued for election of a new Parliament, to meet on May 8, 1661. On April 29, 1661, the name of John Denham, Esq. (his knighthood unnoticed), was certified as that of one of the two burgesses elected from the borough of Old Sarum in Wiltshire.[18] Old Sarum was one of the most superlatively rotten of the "rotten boroughs" in English parliamentary history, and had been so since the late Middle Ages. When it sent Sir John Denham as one of its two representatives to the House of Commons it already consisted of no more than the archaeological site of a monastic town and fortress that had been abandoned at the time of the foundation of New Sarum, or Salisbury; the place still survives as a national

---

[17] Among the young noblemen made knights of the Bath were Philip Herbert, second son of the Earl of Pembroke, Henry Belasyse, son of Lord Belasyse, and Henry Hyde, who was to succeed the Chancellor as second Earl of Clarendon. Among the commoners were John Nicholas, son of Sir Edward Nicholas, secretary of state, and Francis Godolphin, Edward Harley, Francis Popham, and Edward Walpole. Another new knight of the Bath was William Morley, who married Denham's daughter Anne.

[18] House of Commons, *Names of Members returned to serve in Parliament 1213–1885* (Westminster [?], 1878), pp. 519 ff. Denham's fellow burgess from Old Sarum was Edward Nicholas, a son (?) of Sir Edward, the secretary of state. Sir Edward Nicholas had estates in Wiltshire, where he was born and raised; he went to school at Salisbury. His second son, Edward, was baptized in 1624 (*DNB*). One of the two knights of the shire from Wiltshire was Sir Henry Hyde, K.B., and in 1664 the Chancellor's son Edward Hyde was elected a burgess from Salisbury City (New Sarum). What connections exist, if any, between these Nicholas and Hyde elections from Wiltshire and the election of Sir John Denham I have been unable to determine.

monument. In the late eighteenth century it had neither house nor inhabitant, and the same situation in all likelihood prevailed when Denham served Old Sarum in Parliament. The power to se-cure the return of burgesses from Old Sarum depended on secur-ing the suffrages of freeholders who occupied "burgages" in the old city. There was consequently a traffic in burgages, and a fluc-tuation in the nominal electorate, from ten or eleven in 1625 to seven in 1689, ten in 1705, five in 1734 and 1761, seven in 1816, and three in 1831 on the eve of the Reform. How many "voices" were represented in 1661 remains unknown, or who really controlled them. Throughout the seventeenth century the earls of Salisbury exercised considerable influence in Old Sarum, but in 1624, at least, the Earl of Pembroke achieved control of a majority of the burgages, and it is not unlikely that his successor of 1661 may have had a hand in electing John Denham.[19]

When the new "Cavalier" or "Pensionary" Parliament met on May 8, 1661, for the first session of its long existence, Sir John Denham was among the members of Commons present, and he remained an active member throughout the rest of his life. The Parliament convened on a Wednesday, and on the following Satur-day, the 11th, the Committee of Elections and Privileges was formed, to meet on every Tuesday, Thursday, and Saturday at two o'clock. Sir John Denham was nominated to this committee,

---

[19] See the *Victoria County History of Wiltshire*, VI (1962), 66–67, and T. H. B. Oldfield, *Representative History of Great Britain* (London, 1816), pp. 215, 217. During the period when Denham represented Old Sarum, control of the borough seems not to have been completely firm: in the election for the Convention Parlia-ment, *three* burgesses were returned (April 14, 1660). The House ordered the sitting of Seymour Bowman and of John Norden "until the merits of the case be deter-mined." The case remained unsettled when Parliament was dissolved. No dispute arose in 1661, but in the by-election of October 1669, to fill the seat vacated by Denham's death, the election of Sir Eliab Harvy was protested by Sir William Salkeild, and the matter was referred to the Committee on Elections, which ruled, on November 17, in favor of Harvy (*Names of Members returned; Commons Jour-nal*, IX, 97, 102, 107). It is not impossible, of course, that Denham owed his election to the interest of Sir Edward Nicholas, whose son was elected from Old Sarum at the same time, rather than to that of the Earl of Pembroke.

as he was to be at every session of Parliament but one until his death.[20] Parliament remained in session until Tuesday, July 30, and in the meantime Denham had sat on committees to deal with bills concerning drainage of the Great Level of the Fens and the rendering naviagable of two rivers — committees appropriate for the surveyor general — as well as on such less likely committees as one to examine the King's Majesty's revenue, and one to consider repealing an act against temporal jurisdictions by persons in Holy Orders.[21] Of direct concern to him was a bill for "Paving, Repairing, and Cleansing the Streets and Highways of *Westminster*, and other Parts adjacent to *London*," on the committee to consider which he also quite appropriately sat.[22] Before the House rose for the summer it also passed a motion that would ensure Denham's not being idle in the interim. On July 24 the Commons ordered that "it be recommended to Sir *John Denham* Knight of the *Bath*, his Majesty's Surveyor-General of his Works, to take care in this Recess for opening of the Stairs now stopped up, which were formerly used for a Passage to this House; and to prepare a Place for the Clerk of this House, and his Assistant, to write in, and for the Custody of the Books and Records belonging to this House, and all such other Things as may conduce to the better accommodating of this House." [23]

Denham is not heard from again during the parliamentary recess, but after the House resumed its session his name occurs with great frequency in the records. Parliament sat from November 20, 1661, until May 19, 1662, except for brief recesses at Christmas and Easter. Denham was named to no fewer than nine committees during this period in addition to the others on which

---

[20] *Commons Journal*, VIII, 246–247, 436, 534, 567, 627; IX, 2. The exception to the rule of Denham's inclusion on the Committee of Privileges took place during the plague session of Parliament held at Oxford in October 1665 (*ibid.*, VIII, 614).

[21] *Ibid.*, pp. 258, 267, 274, 291, and *passim*.

[22] *Ibid.*, p. 311 ("Jovis, 25 Julii").

[23] *Ibid.*, p. 310.

he continued to serve.[24] Those that seem best to reflect his special interests are the committees to consider bills for restraining and regulating abuses of hackney coaches and for the better relief and employment of the poor in London and Westminster.[25] On Saturday, March 22, 1661/2, a proviso brought in to the bill for paving the streets was committed to Sir John Denham, Serjeant Charlton, and Sir Robert Howard (Dryden's brother-in-law) with the instructions that "they are to prepare a Clause to be added to the Bill . . . to provide how the Surplus of the Revenue of Hackney-Coaches shall be employed for repairing the Highways, or inlargeing the Streets."[26] After some bickering with the Lords, the highways bill was recommitted to its former committee on April 5, 1662, and on April 8 the House ordered that "Sir *John Duncombe,* Sir *John Denham,* Serjeant *Charlton,* Sir *Robert Atkyns,* and Sir *Rob. Howard,* do prepare and draw up Reasons, to be insisted on at the Conference to be had with the Lords, upon the Points . . . wherein this House doth differ from the Lords."[27] After more bickering the bill was again recommitted on April 11, and after still another conference the Lords on April 29 finally capitulated on the remaining differences between the two houses, and the Streets and Highways Act passed the royal approval on Friday, May 2, 1662.[28] Thus the way was cleared for Denham as surveyor general to win the approval of John Evelyn. Denham's official knowledge of structural matters was called on by the House again in this session when he was named one of six members "to view the Room over the House of Commons; and make Report to the House, whether the Records of the King's-

---

[24] These were committees on Norwich textiles (Dec. 2), for restoring sequestered property to the Earl of Derby (Feb. 17), on handicraft skinners (Feb. 28), on fisheries (March 10), on accountants (March 19), in addition to those mentioned in the text (*ibid.,* pp. 323, 338, 345, 346, 366, 375, 383, 390, and *passim*).

[25] *Ibid.,* pp. 338–339, 346.

[26] *Ibid.,* p. 393.

[27] *Ibid.,* p. 400.

[28] *Ibid.,* pp. 403, 405, 407, 413, 416, 417.

Bench and Common-Pleas may, with Conveniency, and without Danger, be brought back, and lodged in the said Room; and to inquire, and report, where the said Records were anciently kept." [29]

Another matter dealt with by the House of Commons during this session, while not affecting Denham directly, must nonetheless have concerned him. On Monday, March 24, 1661/2, the House, upon information that Denham's ancient adversary, George Wither, had been the author and publisher of a "scandalous and seditious Pamphlet . . . to vilify and defame the Members of this House, and to blemish the Honour and Justice of this House," after an examination of the pamphlet and the culprit, and after the latter's defiant confession that "it was but Parcel of what he intended," committed Wither to the Tower, "there to be kept in close Custody, and be denied Pen, Ink, and Paper, and debarred from having any Company to come unto him." [30] Denham must certainly have been interested in this confrontation, where the tables were so radically turned on the former bloodhound of his estates, and perhaps it was really on this occasion that some remark or episode gave rise to Aubrey's legend of Denham's saving Wither from hanging, in order not to be the worst poet in the kingdom. [31]

Outside of Parliament we find Sir John Denham named on February 2, 1661/2, presumably in his official capacity, as having priority to the amount of £6,000 in the receipt of the Voluntary

---

[29] *Ibid.*, p. 416 ("Martis, 29 Aprilis 1662").

[30] *Ibid.*, p. 394.

[31] During this session of Parliament, as well as throughout the session of the preceding Convention Parliament, Sir Allen Apsley was active in the defense and protection of his brother-in-law, the Puritan Col. John Hutchinson, husband of his sister Lucy. Apsley, however, so far as the records reveal, never called upon Denham's help in his efforts, nor was Denham ever appointed to any of the Commons committees named to consider Hutchinson's case. No direct connection therefore appears at this time between Denham and the Hutchinsons by which Lucy Hutchinson might have acquired her copy of Denham's unpublished *Aeneid* translation.

Present in South Wales.[32] On March 14 appears a money warrant for the payment to him of the fees of 2s. a day for himself
and 6d. a day for a clerk for his office of clerk of the works in
the Tower of London and in all His Majesty's "honors, castles,
&c, reserved for his abode." [33] This office of "Clerk of the Works"
it must be assumed was ancillary to that of "Surveyor Generall
of all Our Howses Workes and Buildings." Also it was probably
on March 8, 1661/2, that Denham rounded out his staff by
certifying the fitness of Henry Phillips to fill "the place of Carver &
Sculptor to his Maiesty, [which] hath for a long tyme been
voyd." [34] For the balance of the year the only other record of
Denham survives in the form of a note he addressed on July 24,
1662, to Sir George Lane in the administration of Ireland at Dublin
Castle, recommending to Sir George for the service of the Duke of
Ormonde "my kinsman, Dr. Denham"—probably, from an allu-
sion in the letter to "the body naturall," the physician Dr. Edward
Denham.[35]

---

[32] C.Treas.Bks.: 1660–1667, p. 357.

[33] Ibid., p. 375.

[34] C.S.P.D.: 1660–1661, p. 528. The indication of Denham's knighthood in the
naming of Sir John Denham on this certificate reveals that the entry, dated March 8,
1660/1, has been miscalendared by at least a year.

[35] Historical Manuscripts Commission, Ormonde Manuscripts, n.s. (1904), III,
19–20. The same source lists under "Concordatums and Imprest Warrants" a payment
to Dr. Edward Denham "for his allowance for twelve months ending the 26th of
February 1661, by warrant dated the 14th of August, 1660: £70. 16s. 0d." How this
may be reconciled with a recommendation for employment dated in 1662 I cannot
say. On November 3, 1663, Sir George Downing wrote to Secretary Bennet (both in
Ireland), "Being confined by an indisposition, I send Dr. Denham to convey an
account of an overture that has been made to me" (C.S.P.D.: 1670 / Addenda: 1660–
1670, p. 686). Foster, Alumni Oxonienses, I, 438, lists an Edward Dynham, "a Lon-
doner born," D. Med. from Montpelier of March 19, 1639, incorporated at Oxford
on April 3, 1641, who is probably the same person. Edward Dynham's kinship to
John Denham remains unrevealed, but it was most likely a distant one; possibly
Edward was a descendant of Thomas Dynham, brother of John Denham's grandfather William. Denham also signs himself to Sir George Lane as "your most affectionate kinsman," but his basis for so designating himself remains even more obscure.
Lane was married to Susannah, daughter of Secretary Nicholas, with whom Denham
seems mysteriously connected; perhaps a relationship of godparentage subsisted some-
where to connect these families.

Not until February 1662/3 does Denham's name recur in the public records, but there is no reason to suppose that he was not diligent in the duties of his office in the meanwhile. The Parliament prorogued in May 1662 was not reconvened until February 18, 1662/3, and so the *House of Commons Journals* are silent on the intervening months. Over the next few years his name occurs frequently, but rarely in a way to reveal much about his personal life. He was faithful in attendance at the House, his name never appearing either in the lists of those absent on the occasions of the sporadic roll calls of the membership or among those requesting permission to be away. From the session of Parliament convened on February 18, 1662/3, until that prorogued on March 2, 1664/5, Denham was returned each session to the Committee on Elections and Privileges, and was named in addition to twenty-five other committees. Appropriately to his administrative office, most of these were committees to consider legislation dealing with such matters as highways and rivers, hackney coaches, brick and tile, drainage of fens, painter-stainers and plasterers, and patents for machinery. He also, however, served (with Edmund Waller) on a committee to consider means of hindering the growth of Popery, and on one to devise new remedies against sectaries and nonconformists. In general a catalogue of all these committees would serve little purpose in illuminating his life; a certain piquancy nevertheless may be felt in his nomination, on May 6, 1664, to a committee to review an act to prevent deceitful and excessive gaming.[36]

As surveyor general Denham also kept well occupied during these years. He seems to have had both his working office and his residence in "Sir John Denham's Buildings" in Scotland Yard. Apparently he built these buildings at his own cost, and they appear to have been his personal property rather than merely perquisites

---

[36] Denham's committee assignments are recorded in *Commons Journal*, VIII, 436, 438, 448, 449, 450, 452, 460, 464, 465, 473, 481, 488, 489, 499, 513, 534, 539, 540, 543, 545, 551, 552, 553, 554, 555, 559, 567, 569, 585, 587, 588, 608, and *passim*.

of the surveyor-generalship.[37] They continued to be called by his name after his death, and though their capaciousness was coveted by other departments of the government, the intermittent negotiations throughout Denham's lifetime for occupation of his buildings by others always assumed his receipt of a sufficient compensatory consideration, cash or otherwise.[38] Nonetheless, one of the earliest references to this mysterious proprietorship merely records on December 23, 1663, without mention of compensation, the intention of the Council of Trade to request the King "for remove of the Councell to Sr John Denhams buildings in Whitehall in wch there are 3 or 4 voyd Roomes very Convenyent

---

[37] In his will, Denham speaks of "the lease which I hold by grant from his Majesty of the ground in Scotland yard adjoining to Whitehall (wherein I have att my owne sole costs and charges built a new rainge of brick buildings)" (*Wills from Doctors' Commons*, ed. John Gough Nichols and John Bruce, Camden Society Publications, 83 [Westminster, 1863], p. 120).

[38] An entry in *C.S.P.D.: 1670 / Addenda 1660–1670*, p. 600, records the reference in a letter of December 31, 1670, to a certain house as being near "Sir John Denham's Buildings." The entry was made almost two years after Denham's death.

The buildings are described in "Sir John Denham's Memorial" calendared for 1665 in *C.S.P.D.: 1670 / Addenda: 1660–1670*, p. 706. This "Memorial" has to do with a lease Denham holds from the King, for fifty-one years, of which four are expired, "of certain buildings containing twenty sets of chambers, seven great garrets, and six great cellars, worth in all 1,240 *l.* a year, for which the King has offered him 7,000 *l.*" Denham indicates his willingness to accept this offer, or an annuity of £1,200.

If four years of the lease had expired in 1665, commencement of the lease would have occurred in 1661, a date that appears plausible. It was, of course, the building site that Denham had leased, "at £5 per annum quitt rent to the Crowne" as another document records (S.P. Dom., ser. 29, Vol. 26, no. 66, p. 95). The *C.S.P.D.: 1668–1669*, p. 137, contains a further entry to the effect that Denham's lease has forty-six years to run, which is equal to thirteen years' purchase, and that the buildings should let at £1,240 a year. Denham, however, indicates his willingness to accept the King's offer of £7,000, "provided the receipt of it may be easy." This entry must be miscalendared in 1668, for if the lease has forty-six years to run, only five of the original fifty-one have expired, and the entry therefore must be no more than a year later than that recorded for 1665, and so must properly belong in 1666.

Still a third entry pertaining to negotiations between Denham and the King over sale of Denham's buildings is calendared erroneously in 1660 (*C.S.P.D.: 1660–1661*, p. 458). This undated document, somewhat inconsistently with the preceding, states that "Sr John Denham and his Lady propose to Sell their buildings in Scotland yard to his Matie esteemed according to the particulars hereunto annexed, at the

for that purpose." [39] For staff Denham had during these first years, in addition to "Mr. Cooper, his man," two rivals for his own position. One was John Webb, Denham's assistant in direct charge of the construction work at Greenwich Palace which went on all during Denham's regime, who seems on the whole to have been an easily subdued man who kept his grievances in check. The other was the highly ambitious Hugh May, paymaster of the Works, whose eagerness to succeed if not also to supplant Denham was too ill concealed to avoid giving the latter some uneasiness and to motivate his ultimate thwarting of May's designs. [40] The comptroller of the Works was Francis Wethered, who seems not to have involved himself in any intrigues.

The work conducted or supervised by the surveyor general before 1665 included, besides the construction at Greenwich, extensive repairs to Windsor Castle. Pursuant to additional legislation, in the formulation of which Denham continued to take part, the program of paving, repairing, and maintaining the streets and

---

yearly valew of 617 *l.* 10s., the title being a Lease of about 45 years to come . . . for which they desire an annuity for the life of . . . the longest Liver . . . [of] £1,225 per annum, which they desire may be charg'd upon some certain fonde." The particulars reveal the buildings to have been of three stories, plus garrets and cellars, amounting to fifty-three rooms, nine garrets, and six cellars (S.P. Dom., ser. 29, Vol. 26. no. 66, p. 95). This item cannot belong in the first place to any date earlier than Denham's knighthood of April 1661, and in the second place to any date earlier than his remarriage on May 25, 1665. Furthermore, it must precede the subsequent death of Lady Denham in January 1666/7. These three items, then, despite their scattered positions in the State Papers, must refer to negotiations within a limited period of 1665 and 1666. From the fact that Denham in his will bequeathed his lease to his daughter Elizabeth may be gathered that the negotiations with the King bore no fruit.

Denham's buildings in Scotland Yard are identified as "the East Row" by William Oldys in a MS note to a copy of Gerard Langbaine, *An Account of the English Dramatick Poets* (1691), in the British Museum (shelf mark C. 45. d. 14). Incidentally, the figure of £7,000 twice mentioned as the King's bid for the property coincides with curious exactness with the sum Aubrey asserts Denham got by his place as surveyor.

[39] S.P. Dom., ser. 29, Vol. 86, no. 44, p. 89: "The results of the Councell of Trade Thursday 17th . . ." (*C.S.P.D.: 1663–1664*, p. 386).

[40] May seems to have been a client of Denham's friend the Duke of Buckingham, although after Denham's death he was to complain that the Duke had abandoned him (see Pepys, *Diary*, March 21, 1668/9).

highways in and about Westminster and London was progressively carried on, and extended to sewers in the metropolitan area and to highways in Surrey. The surveyor general also was charged with enforcement of the misconceived Tudor and Stuart policy of limiting the size of the capital by restricting new building. Under the law Denham approved on April 18, 1663, a license for the Earl of Suffolk to build in London, and on June 13, 1664, a plan by his old acquaintance the Duke of Buckingham to rebuild York House.[41] Perhaps there was no peculation involved in the approval of warrantable projects by these responsible noblemen, but the enforcement of the laws against building certainly could have its profitable side. A warrant of about 1663 at any rate provides a commission for Sir John Denham and four associates "to inquire into all such ffynes fforfeitures Summe or Summes of money as have been imposed upon severall persons by force of a late Act for the preventing of Multiplicities of buildings in and about the Citties and Suburbs of London and Westminster," and they were empowered "to levy and recover fines by the late pretended Parliament of one year's rent on houses erected between 1621 and 1657." [42] Nor, in view of prevailing seventeenth-century standards of public morality, is it surprising that on October 1, 1664, a license was issued to Sir John Denham and Sir William Poulteney to build "ten or twelve" houses.[43] Licenses to build were not difficult for the right people to come by, and on February 20, 1664/5, Samuel Pepys walking near Piccadilly observed under construction the "Lord Chancellor's new house, near St. James's. . . . Near that is my Lord Berkeley beginning another on one side, and Sir J. Denham on the other." Sir John Denham's new house was Burling-

---

[41] *C.S.P.D.: 1663–1664*, pp. 114, 612.

[42] S.P. Dom., ser. 29, Vol. 88, no. 23, f. 38 (*C.S.P.D.: 1663–1664*, p. 401). This undated document is calendared under 1663. Denham's associates were "Colonell Daniell O Neale Esqr and Groome of our Bedd Chamber [Daniel O Neill], John Birkenhead Esqr Doctor of the Lawes, William Geery of Grays Inne Esqr, and Huntington Hastings Corney Esqr."

[43] *C.S.P.D.: 1664–1665*, p. 25.

ton House; it was built for profit and not for his own occupancy.

Other functions of the surveyor general probably added nothing to his income. These merely dutiful transactions no doubt included his approval on March 25, 1663, of the petition of Sir John Robinson, Bart., lord mayor of London, for setting up two ferries over the river "at a certain rent payable to the King." Certainly there was no financial gain in an act of Denham's reported on March 17 a year later. On that date Margaret Chaplaine, widow, "whose family suffered for loyalty and who attended the late King to York and Oxford, and his present Majesty into the West, as sempstress to the gentry waiting on his Highness," petitioned for a grant to relieve her poverty, testifying that when her shed was plucked down "she would have been forced to lie in the streets had not Sir John Denham lent her a stable."[44] Whatever moral benefits Denham may have reaped from this act of charity, his office also facilitated his receipt of other intangible, though more worldly, rewards. On May 20, 1663, he was elected, no doubt ex officio, one of the founding Fellows of the Royal Society.[45] Another project carried out under the surveyor general was the construction of the waterways and the Mall in St. James's Park upon which Pepys comments so frequently and which in 1661 elicited its meed of melodious praise from Edmund Waller in his poem *On St. James's Park, as lately improv'd by his Majesty.*[46] Waller

---

[44] S.P. Dom., ser. 29, Vol. 89, no. 75, f. 106 (*C.S.P.D.: 1663–1664*, p. 423). The date "March 17, 1663," means March 17, 1663/4. The "Humble Petition" of "Margrett Chaplin widd:" to Sir Henry Bennet showed that after "she returned to London . . . shee found nothing but ruine and desolation, and within few yeares after hir husband dyed and left [her] with three Children . . . and very much in debt; and at his Maities restauration [she] hath leave to build a sheed adjoyning to my Ld Duke of Ormonds Lodgings . . . was within few moneths by his Majys Commands ordered to be pluct downe . . . and had not Sr Jo: Denham lent hir a Stable for hir Selfe and Children to ly in, they had beene forced to lie in the Streets, In wch Stable Shee did continue untill [Bennet] borowed it of Sr John Denham. . . ." An accompanying petition to the King requests £50.

[45] *The Record of the Royal Society* (London, 1940), p. 376 (alphabetical list of "Original Fellows" under the second royal charter).

[46] On April 5, 1661, Gabriel Bedell and Tho. Collins entered in the Stationers'

173

fails to mention Denham's role in effecting the improvements, nor does he reciprocate Denham's poetical compliment to him in *Coopers Hill*, but he does compliment Denham to the extent that his poem is an effort in the genre initiated by *Coopers Hill*, as Dr. Johnson astutely recognized.[47]

During this period, as Denham testifies in his dedication of the 1668 *Poems and Translations* to the King, he himself "gave over Poetical Lines, and made it [his] business to draw such others as might be more serviceable" to His Majesty. His connections with the literary world appear accordingly to have been peripheral. On March 22, 1662/3, Sir Henry Bennet, principal secretary of state, addressed to Denham a letter directing him that "His Matie being informed y^t there were in a new comedy lately acted at ye Theater [John Wilson's (?) *The Cheats*] many things of a scandalous & offensive nature hath commanded me to signify his Pleasure to you y^t you & Mr Waller immediatly send for ye sd. new Play & reading it over together give joyntly to his Matie. your opinions of it, y^t if there be cause for it it may be supressed."[48] Another instance of Denham's activities on the fringes of literature also concerned Thomas Killigrew. In 1664 a board composed of the Earl of Manchester, the Earl of Lauderdale, and Sir John Denham, responding to "Complaynts made against him by the Company," reported to the King that Killigrew had not exceeded the powers granted him by his patent

---

Register "a booke called *A poem on St James's Parke*, by Edmond Waller." This was published as *A Poem on St. James's Park*, by Edmund Waller, printed for Gabriel Bedel and Thomas Collins (London, 1661) (Wing W504). Almost simultaneously a surreptitious and mutilated piracy appeared, also a single-sheet small quarto, under the title *On the Park at St. Jamese's* [*sic*]. A copy of this piracy, which Wing does not notice, is in the Henry E. Huntington Library.

[47] "The design of *Windsor Forest* is evidently derived from *Coopers Hill*, with some attention to Waller's poem on *The Park* . . . ," *Lives of the Poets*, "Pope." Despite the accuracy of Johnson's remark, Waller's poem has entered hardly at all into critical discussion either of *Coopers Hill*, its predecessor, or *Windsor Forest*, its successor.

[48] S.P. Dom., ser. 44, Vol. 10 (Letter Book 1662 and 1663), p. 54 (*C.S.P.D.: 1663–1664*, p. 83; S.P. Dom., ser. 29, Vol. 70, no. 14, p. 41).

to manage the King's Players at the Theatre Royal in Drury Lane.[49] Yet despite his own abstention from creativity, Denham's fame by no means withered during this interval of years. It was in 1664, in dedicating *The Rival Ladies* to Roger, Earl of Orrery, that John Dryden proclaimed *Coopers Hill* to be "a Poem which your Lordship knows for the Majesty of the Style, is, and ever will be the exact Standard of good Writing."[50]

Others of Denham's associations involved more lucrative forms of enterprise. With Sir Philip Warwick he was the recipient early in 1663 of a demise for sixty years of a piece of land behind Pall Mall. Denham's share is described as "Land under St. James Park-wall, being lately a highway from Charing Crosse to ye Pallace of St. James, 218 foot in length & about 39 in bredth . . . under ye yearly rent of 26 *l.* with lbty to build within 3 years. . . ."[51] This may have been the site of Burlington House. His association with Lord Berkeley of Stratton also went beyond building a house next to the one that Berkeley was building, for on August 8, 1664, a warrant was approved, in response to a petition of April 15 by Lord John Berkeley of Stratton and Sir John Denham, for the lease to them of 2,500 acres of wasteland in Norfolk, for thirty-one years at £12 per annum.[52] On November 12, 1664, a warrant was issued to Anthony Lord Ashley and Sir John Denham to examine into the matter of funds "pretended to bee collected for ye Protestants of Piemont in ye time of

---

[49] S.P. Dom., ser. 29, Vol. 109, no. 74, f. 132 (*C.S.P.D.: 1664–1665*, p. 146). The report, signed "Manchester / Lauderdaill / Jo: Denham," is decidedly in Killigrew's favor: "And Wee doe find that he hath beene soe farr from abusing this power that he hath made very little use of it hitherto."

[50] *The Works of John Dryden*, Vol. VIII, ed. H. T. Swedenberg, Jr., *et al.* (Berkeley and Los Angeles, 1962), p. 100. Dryden's phrase was borrowed by Wood, to whom it is sometimes attributed: "A poem it is which for the Majesty of the stile, is, and ever will be the exact standard of good writing" (*Athenae Oxonienses*).

[51] S.P. Dom., ser. 29, Vol. 70, no. 70, f. 160 (*C.S.P.D.: 1663–1664*, pp. 88, 94).

[52] S.P. Dom., ser. 44, Vol. 17, pp. 51–52 (*C.S.P.D.: 1663–1664*, pp. 558, 661). Lord Berkeley was the former Sir John Berkeley, Denham's companion at Caen, Caversham, and the Isle of Wight.

ye late Vsurpation," the King "being informed that there is a sum of money remaining in ye hands of certain persons, not yet accounted for." [53] In this regard, on May 3, 1665, a warrant was issued to Lord Ashley, then chancellor of the Exchequer, to pay £1,030 to Denham.[54] True, this money belonged to the Crown, but in any such slippery transaction some of the proceeds were expected to enter the pockets of the collectors.

Taken all in all, the public life of Sir John Denham from the Restoration until 1665 or 1666 was a prosperous one. He acquired money, property, and estates without resort to unduly underhanded means, and remained free from scandal. Only sheerest accident caused one item of business handled by his office during this busy period to be a forerunner of evil. That item was merely a petition of the inhabitants of the Isle of Portland, County Dorset, to the King, for a patent to levy (or restore) an impost of 12*d*. per ton on all stone carried away from the island, half the proceeds to go to His Majesty as lord of the manor, the other half to themselves, inasmuch as "their commons for pasturage are much wasted by the digging of quarries." The prized Portland stone was highly valued for the new buildings going up in London, and this petition was referred for consideration to the Lord Treasurer, the Chancellor of the Exchequer, and the Surveyor of Works.[55] How the Portland quarries dramatically entered the life of Sir John Denham belongs to a slightly later part of his story.

Naturally little can be known about Denham's private life in these years, but the pages are not absolutely blank. On the 29th of December 1663, for example, Samuel Pepys and Sir William Warren were discoursing on the bad company Sir John Mennis

---

[53] S.P. Dom., ser. 29, Vol. 88, no. 2, f. 3 (*C.S.P.D.: 1663–1664*, p. 399; *1664–1665*, p. 64). Lord Ashley was, of course, Dryden's Achitophel, Anthony Ashley Cooper, future first Earl of Shaftesbury.

[54] *C.S.P.D.: 1664–1665*, p. 344.

[55] S.P. Dom., ser. 29, Vol. 134, no. 82, ff. 171–172 (*C.S.P.D.: 1663–1664*, p. 618). The date was October 13, 1665.

had fallen into, namely that of Sir William Batten. They spoke, Pepys records, "of some means how to part this great familiarity . . . and it is easy to do by any good friend of Sir J. Minnes, to whom it will be a good service, and he thinks that Sir J. Denham will be a proper man for it, and so do I." However successful Denham may or may not have been in weaning Mennis away from Batten, he did not prevent Mennis from entertaining Pepys on the following August 15 with his tale about curing Denham of the pox.[56] In any event, slight as is this private glimpse of Denham, it shows his character during the early Restoration years to have been in good repute and his way of life to have been adjudged stable. Taken all in all, the tiny scraps of evidence that can be gathered together show Denham at this time as a man sober, prosperous, and benevolent, diligent and competent at his duties, and obviously rising in the world. A man who may be so described is almost always, given the chances and changes of this life, a happy man.

Denham's life may also, however, be viewed in another light. He was a man building his career and making a go of it. If the happiest time of a man's life is that time when he is exerting his energies to most avail, these years were possibly the happiest of Denham's life. But Denham, unlike most men either of our time or of his, was forty-five years old when his career began. The normal course of his life, like that of many of his contemporaries, had been wrecked by the Civil War and its aftermath. When Denham was admitted to the bar in 1639 he was only twenty-four; when *The Sophy* was produced he was twenty-six. Had he elected to pursue a career either at the law or in the theater he would have commenced, in normal times, at a normal and propitious age. Then he had been a married man and a young father, and could have been expected to mature and develop over the ensuing decades. But the war closed down the theaters, and Den-

---

[56] See above, chap. iv, p. 93 n. 24.

ham's appointment as high sheriff of Surrey with some irony terminated his legal career, so that in 1642 both roads upon which
Denham had begun to advance were suddenly closed to him.

When Denham left Egham in 1642 to occupy Farnham Castle
for the King he also in effect, though unintentionally, abandoned
his wife and abdicated his fatherhood. Anne Denham did not
accompany her husband to Oxford, for in May 1643 she was through
the courtesy of Parliament preparing for childbirth at Egham, and
on November 25, 1645, she informed the Committee for Sequestrations that "she hath ever lived in the Parliament quarters,"
and was negatively certified "not [to have] lived in ye Enimyes
Quarters." [57] On January 19, 1645/6(?), the Committee for Compounding had ruled that she was "to hold her husbands Estate
being Sequestred for Recusancy." [58] By December of 1647 she was
already dead, and, since Denham was in prison for the first
months of 1646 and then abroad until July 1647, it is difficult
to see what further married life the two might have enjoyed together. While Denham was running royal errands, his estates
were being confiscated by the enemy and his children put under
the guardianship of another man. His life was exciting, perhaps
important, but certainly abnormal and unstable. Denham need not
be criticized for loyalty to the Crown, which may have been
a high virtue, nor is there any derogation implicit in the observation that the earliest fruit he gathered of that loyalty was to find
himself, when well past thirty-five, footloose and impoverished in
a dissolute and shabby exiled court, his principal employment
the writing of bawdy verses to amuse a twenty-two-year-old who
happened to be his King — "to divert and put off the evil hours
of our banishment."

That Denham like other Royalists was a victim of history fails
to alter the fact that his life for eighteen years consisted of a

---

[57] S.P. Dom., ser. 20, Vol. 2, p. 11.
[58] S.P. Dom., ser. 23, Vol. 77, pp. 502–503. Dated "19 Jan 1645."

regression from normal maturity to a prolonged adolescence. His return from exile in 1653 did not mend matters, for he returned not to a world of the usual adult responsibility, but to the febrile — and as its history indicates, not very realistic — atmosphere of the Royalist underground. That underground was a land of the dispossessed and disenfranchised, of younger brothers and second sons.[59] From it Denham emerged in 1660 to begin again a serious career, twenty years after his first beginning. A man twenty years younger, it is true, could not expect to start out as surveyor general, but a surveyor general who had begun building his career twenty years earlier and had continued uninterruptedly could also have built up a family and a social position that might have saved him from Denham's folly of 1665.

---

[59] The extent to which the Royalist conspiracies of the interregnum were the work of the cadets of Royalist families rather than of those charged with the responsibilities of family estates (who usually preferred the course of passive conformity) is emphasized by David Underdown, *Royalist Conspiracy in England 1649–1660* (New Haven, 1960), pp. 323 ff. and *passim*.

VII: Distress

What subtle Witchcraft man constrains,
To change his Pleasure into Pains,
And all his freedom into Chains?

By 1665 Sir John Denham was well established in his belated career, but he was also fifty years old, limping, and prematurely aged. Nevertheless, on Thursday the 25th of May in that year, at Westminster Abbey, he married the twenty-three-year-old Margaret Brooke, third daughter of Sir William Brooke, also knight of the Bath. Aubrey describes Denham's new wife as "a very beautiful young lady," but adds "Sir John was ancient and limping." The reprehensible Anthony Hamilton later exaggerated the mismatch by reporting the bride's age as eighteen, the groom's as seventy-nine, but Denham clearly must have appeared older than his actual years.[1] The felicity of such a marriage, at the court of King Charles II, was obviously doomed.[2] It was indeed a spe-

---

[1] Anthony Hamilton, *Memoirs of the Comte de Gramont*, trans. Peter Quennell, ed. Cyril Hughes Hartmann (New York, 1930), pp. 169–170.

[2] The precariousness of Denham's wedded situation is emphasized in a set of verses Waller wrote, but apparently never published, on the occasion of Denham's marriage. Yet it is a misreading of these verses to see in them derision of Denham as a cuckold. Seventeenth-century verses on such topics rarely prefer subtle allusion to broad assertion, and the absence from Waller's lines of any direct reference to cuckolds or horns should be taken at face value. The poem emphasizes the disparity between Denham's age and lameness and his wife's youth and beauty; glances hesitantly at one popular theory — that Denham was impotent; warns him of his potential cuckolding; and advises him to submit gracefully to the inevitable. The poem, printed by G. Thorn-Drury (*A Little Ark Containing Sundry Pieces of Seventeenth-Century Verse* [London, 1921], pp. 33–34) alludes to *Coopers Hill* and puns several times upon *Brooke*, the maiden name of Denham's bride. The following excerpt illustrates perfectly the tenor and style of the whole:

cies of madness that precluded John Denham from foreseeing the consequences of marrying the lovely Miss Brooke, but what in fact ensued the wedding needs to be examined with far more care and attention than has ever previously been expended on this turbulent episode of Denham's life.

Denham's second marriage did not last long: on January 6, 1666/7, nineteen months and twelve days after their wedding, his beautiful and troublesome young bride was dead. The briefness of the interlude may excuse the confusion in the memories of contemporary witnesses as to the precise sequence of events in that year-and-a-half-long drama, but it cannot excuse the unexamined repetition of the garbled stores of those witnesses, or the fabrication of further fictions, which has been the established practice for Denham's biographers ever since. So many precisely datable facts about that ill-starred marriage are available in the records as to make almost inexplicable the vast amount of unacknowledged fiction purveyed on the subject. Perhaps the first specific statement therefore that requires mention is that, for all the evidence that appears to the contrary, the first ten or eleven months of the marriage may have been sublimely harmonious.

When Denham remarried in May of 1665 the Parliament was not in session, it having been prorogued on March 2 until June 21. When June 21 came around the Parliament was prorogued once more until the first of August, and on August 1 it was prorogued again until the third of October. The most probable

---

> why should men wounder att this marriage thus
> The prouerb makes the lame man lecherous
> Wisely the nimph has made her choyse of one
> who can not after other bewtys runn
> Suppose he had nor foot nor t'other limbe
> he that can neither stand nor goe may swim
> 'tis said he had the royal leave to woo
> he that asks leaue of right should giue it too
> The course of brookes no person should restrain
> Through seuerall grounds they rowl into ye main . . .
> (lines 7–16)

181

reason for these successive prorogations was that in June the first signs of plague were becoming evident in London, and by August and September the great and memorable plague of 1665 was raging at its highest intensity. On October 3 the situation in London was so fearful that Parliament did not even attempt to meet, although it had been prorogued until that date, and no entry appears for the day in the *Journal* of either House. Word presumably in some way was conveyed to the members, and a Parliament greatly reduced in numbers straggled into a brief session held at Oxford from the 9th to the 31st of October. By reason of the plague public records for most of 1665 are scanty, and little else appears of a nature to carry news of Sir John and Lady Denham. Most likely, however, it was during the tranquil early months of the marriage that a document appeared among the State Papers listing the particulars of Sir John Denham's buildings in Scotland Yard, value £617 10s. a year, "which he and his lady propose to sell to the King, for a grant with survivorship to them of a pension of 1,225 *l.* assigned on some certain fund." [3] This proposal, which bore no fruit, sounds like that of a loving new husband, careful of his young wife's future security. Evidence of Denham's continued aggrandizement occurs on July 17, less than two months after the wedding, in the form of a warrant from the treasurer to the attorney general to prepare a bill for a grant to "Sir John Dinham and Sir William Morley [his son-in-law] of a parcel of waste land and oosey ground in Sussex." [4]

No doubt Sir John and his Lady, like all others who could afford to do so, left London to escape the plague. Where they went first there is no way to know, but perhaps it was to Greenwich, where Denham still had construction work in charge. At any rate on August 15 the King, who was then at Salisbury,

---

[3] S.P. Dom., ser. 29, Vol. 26, no. 66, p. 95 (*C.S.P.D.: 1660–1661*, p. 458); see chap. vi, p. 170 n. 38, above.

[4] *C. Treas. Bks.: 1660–1667*, p. 674.

ordered the Navy commissioners (who by reason of the naval war with the Dutch could not suspend business) because of the increase of infection in and around London and Westminster to remove their office to the manor house at Greenwich, "in rooms to be appointed by Sir John Denham."[5] When Parliament convened in Oxford in October, however, Denham was present, for on Wednesday the 11th he was named to a House committee appointed "to inspect the Act of *primo Jacobi*, concerning the Plague; and to prepare and bring in an Act to supply the Defects of that Act."[6] For the first time since becoming a member Denham was not nominated to the Committee of Elections and Privileges appointed the same day, nor on Tuesday, October 17, was he placed on the committee to consider a bill to prevent the spreading of the infection of the plague, brought forward by the committee to which he had been named on the 11th. For whatever reason, his name in fact appears on that one occasion only in the records of the business of Parliament throughout the three-and-a-half-week Oxford session. He cannot have been ill, absent, or incapacitated for all that time, however, for on Friday the 13th, in conjunction with Lord Ashley and the vice-chamberlain Sir George Carteret, Sir John Denham signed a report on the petition of the inhabitants of Portland for a restoration of their right to receive 12*d.* on every ton of stone quarried in the island. These three officials advised an allowance of 9*d.* per ton to the Portlanders, except on such stone as was brought away for the King's own special use. Accordingly on November 3 a royal declaration granted to the inhabitants of Portland a fee of 9*d.* on every tone of stone re-

---

[5] S.P. Dom., ser. 44, Vol. 17, p. 129 (*C.S.P.D.: 1664–1665*, p. 518): "take order for yᵉ removing of yᵉ sd Office of Our Navy . . . unto Greenwich, there to be held & kept in such Rooms & Lodgeings within Our Mannor house there, as shall be assigned & appointed for that purpose by Our Trusty & Wellbeloved Sʳ John Dinham Knt of yᵉ Bath, Our Surveyor of Our Workes (whom Wee have directed to give effectual & speedy Order therein)."

[6] *Commons Journal*, VIII, 614.

moved from their quarries, except on stone dug for the King by warrant of the surveyor general.[7] The record of Denham's activities for the year 1665 thus closes in November with his involvement in the matter of taxing Portland stone, and the necessity of his issuing special exemptions on stone to be dug for the King, which is to say, on stone to be used in Denham's own operations. How well he knew Portland and its quarries before this time is an open question; obviously his duty required him now, if never before, to make himself familiar with the diggings. By the end of November the plague had died down, and in December London life had returned to its former courses. No doubt Denham and his wife returned to their interrupted life in the city at about the same time as everyone else.

Parliament had been prorogued on October 31 until February 20, 1665/6, but when the latter date arrived the session was prorogued once more until April 23, 1666; therefore the *Commons Journal* cannot serve as an index to Denham's activities in the interim. On February 25, whether or not they remembered or cared, John Denham and Margaret Brooke had been married for nine full months, and so far, despite the distortions of later reminiscences, no breath of recorded contemporary scandal had sullied their marriage beyond the snide gossip at the discrepancy in their ages. But even without scandal Sir John Denham was ancient and limping, his Lady young and alluring; he doubtless suffered psychological strain as the aged husband of a sparkling young beauty who was evidently both flaunting and vain. To have submitted himself voluntarily to play the role of Pinchwife at the Restoration court was sufficient by itself to guarantee that Denham's ego, expanding with his worldly success of the past five or six years, should now be severely bruised, without any private failures of

---

[7] S.P. Dom., ser. 29, Vol. 134, no. 82, f. 172*v* (report signed "Ashley / G. Carteret / Jo: Dinham"); Vol. 136, no. 25, f. 45 (the proclamation) (*C.S.P.D.: 1665–1666*, pp. 12, 40–41).

rapport he may be conjectured to have suffered in personal encounters with his wife.

Meanwhile in Ireland a new ninety-day wonder had arisen. A preacher named Valentine Greatrakes found himself possessed of the power to cure the King's Evil by touch, and soon advanced to the treatment of other afflictions. He cut a wide swath through Irish society, healing by the laying on of hands — or "stroking" — and by prayer. Early in 1665/6 the "Irish Stroker" ventured to England on his healing mission, but found English air less conducive to the exercise of his miraculous powers. Although highly recommended by the Irish nobility, Greatrakes produced no spectacular successes in the more affluent country. Nevertheless the skeptical Charles II invited the Stroker to perform at court.[8] On Saturday, March 3, 1665/6, Sir George Rawdon at Dublin wrote to Viscount Conway and Killulta to report the latest from England on Greatrakes' progress. The Lord Lieutenant, wrote Rawdon, "had heard from Court that the King had sent for him for Sir John Denham."[9] The letter does not specify for what ailment Greatrakes treated Denham, but a reference in another source to Greatrakes' "striking upon his limbs" makes virtually certain that the treatment was intended for Denham's long-chronic lameness.[10] Whether the notorious limp had recently grown worse,

---

[8] See the account of Greatrakes' career in *DNB*.

[9] *Calendar of State Papers, Ireland: 1666–1669*, ed. R. P. Mahaffy (London, 1908), p. 52.

[10] Denham had been seeking treatment for his lameness as long previously as July 1659, as we have seen. The interpretation of Denham's treatment by Greatrakes as an endeavor to cure his madness is contradicted not only by considerations of chronology but also by every other consideration. In the first place, Greatrakes did not pretend to cure afflictions of the mind, but only those of the body (besides the King's Evil he seems to have specialized in ague [*DNB*]); in the second place, supposing him to have made an exception of Denham, "striking upon his limbs" would have been a bizarre approach indeed to a mental cure; in the third place, the treatment by Greatrakes was by some contemporaries considered to have been the precipitating cause of Denham's madness, a perverse sort of logic on their part had the treatment been intended also to mend the madness.

or King Charles merely regarded it as a conveniently available ailment on which Greatrakes might test his abilities, Denham would certainly have welcomed its alleviation, and perhaps allowed himself to hope for a cure as a restorative of youth to benefit his marriage. No immediate results of the treatment are recorded, a fact that may safely be construed as a record of its failure, and Denham certainly afterward was still afflicted with his limp.[11]

Denham's treatment by Greatrakes took place sufficiently before March 3 for the news to have reached Dublin by that date. Whatever Denham's condition at the time, he was not incapacitated, for on Thursday, March 8, we find him as surveyor of Works certifying the payment of a sum of money for some minor repairs and improvements effected by Jervase Price, the underkeeper of St. James's Park.[12] On Wednesday, March 28, 1666, Denham joined with four others to defend themselves in a legal altercation concerning the river Wey in Surrey.[13] Shortly thereafter, about the beginning of April, Denham took a journey to the west. If Aubrey can be relied upon, it was a trip to Portland to inspect the stone quarries there, a project perfectly reconcilable with the special responsibilities regarding Portland stone placed on Denham's shoulders the preceding November; but in fact Denham is next heard of apparently in Somerset. Exactly what brought him to that county is a mystery, for, although Somerset is quite easily accessible from the Isle of Portland, it lies by no means on the direct

---

[11] On April 9, 1666 (by coincidence the date upon which another correspondent commenced a letter to Henry Slingesby which contains the first recorded notice of Denham's madness), Sir R. Moray wrote to bring Slingesby abreast of the career of Greatrakes: "I can tell you little of the stroaker that is worth the writing. Some say they are the better for his stroaking, others worse. The King is far from having a good opinion of his person or cures. Printed books talk things of him, that I have not yet taken the pains to read" (*Sixth Report*, p. 339).

[12] *C. Treas. Bks.: 1660–1667*, p. 719.

[13] S.P. Dom., ser. 44, Vol. 18, p. 199 (*C.S.P.D.: 1665–1666*, p. 321). Sir Ed. Turner, Sir John Denham, Sir George Ayscue, and Sir Robert Parkhurst desire the King to order "Mr Atorney to forbear any proceedings or prosecution upon an information of one Radcliffe agst ye petitioners relating to ye River Wey."

road between that place and London.[14] Denham might perhaps have been moved to the house of a Somerset friend, or have previously on his own digressed for a visit; but whatever brought him to Somerset, he had been seized suddenly on his western journey by a strange and violent affliction.

On Monday, April 9, 1666, Sir Paul Neile at Whitehall, beginning a letter to Henry Slingesby in the country, imparted first the news that "Sir John Denham is very sick, if not dead, in Somersetshire. His wife went hence late on Saturday night to travel night and day to see him before he died if she could." Saturday had been, of course, April 7, and Denham's affliction therefore had befallen him as long before Saturday as it would have taken a swift messenger to bring word of it to London. Lady Denham's response — charity requires the acknowledgment — was that of any proper wife, and perhaps it should also be noticed that Neile fails to hint any fault. A day or so later Neile finished his letter: "Thus far was written on Monday, and since then there is nothing new; for we hear nothing more of Sir John Denham, and therefore I hope he will scape the fit." [15] News of Denham's nearly fatal seizure also trickled to Oxford, for in the notebooks of Anthony Wood occurs the following entry: "About the 8 of Aprill, Su[nday], Sir John Denham the poet and the King's Surveyor died. (Not yet dead, but distracted.)" [16] The

---

[14] Examination of the Ordnance Survey *Map of XVII Century England* (Southampton, 1930) suggests that the usual route from London or Westminster to the Isle of Portland (i.e., to Weymouth) would have followed the road westward to Salisbury, and then turned off into Dorsetshire through Cranborne, Blandford, and Dorchester to Weymouth. It was possible to take an alternate, more circuitous route from Salisbury to Weymouth, which did indeed enter Somerset, and it cannot be stated for certain that Denham did not in fact take that longer way, whether for condition of the roads or for some other reason now not recoverable. This route passed from Salisbury through Shaftesbury and Sherborne in Dorsetshire, then to Yeovil and Crewkerne in Somerset before turning back toward Weymouth through Frampton in Dorset.

[15] *Sixth Report*, p. 339.

[16] *The Life and Times of Anthony Wood*, ed. A. Clark, Oxford Historical Society Publications No. XXI (Oxford, 1892), II, 75.

point of Wood's correction appears in the next word about Denham, a letter written on Saturday the 14th by Sir Stephen Fox to Sir George Lane in Dublin: "Sir John Denham, that great master of wit and reason, is fallen quite mad, and he who despised religion, now in his distraction raves of nothing else. I pray God divert his judgments from us and send us health, which I wish you." [17]

On Monday, April 16, a week after Neile had first written of Denham's affliction, official cognizance was taken of his incapacitation by the issuance of a warrant for Hugh May, paymaster of Works, "to execute the office of surveyor of Works, during the indisposition of Sir John Denham." [18] On Tuesday, the 24th of the month, accordingly, Neile wrote once more, this time to tell Slingesby that "Sir John Denham did not die, but is fallen violently mad, and so is likely to continue: he is now at one Dr. Lentall's house at the Charter House. The doctor is one that pretends to cure those in this condition, and to him Dr. Fraiser and the rest sent him: what that means you can safely imagine. Hugh [M]ay execute[s] his place during his infirmity, and it is no hard thing to guess at the meaning of that neither." [19] Denham's madness was no longer news to Slingesby, however, for a full week earlier, on the 17th, his cousin George Walsh had written to inform him that "Sir John Denham is now stark mad,

---

[17] Historical Manuscripts Commission, *Ormonde Manuscripts*, n. s. (1904), III, 217.

[18] S.P. Dom., ser. 29, Vol. 153, no. 129, f. 247 (*C.S.P.D.: 1665–1666*, p. 354): "Being informed of the unhappy indisposition and distemper of minde which hath of late seized Our Trusty and Wellbeloved Sr John Denham Knt of the Bath Our Surveyour of Our Workes whereby he is rendred uncapable for the present of executing the said Place and Office, Wee reposeing especial trust and confidence in the fidelity, good abilityes & discretion of Our Trusty and Wellbeloved Hugh May Esqr Our Paymaster of Our said Workes have thought fitt to constitute & appoint, & accordingly Wee doe . . . constitute & appoint him the said Hugh May to execute the said Place & Office of Surveyour of Our Workes for and dureing the indisposition & distemper of minde of the said Sr John Denham. . . ."

[19] *Sixth Report*, p. 339. The opening of the last quoted sentence is transcribed, "Hugh may execute his place . . . ," although clearly the reference is to Hugh May. I have amended the reading accordingly.

which is occasioned (as is said by some) by the rough striking of Greatrakes upon his limbs: for they say that formerly having taken the fluxing pills in Holland, and they not working, they rubbed his shins with mercury: but that neither causing him to spit, they supposed it lodged in the nerves till the harsh strokes caused it to sublimate."[20] For what ailment Denham was treated in Holland is not stated, and, although it is permissible to guess that it was for syphilis, the fact should be noted that "fluxing pills" of various kinds, and mercury, were used as specifics in the treatment of a range of disorders. Only Sir John Mennis' boast to Pepys specifically connects Denham with a venereal disease.[21] Clear notice, however, should be taken that at the time of the onslaught of Denham's madness the only recorded theory of its cause was that of "sublimation" of mercury.

Compact within a period of just over two weeks (Monday, April 9, to Tuesday, April 24) occur all the surviving directly contemporary records of Sir John Denham's famous madness. Only one of these writers reports a supposed cause, and that a purely physical one; perhaps within a year Andrew Marvell advanced a different but analogous theory — that Denham was brained by a brickbat.[22] Most remarkably, Samuel Butler mentions no cause at all for Denham's madness, though he vaguely implies the madness may have been a time of happy delusion for Denham.[23]

---

[20] *Ibid.*

[21] Mennis may have been telling the truth, or he may have been indulging in a tall tale. At any rate his is the only testimony to Denham's ever having been afflicted with the pox; what Banks interprets as a self-reference on Denham's part (in "On Mr. Tho. Killigrew's Return from his Embassie from Venice, and Mr. William Murray's from Sotland") is no such thing (see chap. v, p. 94 n. 25, above). It *may* have been for the pox that Denham was treated with mercury; it *may* have been as a result either of the disease or of its treatment that he became lame; it *may* have been a consequent paresis that attacked him in 1666 — but all is conjecture based ultimately on Mennis' story to Pepys.

[22] In *Clarendon's House-Warming*, stanza vii.

[23] *A Panegyric upon Sir John Denham's Recovery from His Madness* (ca. 1666, see any edition of Butler's *Works*): "All this was done before those days began / In

But when John Aubrey prepared his notes on Denham's life for the use of Anthony Wood he put forward the story that has been so often repeated, and believed in itself, or believed to have been the contemporary belief, that Denham went mad out of jealousy of his wife. Aubrey in fact is the sole source of this story, and Aubrey is also alone in reporting, somewhat ambiguously, three psychopathological symptoms. Here is Aubrey's report:

Anno Domini 166_ he maried his 2d wife. . . . The duke of Yorke fell deepely in love with her. . . . This occasioned Sir John's distemper of madness in 166_, which first appeared when he went from London to see the famous free-stone quarries at Portland in Dorset, and when he came within a mile of it, turned back to London again, and ~~then would~~/did not see it. He went to Hounslowe, and demanded rents of lands he had sold many yeares before; went to the king, and told him he was the Holy Ghost. But it pleased God that he was cured of this distemper, and writt excellent verses . . . afterwards.

The difficulties of fitting this account into what is factually known of Denham's madness are plain. Aubrey says that Denham's madness *first* appeared when he went to Portland, and this part of the story comports well enough with the record of his seizure in or near Somerset. The correction at the end of the sentence, however, is by no means insignificant: Did Denham refuse to go to Portland, as Aubrey's first version implies, or was he merely unable to go on, as the correction indicates? If the correction stands, then Aubrey's story so far conforms with the contemporary letters, adding only the detail that Denham was smitten on the road to Portland, not on his return — but the account thus loses one psychopathic symptom. The two other anecdotes continue to retail convincing symptoms, although with these a chronological difficulty arises: If Denham was removed from Somerset to confine-

which you were a wise and happy man: / For who e'er liv'd in such a paradise, / Until fresh straw and darkness op'd your eyes?" (lines 51–54).

ment at Dr. Lentall's private asylum, when did he have the opportunity to go out to Hounslowe to collect rents or to reveal himself
to King Charles as the Holy Ghost?[24] Perhaps these stories have
their basis in a less dramatic but equally pathological desire *expressed*
by Denham to his keepers to perform each of these acts, from
which he would have been restrained. His announcement that
he was the Holy Ghost may perhaps be related to that raving on
religion mentioned in Sir Stephen Fox's letter.

Wood's account of the madness is merely a condensation of
Aubrey's, and carries no additional authority. "Upon some discontent arising from a second match," Wood narrates, "he became
craz'd for a time, and so consequently contemptible among vain
Fops. Soon after being cured of his distemper, he wrot excellent
verses. . . ." Wood's allusion to the contempt of fops is governed
by his assumption that Denham's madness was caused by his
marriage, and that the contemptuous fops had taken the same
view. Certainly verses were written ridiculing Denham's marriage,
but only Andrew Marvell alludes both to the marriage and to
the madness, and then does not connect the two. Samuel Butler's
Panegyric upon Sir John Denham's Recovery from his Madness
sets out deliberately not only to ridicule Denham's mental affliction, but to pour its vitriol upon every susceptible weakness of
Denham's, real or imaginary. No sense of delicacy could have
withheld Butler's hand, and the interesting lack in this poem of
any slightest aspersion on the marriage can be accounted for only
if Butler was unaware that Denham's marriage also left him open
to derision. One statement of Wood's, however, far too frequently

---

[24] An incident of some sort at Hounslowe could have been, it must be noted, an
episode of the journey, either westward toward Portland or homeward once more to
London. The main road toward Salisbury, which was undoubtedly the road traveled
by Denham in either direction, passed westward out of the capital through Turnham
Green, Brentford, and Hounslowe before crossing the Thames at Staines. Therefore
Denham would have passed through Hounslowe while journeying toward his massive
collapse in Somerset or Dorset, and he would have been brought back through Hounslowe on his return.

191

overlooked, is absolutely correct: that Denham was soon cured. Although Denham was confined in Dr. Lentall's in April, by the following September, when his activities are once more clearly recorded, he appears to be functioning in every respect quite as well as ever he did, so that the very utmost duration of his "indisposition" could have been no longer than five months.

The question must now be raised, although it cannot with certainty be answered: What was the actual nature of John Denham's affliction and madness? The evidence is far too scanty to allow more than conjecture, but conjecture may be ventured. Although Banks, despite having on hand the evidence to the contrary, allows the notion derived from Aubrey to prevail, that contemporary opinion generally held jealousy to have been the cause of Denham's madness, he himself opts for a different cause: "There is little doubt that his insanity was due to a form of paresis, arising from early excesses. Yet the opinion seems to have been general that he went mad through jealousy of his wife's intrigue with the Duke of York, the coincidence in dates making this interpretation natural." [25]

Paresis as a cause of Denham's bout of insanity cannot be absolutely ruled out, but it is on several grounds improbable, and rendered even more improbable by the complete remission of the symptoms for the balance of his life.[26] As an alternative an-

---

[25] *Poetical Works*, p. 23. Sir Sidney Lee says (*DNB*), "His illness, commonly attributed to the scandalous conduct of his wife, was due, according to Marvell, to an accidental blow on the head."

[26] In the first place, the evidence that Denham had ever contracted syphilis is by no means clear cut, and syphilis in any event does not inevitably lead to paresis. In the second place, Denham's stated delusions compel any diagnosis of paresis to specify his attack as of the "expansive type," but, paradoxically, the characteristic symptoms of that type of paresis are far more grandiosely florid than Denham's. His reported attempt to collect rents at Hounslowe, for instance, is far too realistic to be typical; he had, after all, at one time owned the properties involved. In the third place, the rapid and total remission of his symptoms necessarily restricts any diagnosis to the statistically rare, temporarily remitting form of the disease. In such cases remission is never permanent, and recurrence of symptoms is followed by irreversible degener-

other explanation of Denham's insanity may be put forward on the basis of the limited remaining evidence, which can account as well or better for the described configuration of Denham's affliction. This would be the hypothesis that Denham suffered in March and April of 1666 a psychological functional breakdown, and may be considered in some respects a return to the "jealousy" theory, but with important modifications. The major weakness of this diagnosis may be conceded at once: it depends to a considerable degree on a species of long-range psychoanalysis of Denham. But the materials for an analysis of Denham's character, if not of the inner recesses of his psyche, certainly are not lacking.

In some ways, perhaps, the notion that sexual jealousy was an inciting factor in Denham's mental breakdown might be easier to substantiate were "the coincidence in dates" of his madness and his wife's intrigue with the Duke of York more striking than in fact it is. The dates are close enough together to explain the merging of the two events in the memory of John Aubrey, recalling the story after an interval of fifteen or twenty years, but the sequence noted at the time is just the reverse of the usual assumption. Curiously enough an appeal to the calendar might be used to support a contention that the growth of Lady Denham's affair with the Duke of York coincided rather closely with Denham's *recovery* from his madness. Or a plausible argument might be

---

ation and death. Denham's death, however, although it took place only three years after this affliction, was clearly absolutely free of paretic indications; he was of completely sound mind although failing physically at the end, and perfectly aware of the imminence of his death, as is shown below. Careful study of the chapter on paresis in such an authoritative handbook as Arthur P. Noyes, M.D., *Modern Clinical Psychology* (4th ed.; Philadelphia and London, 1954), suggests that the allegation of Denham's paresis is distinctly unprovable, and that if he did suffer from the disease his case was a highly unusual one.

For this and the following examination and attempted diagnosis of Denham's madness I am deeply indebted to Dr. Gerald A. Mendelsohn, Department of Psychology, University of California, Berkeley, with whom I have enjoyed several fruitful discussions of Denham's case. Ultimate responsibility for the present interpretation must, however, remain mine, and under no circumstances should Dr. Mendelsohn be held accountable for a layman's errors.

advanced that it was her husband's collapse and confinement that drove Lady Denham into the arms of the Duke. Whatever the truth, the very earliest surviving reference to the notorious affair comes from Sunday, the 10th of June 1666, two months after Lady Denham's frantic journey to Somerset to see her husband before he might die, and seven weeks later than the last report that Denham had been committed to the care of Dr. Lentall. The entry in Samuel Pepys's *Diary* for June 10 which carries the first written notice of the affair suggests two things: first, that although the liaison was by that date already established, its origin was still very recent; second, that Denham himself was not on the scene (and so probably still under Dr. Lentall's care): "Pierce the surgeon . . . tells me further, how the Duke of Yorke is wholly given up to his new mistresse, my Lady Denham, going at noonday with all his gentlemen with him to visit her in Scotland-Yard; she declaring she will not be his mistresse, as Mrs. Price, to go up and down the Privy-stairs but will be owned publicly; and so she is. Mr. Bruncker, it seems, was the pimp to bring it about." (It is true that this affair is glanced at in a poem, the *Second Advice to a Painter*, ostensibly dated "April 1666," but the first recorded notice of that poem is in December. For a discussion of that poem, which is conceivably by Denham himself, see the next chapter; April is probably an ideal date, rather than the real time of composition.) The further progress of this liaison remains without dated notice until the following September, by which time Sir John Denham had wholly recovered from his affliction and was engaged once more in a full round of business and other activities. The continuance of Lady Denham's amorous adventure and her husband's apparent reactions to it may perhaps shed a little more light on Denham's psychological makeup, but a clearer picture of the possibility that his insanity was of a functional nature requires first a review of the personality delineated by his actions thus far in his life.

Denham's character throughout his life shows a remarkable consistency with itself. Samuel Johnson, with his extraordinary acuity, in two judgments of contrary tenor effectually summarizes that character: "[Denham] appears, whenever any serious question comes before him, to have been a man of piety"; and "he appears to have had . . . the ambition of being upon proper occasions *a merry fellow*." [27] Johnson has no difficulty in supporting his judgments with instances, for the two kinds of behavior reveal two sides of the single most dominant trait in Denham's character: compliability or amenability. All during his life this trait is prominent, and his psychological history consists of a series of adjustments and accommodations of this trait to several other traits, and to circumstances. The other important traits that appear consistently in Denham's character may be grouped under three general heads: impetuous generosity or loyalty; irresolution and weakness of will; and self-regard in its various forms of self-preservation, self-indulgence, and self-aggrandizement. To move from generalities to the details of Denham's career, these traits may be seen manifest in his early compulsive gambling and concurrent production of a book, to conciliate his father, on the evils of gaming. They may be seen in his gallant and impetuous acceptance of the defense of the forlorn Farnham Castle, and in his ignominious surrender. Courage, moral or physical, was never strong in Denham. Denham served subsequently in the garrison of Dartmouth; and was instrumental in its surrender. A consistent Royalist, he nonetheless at once made a friend of his fire-breathing Puritan captor, Hugh Peters, a man whose notorious virulence alone led to his post-Restoration execution. But Denham was the sort of man who would always fraternize with the enemy. During the interregnum he was constantly engaged in Royalist conspiracy, but on good social terms with members of the Council of State; he was arrested, but treated with special favor. Denham engaged in dangerous royal correspondence in 1648, but took alarm and fled before any

---

[27] *Lives of the Poets*, "Denham."

move was made to apprehend him. On the occasions of two armed Royalist insurrections he was visible in the background, but he never took up a weapon.

Within the Royalist camp Denham proposed extravagant results to come from his own efforts, and attempted to ingratiate himself with Hyde; to do so he disclaimed all connection with the Louvre, but kept up relations with his patently Louvrist friends. Quite unrealistically he attempted to unite the Louvre and the Sealed Knot factions against Mordaunt, yet in the event does not seem to have made a lasting enemy of Mordaunt. On a more personal plane something of the same temporizing may be seen in Denham's relations with his sovereigns. When Charles I expressed the priggish hope that Denham would write no more verses in such grave times Denham not only acceded, but seems almost to have suppressed his own knowledge that his obedience had its limitations. Even if Denham be relieved of the authorship of "Verses on the Cavaliers," the *Panegyric on Monck*, and the *Prologue to his Majesty*, he wrote more poems between 1647 and 1667 than he acknowledged to Charles II. Further similar illustrations of the crossed strands in Denham's character — compliance with others and service of self — may be multiplied freely. His acceptance of his rival John Webb as his assistant, but his care that Webb's reversion should not pass the Great Seal, might also be instanced.

From 1660 until 1665 the elements of Denham's character could reside together in perfect harmony. The powers in the state to whom prudence dictated compliance were also his King and his Royalist friends; there was no longer any conflict of conscience when God and Mammon were, so to speak, one and the same. With his lucrative office and his seat in the Commons Denham could afford to steer his way without appreciable difficulty among the rocks and shoals that, in the Royalist high tide, still obtruded from the former conspiratorial factions. Until the very last moment it is difficult to place Denham in, for instance, any of the parties

196

that arose during the controversies over Clarendon. Sir John Denham was an important man, growing rich albeit also old, when
he married Margaret Brooke.

However successful any man may be, he is liable to suffer
psychological strain as he passes beyond middle life and feels his
powers beginning to fail. The stresses John Denham became subject
to at fifty were exceptionally severe. He was aging prematurely; he
had to limp about on a crutch.[28] His time of success had been
very belated, and so could not give him sufficient consolation. Just
at this unpropitious moment, perhaps in a deluded grasping at
youth, he took to himself the burden of a delectable and flighty
young wife. The marriage, of course, was unsuccessful, and Greatrakes' recent failure to amend his lameness may have unsettled
Denham's mind. It is unnecessary to conjecture what particular private incident especially disturbed Denham at his departure
from London to inspect the Portland quarries; perhaps there was
none, but possibly leaving his wife alone and unwatched amid
the gathering seducers, perhaps for the first time, proved more of
a strain than he could bear: when the collapse came, maybe Denham at a crucial moment actually did refuse to go on to Portland —
farther away from London — as Aubrey at first recorded. Whether
Denham's brooding on his condemnation to old age or agitation
about his wife was triggered into psychic collapse by some perhaps
tiny incident of his journey can never be known, but a total functional collapse might at first so derange the responses as to give
rise to the initial assumption that Denham's unspecified symptoms were the product of physical affliction. All the later psychotic
symptoms fit completely the picture of functional disorder.

---

[28] References to Denham's lameness abound in contemporary and later writings.
Aubrey says that Denham at the time of his second marriage was "ancient and
limping"; a poem written by Waller on the occasion refers to Denham as "the lame
man" and "him who downright halts"; and the anonymous "The Session of the Poets,"
printed in *Poems on Affairs of State* (1697), I, 210, refers to Denham as "the limping
old Bard."

Religious ravings arising from feelings of inadequacy and guilt would be sufficiently typical, but in the absence of details not much can be made of them. Denham's claim to be the Holy Ghost, however, would be a fairly commonplace delusional assertion of omnipotence designed to compensate for a devastating feeling of impotence. Free conjecture may be carried too far, of course, but in the light of peripheral gossip about Denham's second marriage, the possibility may also be considered that Denham's claim to be the Holy Ghost was not unconnected with the peculiar relationship asserted by theology to have subsisted between the Holy Ghost and the Virgin Mary. Most interesting psychologically of the reported symptoms, however, is Denham's alleged attempt to collect rents for properties he had once owned but long ago lost. This enactment of a refusal to acknowledge that what was once his valuable possession has now irretrievably passed from him provides so pathetic a parable of Denham's distress at the irrecoverable loss of his youth and vigor as almost in itself to decide the question of the true nature of his insanity. His rapid recovery and the further progress both of Lady Denham's affair with the Duke of York and the resultant scandal are all perfectly concomitant with the theory of functional breakdown as the cause of Denham's illness, and with the underlying qualities of his character.

Middle-aged men who suffer psychic distress at the decline of their vigor, energy, and competence usually adjust in time to the facts of maturity and enter old age with renewed serenity. Even John Denham, whose crisis was unusually severe, adjusted himself in time to the facts, even though the facts he had to adjust to were somewhat more unpalatable than most. His whole lifetime, however, had conditioned him to compliance with more powerful adversaries, while retaining his own private world of opposition or conspiracy. He labored hard to please his father on the matter of gambling, but went on gambling; he agreed with the King that he should not write verses, and went on writing verses; he made friends among Cromwell's councillors, and persisted in

198

Royalist conspiracy; he swore to Hyde he had no connections with the Louvre, and continued his friendship with the Ashburnhams. Now, in 1666, he apparently found it possible to adjust himself to the fact that his wife had become the mistress of the Duke of York. He became the butt of vain fops, perhaps; certainly many verses were printed, and more written, deriding him as a cuckold. But obsessed biographers have failed to notice that the verses never suggest any jealousy on his part, never speak of any frenzy: on the contrary, Denham is derided as a wittol, a husband acquiescent in his wife's infidelity.[29]

The affair itself was notorious, and must now be charted to its end as a significant episode in Denham's life. After Pepys's reference on June 10, Denham himself makes his reappearance before Lady Denham and the Duke are next heard of. Sometime, perhaps in June, Denham signed a document, an accounting by him and two other officers of the Works of the monthly disbursements of his office from June 1660 to the end of May 1666. This covered the entire period of his stewardship, and may have been occasioned by the temporary appointment of Hugh May to fill the place.[30]

---

[29] Of verses specifically referring to Denham's cuckoldry two may be instanced. The Reverend Robert Wilde composed some versified remarks on contemporary poets which he sent to his friend Nathaniel Wanley; he categorizes Denham as one who wears his horns with pride: "Jack Denham tempting laurel scornes / Since greater pride his brow adornes . . ." (the MSS of F. Bacon Frank, Esq., catalogued in *Sixth Report*, p. 458). Marvell, in his *Last Instructions to a Painter about the Dutch Wars, 1667*, adopts a similar view:

> Of early wittols first the troop marched in,
> For diligence renowned, and discipline;
> In loyal haste they left young wives in bed,
> And Denham these with one consent did head.
>
> (lines 151–154)

[30] S.P. Dom., ser. 29, Vol. 157, no. 90, ff. 171–172 (*C.S.P.D.: 1665–1666*, p. 423). Against the view that this accounting was *ad hoc*, and occasioned by Denham's distemper, must be set the fact that the accounting itself clearly reveals the surveyor's fiscal year to have run from June to May; this accounting covers precisely seven years, with annual subtotals of the monthly disbursements, and may in fact have been some kind of sabbatical or jubilee accounting. Moreover, this accounting bears Denham's own undoubted signature, along with those of "Edw. Marshall" and "John

Denham doubtless played small part in compiling this accounting, but his signature to it alone testifies to the amelioration of his affliction, and his next appearance was in his own person. The Oxford Parliament of 1665 had been successively prorogued to February and April, and finally to Tuesday, September 18, 1666. On that day it resumed its sittings, once more back in Westminster, and promptly adjourned to the following Friday, the 21st. On Friday the usual Committee of Elections and Privileges was named, and just as if nothing untoward had occurred since the last session, the name of Sir John Denham appeared once more on the list. But in fact more had occurred in the interim of Parliament than John Denham's madness and recovery: two weeks before the session began the Great Fire of London had broken out, on Sunday, September 2, 1666, and had swept through the ancient City. Quite predictably, the Member who also happened to be surveyor of Works was appointed on Saturday the 22d to the Commons committee set up "to consider of and prepare Proposals, to be tendered to the House, for Relief of the City of *London*."[31] The following Monday, the 24th, Denham was appointed to still another committee. Obviously he was no longer considered mad, and had been liberated for some time from Dr. Lentall's private care. Nor does his functioning as an M.P. appear to have been the least impaired by his wife's flagrant entanglement with the Duke of York.

On Wednesday, September 26, two days after Denham's most

Davenportt," disclosing a certain degree of competence on Denham's part at the time of signing. The disbursements of the Office of Works "upon their Ordinary and all Extraordinary besides the new Building of Greenwich" amounted to £86,276 17*s.* 7½*d.* over seven years, against receipts of £75,288 6*s.* 4*d.*, leaving a deficit of £10,988 11*s.* 3½*d.*

[31] *Commons Journal*, VIII, 626. Denham, moreover, appears to have been once more in possession of his "buildings," and presumably of his office, at the actual time of the fire. Such at least is the implication of his later contention (see chap. viii, p. 230 n. 23, below) that he was promised reimbursement for allowing his buildings to be unroofed as a means of checking the fire. Therefore not only is it certain that Denham had recovered from his affliction of madness by September 18, 1666; it seems probable he had already recovered before September 2.

recent appointment to a committee of Commons, Pepys once again reports the scandalous romance. Even now the affair was still so apparently fresh that Lady Denham is to him an object of curiosity: "[at Whitehall] I had the hap to see my Lady Denham: and at night went into the dining-room and saw several fine ladies; among others, Castlemayne, but chiefly Denham again; the Duke of Yorke taking her aside and talking to her in the sight of all the world, alone; which was strange, and what I also did not like. Here I met with good Mr. Evelyn, who cries out against it, and calls it bitchering, for the Duke of Yorke talks a little to her, and then she goes away, and then he follows her again like a dog."

The following Monday, October 1, Denham's name appears again on a committee of Commons,[32] and just a week later, on Monday the 8th, Pepys noted, "The Duke of Yorke is wholly given up to this bitch of Denham." On Saturday the 13th Pepys went again to Whitehall and saw there "the Duke of York (who is gone over to all his pleasures again, and leaves off care of business, what with his woman, my Lady Denham, and his hunting three times a week)." Two days later he has some further news of the affair, with unrecognized political overtones: he walked to Westminster Hall with Sir Henry Cholmley, "in our way talking of matters and passages of state, the viciousness of the Court; the contempt the King brings himself into thereby . . . the Duke of York becoming a slave to this whore Denham, and wholly minds her. . . . He tells me, what I wonder at, but that I find it confirmed by Mr. Pierce . . . that Sir W. Coventry is of the caball with the Duke of York, and Bruncker, with this Denham; which is a shame, and I am sorry for it, and that Sir W. Coventry do make her visits; but yet I hope it is not so."

The affair was about to take a dramatic new turn, but Denham himself throughout these events apparently retained a perfect composure. At any rate, his predicament did not interfere with his

---

[32] *Commons Journal*, VIII, 629.

work. On October 26 he wrote to an assistant concerning repairs on Windsor Castle, and discussed the corruption of officials there. As the letter more nearly resembles a personal communication than most of the surviving documents to which Denham's signature is affixed, it deserves reproduction at length:

Sir,

I could not see you this day, having taken Physick wch confines me to my Chamber, but if you see my Ld Arlington before I do you may please to putt him in mind y^t 2 or 3 daies since I told him y^t ye King had bidden me speake to his Lshp to gett a warrant for his Matie to signe, to the receiver of ye rents of Windsor who hath money in his hands for ye repayre of y^t Castle and y^t his Matie thinks ye best way of beginning y^t worke is to putt out ye Surveyor there, for having cheated him to such a degree y^t it goes beyond all, y^t any accountant ever made, (according to y^e proportion) (except Prettyman) nay more than y^e Parliament libellers say of others, or those who made y^t libell cann so much as support. The receivers name is Dudley Reuss Esqr, and y^e summ hee is to lay downe is 100 $l.$ to carry on y^e suite begunn agst him in y^e Exchequer, by Mr Attorney upon a Scire facias. The money pd to my Ld Mordant [now become Governor of Windsor Castle; see next chapter] or y^e Sollicitor Mr Gerard, for I desire not to touch it, when y^e warrant is signed you may give it me to send to my Ld Mordant ffor Parsons Green or to give it him at ye Lds house. I did not thinke to bee so prolix to a man off so much busines.

y^r servant JoDenham.[33]

One searches this letter in vain for evidences of paresis, functional breakdown, or even of marked anxiety or confusion. On the 8th of November Denham was named to a House of Commons committee to study a bill "for making Provisions for such as shall

---

[33] S.P. Dom., ser. 29, Vol. 176, no. 43, f. 66 (*C.S.P.D.: 1666–1667*, p. 220). The letter is addressed to "my worthy Friend Mr Williamson at My Ld Arlingtons Lodging," and is a very useful sample of Denham's autograph. Williamson has been identified as clerk of the Works at Windsor.

be infected with the Plague."[34] Even the grant on November 21 of somewhat greater autonomy to John Webb as Denham's assistant at Greenwich, specifically a power to grant warrants for Portland stone, does not reflect a decline in Denham's position, for the warrant specifically emphasized Denham's possession of this power, and Webb's position as his assistant.[35]

Meanwhile on Saturday, November 10, Pepys had a stimulating piece of news to confide to his Diary: "This afternoon Creed comes to me, and by him, as also my Lady Pen, I hear that my Lady Denham is exceeding sick, even to death, and that she says, and every body else discourses, that she is poysoned." So began what was to be the great scandal of the winter season of 1666. On Monday Pepys records again: "Creed . . . and I . . . talking of the present ill condition of things . . . and particularly of my Lady Denham, whom everybody says is poisoned, and he tells me she hath said it to the Duke of York; but is upon the mending hand, though the town says she is dead this morning." Her recovery from this bout continued, for by Thursday (November 15) H. Muddiman, in a newsletter dispatched to George Powell of Pembroke, reported: "Lady Denham is recovering; some have raised strange discourses about the cause of her sickness, but the physicians affirm it to have been *iliaca passio.*"[36] No more is recorded for a month, but on Wednesday, December 12, she was apparently still ill, though probably not severely so. On that day Pepys noted the conversation at a dinner party he attended: "They talked . . . that the Duke of York do not haunt my Lady Denham so much; that she troubles him with matters of State, being of my Lord

---

[34] *Commons Journal*, VIII, 646.

[35] S.P. Dom., ser. 44, Vol. 14, ff. 106–107 (*C.S.P.D.: 1666–1667*, p. 286): "Mr Webb Surveyor Assistant to Sir John Denham in bldg Our Palace at Greenwich with the same power of Executing, acting, proceeding therein and granting of warrants for stone to be had from Portland to all intents and purposes as the said Sir John Denham. . . ."

[36] S.P. Dom., ser. 29, Vol. 178, no. 69, f. 104 (*C.S.P.D.: 1666–1667*, pp. 262–263; dated from Whitehall). *Iliaca passio* is seventeenth-century medical jargon for colic.

Bristoll's faction, and that he avoids; that she is ill still." This entry does not make clear whether the Duke's aversion was from being troubled with politics by his mistress, or specifically from the politics of the Earl of Bristol. George Digby, the second Earl, with whom Lady Denham could trace a connection by marriage, had as early as July 1663 accused Clarendon of high treason. The charge had been leveled before the political moment was ripe and the King had ordered Bristol's arrest.[37] Consequently Bristol had had to hide for two years. By 1666 the tide of opinion against Clarendon had become sufficiently strong to encourage the reactivation of Bristol's faction, although he himself did not dare as yet resume his seat in the Lords. The Duke of York lavished little love on Clarendon, although his Duchess, Ann Hyde, was the Chancellor's daughter. The Duchess, accordingly, would have a double reason to dislike Lady Denham: as a rival for her husband and as an antagonist of her father. In view of Lady Denham's relationship with the Earl of Bristol, and her partisanship with his faction, it is interesting to find Denham himself visiting the Earl the following year, and later dedicating a poem to him. The implication would seem to be that Denham shared his wife's partisanship for Bristol.

For the last three weeks in December the Parliament was in Christmas recess, but regardless of his wife's illness Denham had served in the earlier part of the month on two other committees: one regarding "Utensils for the speedy Quenching of Fire," and one on "regulating the Making of Brick and Tile," both appropriate for the surveyor of Works.[38] After the recess, on January 4, 1666/7, he was predictably appointed to a committee to consider a bill for rebuilding the devastated City of London, and the committee was instructed to meet the following day, Saturday the 5th, at two in the afternooon.[39] Whether Denham attended that

---

[37] See *DNB* for details of Bristol's career.
[38] *Commons Journal*, VIII, 656, 657.
[39] *Ibid.*, pp. 670–671.

meeting or not is unknown, but a crisis was coming on at his home. On Monday Pepys reports on Lady Denham once more: "At noon . . . with my Lord Bruncker by coach as far as the Temple, in the way he telling me that my Lady Denham is at last dead. Some suspect her poisoned, but it will be best known when her body is opened, which will be today, she dying yesterday morning [i.e., Sunday, January 6]. The Duke of York is troubled for her; but hath declared he will never have another public mistress again; which I shall be glad of, and would the King would do the same." The medical men once more obdurately refused to find any evidence of poison, for on January 25 Lord Orrery, reporting on the results of the autopsy in a letter to the Duke of Ormonde, says: "My Lady Denham's body, at her own desire, was opened, but no sign of poison was found." [40] On the very day following the autopsy Pepys skeptically recorded a more piquant product of that operation, which was to give rise to its own tradition. For January 8, 1666/7, he wrote in his *Diary*: "Sir Richard Ford did this evening at Sir W. Batten's tell us that upon opening the body of my Lady Denham it is said that they found a vessel about her matrix which had never been broke by her husband, that caused all pains in her body. Which if true is excellent invention to clear both the Duchesse from poison or the Duke from lying with her." [41] This is the only hint dropped by Pepys

---

[40] This citation, from the *Orrery State Papers* (1742), p. 219, is given by Wheatley in his edition of Pepys's *Diary* as a note to the entry for January 8, 1666/7, quoted in the text above immediately after this present quotation.

[41] This tradition, of Denham's impotence and the Duke of York's carnal innocence, on the one hand reflects the insinuations of Waller's poem on the marriage, and on the other hand is reflected in Aubrey's statement in his notes on Denham: "The duke of Yorke fell deeply in love with [Lady Denham], though (I have been morally assured) he never had carnall knowledge of her." A contrary tradition implicitly contradicts this one. That is the tradition reported by Sir Sidney Lee in *DNB* to the effect that Denham had practiced a "loathsome" method of revenge on the Duke. Lee's source is a manuscript addition by William Oldys to a copy of Gerard Langbaine's *An Account of the English Dramatick Poets* (Oxford, 1691), p. 125, now in the British Museum (shelf mark c. 45. d. 14). Oldys' note reads: "The tradition of the Duke of York's lying with Sir John's Wife; and his getting the Pox

that he had ever heard anyone specifically accused of the poisoning, but other pens were not so reticent. Despite the autopsy report, Lord Conway wrote on that same day, Tuesday, January 8, to inform Sir George Rawdon that "My Lady Denham died poisoned, as she said herself, in a cup of chocolate." [42] The received version apparently held the Duchess of York to be the culprit, a cup of poisoned chocolate her means. Marvell several times insinuates as much. About the Duchess in one place he writes:

> Express her studying now, if *China* Clay
> Can, without breaking, venom'd Juice convey;
> Or how a mortal Poison she may draw
> Out of the Cordial Meal of the *Coca*. . . .
> Not unprovok'd she tries forbidden Arts . . .
> And her self scorn'd for emulous *Denham's* Face,
> And nightly hears the hated Guard, away
> Galloping with the Duke to other Prey.

Later in the same poem the poor young victim is made to figure in an extended simile dealing with the Duchess' father:

> What Frosts to Fruits, what Arsnick to the Rat,
> What to fair *Denham* mortal Chocolat;
> What an Account to *Carteret*, that and more,
> A Parliament is to the Chancellor.[43]

Once more in a similar context Marvell alludes to the separate mis-

---

purposely that she might give it the Duke: for so I have read it in a note upon a MS Vol. of Satyres in the Harleian collection." The only nearly contemporary reference to this allegation I have been able to find occurs in "An Historical Poem" (*ca.* 1680), a satire on Charles II formerly attributed to Marvell: "But now York's genitals grew over hot / With Denham's and Carneig's infected pot" (lines 46–47). Around 1668 Robert Carnegie, Earl of Southesk, whose Countess had become the Duke's mistress, was widely believed to have practiced the same mode of revenge.

[42] John Bramshall, *The Rawdon Papers, consisting of Letters . . . to and from Dr. John Bramshall* (1819), p. 227, cited by Banks, *Poetical Works*, p. 24.

[43] *The Last Instructions to a Painter about the Dutch Wars, 1667*, lines 65–78, 341–344.

fortunes that befell Lady Denham and her husband. In *Clarendon's House-Warming* (stanza vii) he writes thus of the Chancellor:

> Thus daily his Gouty Inventions he pain'd
>   And all for to save the Expences of Brickbat;
> That Engine so fatal, which *Denham* had brain'd,
>   And too much resembled his Wife's Chocolat.

According to one story, the Duchess of York was soon thereafter "troubled with the apparition of the Lady Denham, and through anxiety bit off a piece of her tongue."[44] No other candidate seems to have been advanced by contemporary gossip, although in aftertimes suspicion was also directed elsewhere. Aubrey is unsupported in his allegation that Lady Denham "was poysoned by the hands of Co[untess] of Roc[hester] with chocolatte." The basis of this charge is totally obscure.[45] The beginning of the following century even saw the charge, in Anthony Hamilton's *roman pretendu historique* called *Memoirs of the Comte de Gramont,* that Denham himself was the guilty party.[46] Denham cannot be con-

---

[44] Reported by Sir Sidney Lee (*DNB*) who names Henry Newcome as its source. Newcome (1627–1695) began in 1646 a diary which he kept up to the end of his life. The portion from September 30, 1661, to September 29, 1663, was published by the Chatham Society in 1849, and, of course, does not cover the period of the Denham scandals. An abstract of the entire diary, entitled *The Autobiography of Henry Newcome, M.A.*, was published in two volumes by the Chatham Society (Manchester, 1852), but fails to mention this anecdote.

[45] Thorn-Drury (*A Little Ark Containing Sundry Pieces of Seventeenth-Century Verse,* p. 34) says that the "Countess of Rochester, acting for and on behalf of the Duchess of York," was suspected of the murder, but fails to indicate his authority for the statement, which may therefore be no more than the product of his own amalgamation of the general gossip about the Duchess with Aubrey's isolated accusation of the Countess. The source Thorn-Drury cites, *Vox & Lacrimae Anglorum: Or, The true Englishmens Complaints* (1668), merely repeats the standard allegation about the Duchess of York, as a parallel to the destruction of Rosamond, "Par amour to Henr. II., whom the Queen, finding in her labyrinth, dispatched, as the Dutchess served Madam Denhan [*sic*] lately."

[46] Hamilton, *Memoirs of the Comte de Gramont,* pp. 191–192: "Old Denham, who was naturally jealous, became more and more so, and grew convinced that his suspicions were not without basis. His wife was young and beautiful; himself was old and unappetizing . . . he had not a country-house where he could incarcerate

victed of wife murder on evidence such as that, and every other record disagrees flatly with the *Memoirs'* statement that Denham was suspected at the time.[47] In sober fact, from all the evidence presented, including the autopsy report, a most probable guess is that the unfortunate lady actually died of appendicitis.

---

the unfortunate Lady Denham. Thus the old ruffian arranged that she should take a far longer journey, while never leaving London; pitiless death cut her off among her fairest hopes and in the flower of her age. Nobody doubted but that he had poisoned her, and the rabble near where he lived determined to stone him as soon as ever he showed his nose out of doors. Denham, however, kept his house, the better to lament his wife's decease, till such time as their fury had been allayed by a magnificent funeral, at which he distributed to people four times greater quantity of burnt wine than had ever yet been drunk at any obsequies in England." The editor of this edition of Hamilton points out several inconsistencies and anachronisms in this highly fanciful tale. Hamilton never alludes to Denham's madness.

[47] I do not know on what grounds, other than Hamilton's gossip, Sir Sidney Lee (*DNB*) asserts that the reputation of Denham's guilt was general. Lee is absolutely wrong in his statement that Pepys shared Hamilton's view. On the contrary, as we have seen, Pepys never accuses anyone, but alludes only to the commonest rumor — that the Duchess of York was the poisoner.

VIII: Serenity

My early Mistress, now my Antient Muse,
That strong Circaean liquor cease t'infuse,
Wherewith thou didst Intoxicate my youth,
Now stoop with dis-inchanted wings to Truth.

LADY DENHAM was buried by her husband in St. Margaret's, West-minster, on January 9, 1666/7, three days after her death, and by the 22d of the month at least he was in attendance once more at the House of Commons.[1] On that day he and three other members were granted permission by the House to attend upon the Lords as material witnesses for the defense in the trial of Viscount Mordaunt. Mordaunt had been rewarded for his Royalist conspiracies with the minor sinecure of the governorship of Wind-sor Castle; at this session of Parliament he had been impeached by the House of Commons for alleged irregularities and petty tyrannies in his conduct of that office. Mordaunt had many ene-mies, among whom Denham certainly at one time had been num-bered; Denham's call as a witness on Mordaunt's behalf is therefore worth comment. Since one of the crimes of which Mordaunt stood accused, however, consisted of the eviction of certain statu-tory tenants of quarters in Windsor Castle, perhaps Denham's prospective function as a material witness was merely to testify, as surveyor general, as to the correct allocation of space in the castle. The attack on Mordaunt, however, was no doubt politically rather than personally inspired, and served as a rehearsal for the impeachment of Clarendon which was to take place the following

---

[1] *Commons Journal*, VIII, 681; see also *Lords Journal*, XII, 84.

winter. What Denham would have testified can never be known, for the King terminated the proceedings against Mordaunt by suddenly proroguing the Parliament on February 8.[2]

The year following the death of his wife was a busy one for John Denham. He was active in his office, in Parliament, and, for the first time in many years, active once more as a poet. He himself later assured the King that his resumption of verse writing took place only that summer, the summer of 1667, "at the Wells."[3] Perhaps he was truthful in this assertion, and certainly his release from the stress of his marriage affected Denham for the better. What he wrote during the remainder of his life is marked by a dignified valedictorian tone which indicates he was at last resigned to grow old in grace and serenity. The period from 1667 to 1668 was for Denham a period of poetic productivity unequaled in his life since the years 1641 and 1642. But perhaps he was not entirely truthful in his assertion to the King, and his *annus mirabilis* began with his recovery from insanity in 1666.

Denham's recovery coincided quite closely with that other *annus mirabilis* celebrated by John Dryden, the extended year from the outbreak of war with the Dutch, and the early British naval victories, in 1665 (which coincided roughly with the outbreak of plague in London), to the less successful naval campaign of 1666 and the

---

[2] *DNB* should be consulted for the background and consequences of the proceedings against Mordaunt. The parliamentary moves can be followed in the *Commons Journal* sporadically, and in the *Lords Journal*, XII, 84, 92, 94, 96, 98, 99, 100, 101, 103, 104, 105, and 106–107. On January 31, 1666/7, Denham was appointed to another committee, one to consider adding a proviso concerning St. Paul's Cathedral and two other churches to be added to a bill for the rebuilding of London (*Commons Journal*, VIII, 687).

[3] Dedication "To the King" in *Poems and Translations* (1668). Denham writes that at the behest of Charles I he had given over "Poetical Lines, and . . . since that time I never disobeyed my old Masters commands till this Summer at the Wells. . . ." The same volume contains a similar statement in the preface to Denham's translation of Mancini: "Going this last Summer to visit the *Wells*. . . ." The "Wells" would have been either Epsom or Tunbridge Wells. Both resorts were becoming popular, but Denham's visit may have been simply for the purpose of alleviating his lameness.

Great Fire. Denham's recovery may with virtual certainty be dated before the fire, that is, before the beginning of September. When Denham's mental balance was restored and he emerged from Dr. Lentall's house, he had to confront the fact that his wife was the open and acknowledged mistress of the Duke of York, the second most important person in the kingdom. His characteristic response was to comply with the reality of power, and thereby earn for himself contempt as a wittol. There is no reason to suppose Denham enjoyed this role, and the history of his reactions under analogous circumstances in the past leads readily to the supposition that he would seek some concealed means of reasserting his own self-regard, his *amour-propre*. Gossip has spontaneously generated stories that in fact he found such means; the allegation that he poisoned his wife is only one response to an instinctive evaluation of his character.[4] One substantial piece of evidence indicates that he may have found a more subtle means of redressing the balance, in a poetic attack on his rival.

The Duke of York had been a principal actor in the international events celebrated in Dryden's *Annus Mirabilis*. At the opening of the Dutch War he had commanded the fleet at the essentially indecisive battle of Lowestoft, which had been, however, claimed as a British victory. In March 1665/6, just before Denham's collapse, the inveterate courtly flatterer Edmund Waller published a poetic eulogy on the Duke's conduct under the title of *Instructions to a Painter for the Drawing of the Posture and Progress of His Maties forces at Sea under the Command of his Highness Royal. Together with the Battel and Victory obtained over the Dutch, June 3, 1665.*[5] A year later, under the im-

---

[4] The "Historical Poem"–Oldys revenge story is based on a parallel estimate.

[5] Published as a broadsheet under date of 1665 (Wing W499), and as a folio under date of 1666 (Wing W500), by Henry Herringman. Herringman registered the poem in the Stationers' Register on March 1, 1665/6, as "*a booke intituled Instructions to a painter for ye drawing of ye posture & progresse of his Mats forces at sea under ye comand of his highnesse royall togeather wth ye Battell & victory obtained over the Dutch, 30 Junii 1965*, by Edm: Waller Esq." Somewhat puzzlingly,

print date of 1667, and without a printer's name, a second poem appeared titled *The Second Advice to a Painter, for Drawing the History of our Navall Business; In Imitation of Mr. Waller. Being the last Work of Sir John Denham.*[6] This is a 340-line poem satirizing both Waller's eulogy and the Duke of York, and also slighting the naval conduct of the Earl of Sandwich in August 1665. This mock eulogy was the first of a sequence of five "Instructions to a painter" satirizing the entire course of the Dutch War, as well as progenitor of an untold number of offspring in what became recognized by the end of the century as a satiric genre. Four of the "instructions" on the Dutch War were attributed by their title pages to Denham; the fifth is known to have been written by Andrew Marvell. Denham's authorship of any of these "instructions" has been questioned, however, and Banks has excluded all of them from Denham's canon.

Arguments for the exclusion of all these so-called painter poems are not hard to find. In the first place, Denham's authorship of the satires was early doubted. Wood says of the surreptitious pieces, "Sir *John Denhams* name is set, yet they were then thought by many to have been written by *Andrew Marvell* Esq."[7] The editors of *Poems on Affairs of State* (1703) note in the table of contents of the volume that reprints these poems that they are "said to be written by Sir *John Denham,* but believ'd to be writ by Mr. *Milton.*"[8] In the second place, Denham certainly did not ac-

---

Herringman had already entered, a year previously, on March 10, 1664/5, "a paper intituled *Instructions to a Painter for drawing of a picture of the state & posture of the English Forces at sea under the Comand of his highnesse royall in the conclusion of the yeare 1664,* by Edmund Waller Esqr." So far as I can find, this "paper" was never separately published, and the poem published in 1666 was therefore probably a reworking of a poem written or projected months before the battle of Lowestoft, altered to center on the battle.

[6] Wing D1008. Breda has been suggested as the place of printing of this 8vo pamphlet, despite Wood's vague report that a printer was stood in the pillory for printing this or another set of similar "directions."

[7] *Athenae Oxonienses.*

[8] Perhaps "Milton" is a blunder for "Marvell."

212

knowledge the poems, and it has been held that his writing of them would have been an act of gratuitous recklessness. Other piecemeal arguments need not for the moment be considered. But before the other side of the matter is examined, the point should be emphasized that establishing the authorship of any one of these pieces does not establish the authorship of any other. No prudent author would willingly publish any of the satires under his own name, and, when once the first had come out attributed to Denham, it was only natural that further accruals to the series should carry the same name. Each of the mock "instructions" must be analyzed separately for traces of authorship; a wholesale approach to the entire sequence can only be self-defeating. Accordingly the real question is not did Denham write all five painter poems, but did he write any. Logically that question narrows to this: Did he write one of these poems and, specifically, did he write the first?

So far as Banks's arguments against Denham's authorship of the *Second Advice to a Painter* may be separated from his general argument against Denham's authorship of the entire group of poems, they may be listed as follows: (1) it is incredible that Denham, holding the office of surveyor-general, should have openly published under his own name a poem attacking state policies and high officials; nor could Denham have written the poem without intending its publication for such a proceeding would have been not only dangerous, but pointless, as the very *raison d'être* of such political satires is publicity; (2) Denham's insanity may have lasted until as late as June 1667, so that he may have been insane at the time the poem was written or published; (3) the poem contains a reference to Lady Denham as the Duke of York's mistress, and, "although Denham was perhaps a complaisant husband, it seems impossible that he should thus refer to his wife's infidelity." [9] In favor of Denham's authorship Banks concedes the evidence of style, which he finds compatible with his

---

[9] *Poetical Works*, pp. 329–331.

judgment of the manner in which Denham wrote.[10] And of his counterarguments only two need be considered, for, although he allows his second point — Denham's madness — to stand in his text, he withdraws it in a footnote, acknowledging its erroneousness and lack of value.[11] As for Banks's first argument, it involves almost as great a misconception as the second. Certainly Denham would not "openly publish under his own name" an attack on the Duke of York; obviously Denham did not authorize the printing of the *Second Advice* even if he did write it, still less cause his name to be affixed to the printed pamphlet. But that fact has no bearing on his authorship. Nor does agreement that early "publication" was no doubt intended by the author of the satire at all support Banks. What the author sought was circulation of his satire through "the Town," and the standard way to accomplish that end in the seventeenth century was by dissemination of manuscript copies. Often a satire was not printed until years after its composition; some written in the period have not been printed even yet.[12] When such a piece did see print, more often than

---

[10] *Ibid.* Throughout this work I have rejected subjective evaluation of style as a valid criterion of authorship.

[11] *Ibid.*, p. 330n. Banks seems to have written his Appendix B, in which he discusses the authorship of the various "instructions to a painter," some considerable time before his book went to press. His general introduction takes cognizance of the fact, first pointed out by T. W. Baldwin ("Sir John Denham and *Paradise Lost*, *MLN*, 42 [1927], 508), that Denham had fully recovered from his madness by September 1666. Yet the Appendix, continuing to assert that after Denham's seizure "we hear no more of him until June, 1667," stands unrevised except for this footnote retraction. Since the argument based on insanity forms an integral part of Banks's chain of reasoning which leads him to reject all the *Advices* as spurious, it is surprising that he does not review his case to see how it stands after the withdrawal of that part, and restate his arguments. To illustrate the effect of such a revision we may instance Banks's summary of his reasons for rejecting the *Second Advice*: "the *Second Advice*, judged merely by its style, might possibly be by Denham . . . but his authorship is made very doubtful by (1) the fact that he may have been insane at the time the poem was written or published, and (2) the reference to his wife's intrigue" (*Poetical Works*, p. 331). Had Banks revised his Appendix in the light of his later knowledge, his summary would have to read thus: "the *Second Advice*, judged merely by its style, might possibly be by Denham . . . but his authorship is

not it did so as a result of the enterprise of some printer who published a manuscript he had acquired for the benefit of those outsiders who had no access to the manuscript circulation. The *Second Advice to a Painter* was surreptitiously published, the printer carefully suppressing his own name although identifying Denham as the author; the attribution, if correct, probably came to the printer by rumor. He would feel no compunction about embarrassing Denham, and whatever the truth of the authorship Denham without doubt would deny it. Perhaps that is why Denham was so careful to insist to the King the following year that he had drawn none but architectural lines until the summer of 1667. Moreover, Banks's argument turns on itself: the printed *Advice* bears the date of 1667, yet the poem must have been written in 1666, so that it was *not* printed shortly after composition.

The third objection, that Denham could not have referred to his own wife's infidelity, depends not only upon an interpretation of his character, but on a consideration of the allusion itself. Near the end of the poem, which has derided almost all the principals in the naval actions of 1665 and concluded with the futility of the Duke of York's activity, these six lines occur:

> Now many Historians argue *con* and *pro*:
> *Denham* says thus; tho always *Waller* so: [13]

---

made very doubtful by the reference to his wife's intrigue." On that solitary point of doubt opinions might certainly differ.

[12] Marvell's *Last Instructions to a Painter*, for instance, was apparently not printed until 1689, though certainly it circulated widely earlier. The verses addressed by Robert Wilde to his friend Nathaniel Wanley, which contain a passage on Denham's cuckoldry (see chap. vii, p. 199 n. 29, above), so far as I know have never been printed in full. Every large manuscript collection from the seventeenth century contains copies of contemporary verses, many not printed for years or centuries afterward, many still not printed. Banks seems not to have understood the nature of manuscript dissemination of literature in the seventeenth century, a fact that leads him into several misconceptions, as, for instance, of the early relations between Denham and Waller, or of the genesis of *Coopers Hill*.

[13] Concerning this direct reference to Denham, Banks says (*Poetical Works*, p. 329), "the appearance of Denham's name in the text might under other circumstances be considered a bit of evidence supporting his authorship, but here it seems

And he, good Man, in his long Sheet and Staff,
This Penance did for *Cromwel's* Epitaph.
And his next Theme must be o' th' Duke's Mistress;
Advice to draw Madam *l'Edificatress*.

(lines 331–336)

No one can seriously quarrel with Banks's identification of "Madam l'Edificatress" as Lady Denham, wife of the surveyor general of Works. But about this reference may be observed: first, it is a sneer at the Duke (framed in a sneer at Waller), not at either Denham or his wife directly. The poem contemptuously shares Pepys's dismayed criticism, recorded on October 13, that after the Duke's naval fiasco in 1665 he had abandoned responsibility and "gone over to all his pleasures again, and [left] off care of business, what with his woman, my Lady Denham."[14] Second, the reference is remarkably oblique, even though unambiguous. To write an attack on his rival would no doubt yield satisfaction to Denham, yet it would be hard to write an attack without reference to the provocative rivalry. The minimum and muffled reference by means of allusive French ("Madame l'Edificatress") in place of a name could be the verbal equivalent of the gingerly touching of a sore; it fits the psychology of a man who has accommodated himself to the fact of his wife's public infidelity, but still finds his situation painful.

If Banks's arguments against Denham's authorship of the *Second Advice* are at least nullified, what remain for consideration are the contrary indications. Stylistic evidence and the psychological aptness just discussed may be allowed to be inconclusive. A positive

---

merely put in as a blind." My interpretation of the reference would be just the reverse: I would take the third-person naming of Denham as a normal indication that the poem was *not* written by him, and account for its presence as a blind to distract attention from the possible truth that he *did* write it.

[14] The *Third Advice to a Painter*, seeking to establish continuity with the *Second Advice*, begins by a reference to this same dalliance of the Duke's. Before moving on briskly to the events of 1666, it opens by dismissing the two chief actors of the *Second Advice*: "*Sandwich* in *Spain* now, and the Duke in Love."

argument for Denham's authorship may, however, be con-
structed out of Banks's abandoned and untenable second argument:
the matter of Denham's insanity. The primary events discussed
in the poem occurred in the summer of 1665 (although the allusion to Lady Denham as the Duke's mistress belongs to a year
later). Waller's eulogy on the Duke, the mock model for the
Second Advice, came out early in March 1665/6. The *Second
Advice*, on the other hand, is not heard of until December 1666,
and was ultimately printed under date of 1667. The first notice of
the poem, not surprisingly, occurs in Pepys's *Diary* for December 14, 1666: "here I met with, sealed up, from Sir H. Cholmly, the
lampoone, or the Mocke-Advice to a Paynter, abusing the Duke of
York and my Lord Sandwich, Pen, and every body, and the King
himself, in all the matters of the navy and warr. I am sorry for
my Lord Sandwich's having so great a part in it." [15] Almost without question this is the *Second Advice*, and very probably what
Pepys received from Cholmley was a manuscript transcript, not
the printed octavo pamphlet of 1667. [16] Once the *Second Advice*

---

[15] Pepys, *Diary*, VI, 101–102. The only detail of this description which fails exactly to fit the *Second Advice to a Painter* is Pepys's statement that it abuses "the
King himself." The *Second Advice*, unlike later exercises in the genre, contains no overt
criticism of the King. Perhaps Pepys is referring to the brief dedication "To the King"
accompanying all the printed editions of the *Second Advice*. This dedication also is
not overtly critical, though, of course, it is implicitly highly critical of the King's failure
to prevent the disastrous policies described in the *Advice* from coming into effect.

[16] The identity of the *Second Advice* with Pepys's "Mocke-Advice" is virtually
certain. Aside from the identity of content discussed in the preceding note, these
facts may be considered: (1) the *Second Advice* was undoubtedly the earliest of the
series of mock advices on the Dutch War; (2) the *Third Advice* stands self-adver-
tised as the successor to the *Second Advice*; (3) on January 20 Pepys received a copy
of the *Third Advice*, which he identified both by that title and by content, and noted
that he had already a copy of "the former"; (4) "the former" could be no other than
the *Second Advice*, and the only previous Advice noted by Pepys as having come
into his possession was the "Mocke-Advice" on December 14; consequently the
"Mocke-Advice" and the *Second Advice* must be one and the same; (5) all other
known mock *Advices* or *Instructions* could not have been written until after July
1667.

Pepys's entry is not specific about the nature of the "Mocke-Advice," whether
printed or manuscript. His failure to use the printed title, however, may be taken as

had shown the way, similar satires on episodes of the Dutch War followed hard on the events. By January 20, 1666/7, Pepys had a copy of the *Third Advice to a Painter*, lampooning the summer campaign of 1666, and two further entries in the series, dealing with occurrences as late as August 1667, were in print within the same calendar year.[17] What is striking, therefore, about the *Second*

---

one indication that his copy was not a printed one. A stronger illustration of the probability that he received a manuscript, as well as of the procedure by which a poem circulated in that period, is to be found in his record of receiving the *Third Advice*: "I took it home with me, and will copy it." Clearly what Pepys retained was a manuscript transcript of the poem, and undoubtedly that also is what he received. The *Third Advice* was not printed separately, but together with the *Second* in a single quarto under the title *The Second and Third Advice to a Painter, For Drawing the History of our Navall Actions, The two last Years, 1665 And 1666.* Had this volume been what Pepys received we should expect his entry in some way to reflect that fact, unless we suppose him to have received a dismembered fragment containing only the second poem. His uncomplicated entry suggests he received an uncomplicated copy, and that copy was probably a manuscript. Moreover, he mentions no presumptive author for either *Advice*, and he could hardly have failed to react to the title-page attribution to Denham in both printed volumes.

[17] Pepys records on January 20: "met Mr. Brisband, with whom good discourse, to White Hall towards night, and there he did lend me 'The Third Advice to a Paynter,' a bitter satyre upon the service of the Duke of Albemarle the last year. I took it home with me, and will copy it, having the former, being also mightily pleased with it" (Pepys, *Diary*, VI, 137). That a loyal civil servant like Pepys, a close adherent of the persons lampooned in the *Second Advice*, could nonetheless find both satires highly pleasing may also tell against the notion that the courtier Denham could have written neither.

The sequence of printed editions seems to reflect the probable sequence of composition of the poems. The *Second* and *Third Advice*, in imitation of Waller's *Instructions*, each bore a date, "April 1666" and "October 1st, 1666," respectively (as does also Marvell's *Last Instructions*: "September 4th, 1667"), but these are probably ideal dates rather than genuine dates of composition. Each new volume reprinted the preceding members of the series: (1) *The Second Advice to a Painter:* "Nay Painter, if thou dar'st design that Fight" (Wing D1008); (2) *The Second and Third Advice to a Painter:* (*a*) "Nay Painter, if thou dar'st design that Fight," (*b*) "Sandwich in Spain now, and the Duke in Love" (Wing S2258); (3) *Directions to a Painter for Describing our Naval Business . . . Whereunto is annexed, Clarindon's [sic] House-Warming by an Unknown Author* [Marvell]: (*a*) Nay Painter, if thou dar'st design that Fight," (*b*) "Sandwich in Spain now, and the Duke in Love," (*c*) "Draw England ruin'd by what was given before," (*d*) "Painter, where was't thy former Work did cease?" (*e*) *Clarindon's House-Warming:* "When *Clarendon* had discern'd before-hand" (Wing D998). *The Second Advice* and *Directions* are both octavo, *The*

Advice is the apparent time lag between the events it lampoons and its own composition. Written during the time of the Duke of York's idle dalliance with Lady Denham — roughly, that is, within the last half of 1666 — it ignores the naval events of 1666 (treated in the *Third Advice*), to concentrate on those of 1665 and on Waller's poem of March 1665/6. Now Denham was afflicted in April 1666 and remained out of view until the beginning of September; during most of this time he may be presumed to have been undergoing treatment, and to have in effect dropped out of time. Upon his release from Dr. Lentall's he found himself cuckolded by the Duke of York who just before Denham's interval of chaos had been poetically praised by Waller. For Denham thus belatedly to ridicule the Duke's year-old heroics and to burlesque Waller's paean makes a perfect kind of sense which the same act by any other writer would not make.

The poet of the *Second Advice* shows no special animosity toward the Earl of Sandwich whose indecisive conduct before Bergen in August 1665 (an essential part of the naval failures of that year which led to his "banishment" to an embassy in Spain) is also inescapably treated in the poem, as it is by all writers at the time. But he does demonstrate considerable dislike for the comparatively minor personages Brunker and Sir William Coventry. It will be remembered that Pepys characterized Brunker as "the pimp to bring [the Denham-York liaison] about," and also noted that "Sir W. Coventry is of the caball with the Duke of York, and Bruncker, with this [Lady] Denham," facts not likely to endear either to Sir John Denham. Other feelings within the poem which comport with Denham's authorship are a strong dislike for the Earl of Clarendon, though this was becoming a universal passion, and partisanship with the Earl of Bristol, which

---

Second and Third Advice a quarto; all three volumes bear the imprint date of 1667, no place, and no printer's name. The third and fourth poems in the *Directions* volume are titled the "Fourth Advice" and "Fifth Advice," respectively.

was not. Unlike most attacks on Clarendon, however, this one emphasizes his connection with the Duke of York, and makes Clarendon's responsibility for the Dutch War a diversionary reaction to Bristol's attacks on himself:

> But damn'd, and treble damn'd be *Clarendine*,
> Our Seventh *Edward*, with all his House and Line!
> Who to divert the danger of the War
> With *Bristol*, bounds us on the *Hollander*:
> Fool-coated Gown-man! sells to fight with *Hans*,
> *Dunkirk*; dismantling *Scotland*, quarrels *France*;
> And hopes he now hath bus'ness shap'd, and Power
> T'out last our Lives or his, and scape the Tower;
> And that he yet may see, e'er he go down,
> His dear *Clarinda* circled in a Crown.[18]

The Chancellor's "dear Clarinda" is, of course, his daughter Ann, Duchess of York.

Denham's authorship of the *Second Advice* cannot, of course, in the final analysis be proved, but one interesting and rather frantic contemporary denial of it by no means constitutes disproof.[19] Most

---

[18] Lines 141–150; these lines are part of a speech put into the mouth of a seasick gentleman in the English fleet. The "War with Bristol" is, of course, the political struggle by Bristol's faction to overthrow the Chancellor.

[19] Christopher Wase, *Divination,* in *Poems on Affairs of State: Augustan Satirical Verse, 1660–1714,* Vol. I, ed. George deF. Lord (New Haven and London, 1963), pp. 54–66. Professor Lord, who has printed this poem for the first time, regards it as an "unanswerable argument against Denham's authorship of *Second Advice*" — on what evidential grounds he fails to say. *Divination* is a well-intentioned brief for the defense, but is totally lacking in authority; moreover, it is often so impenetrably obscure in its wording as to defy interpretation. As Lord himself says, the style of the poem "is often elliptical to the point of incoherence," and as its editor he can arrive only at such unsatisfactory formulations of its purport as that it "seems to hint at the Duke of Buckingham" as the true author of *Second Advice.* Lord rejects the authority of this seeming hint chiefly because he believes Marvell to be the true author, so perhaps it is the same commitment that leads him to accept Wase's passionate exculpation of Denham as "unanswerable."

The obscurity of *Divination* and the extravagance of the annotational exegesis into which it has lured Lord may be illustrated by one example. Lines 83–84 contain the remark, "a skilful lapidary . . . parts the diamond from the Bristol stone,"

likely early in 1667 Denham's old admirer Christopher Wase produced a poem, or rather a set of 286 crabbed and cryptic verses,
with the multiple intention of refuting the *Second Advice*, of vin-
dicating Waller, and of asserting loyalty not only to the King but
also to those of his agents who were attacked in the *Advice*.
Above all Wase seems concerned in this piece, which he called
Divination, to free his idol Denham from the imputation of having
written the *Advice*. Despite the cryptic allusiveness of his verses,
Wase reveals no inward knowledge of the true authorship of the
Advice or of the circumstances of its composition, nor is there
any reason why he should have any. Throughout most of his
life he was a somewhat retired scholar; at the time of the *Advice*
and *Divination* he was headmaster of Tonbridge School and unlikely to be privy either to court gossip or to solid information.
His motive in fact for writing *Divination* was outraged loyalty
and a protective concern for Denham's reputation. It is intriguing,
however, to notice that Wase almost unwittingly suggests that
Denham might have had precisely the motive for writing the
Second Advice which has been advanced here, namely, revenge on
the Duke of York and his pimps:

> Denham accus'd would make a statue speak,
> And melting rocks into soft numbers break:
> Whose brains, though strong, by stronger passions rack'd,
> May yield, but's loyalty was never crack'd.
>
> (lines 59–62)

---

to which Lord has attached the following note: "*Bristol stone*: A kind of rock crys-
tal. Supposing Buckingham to be the suspected author of *Second Advice*, the line
may refer also to the alliance of Buckingham and George Digby, Earl of Bristol, in
opposition to Clarendon." Whether the substance of this note derives genuinely from
Wase's poem, or only from Lord's intuition, it betrays unawareness that Denham
cannot be readily dissociated from either Buckingham or Bristol. During the interregnum Denham alone was supposed to have influence over the unstable Duke, and
his affiliation with Bristol was soon to be publicly signalized in his *Poems and Translations* of 1668. In that volume Denham not only mentions a visit he paid to the
Earl in the summer of 1667 (that is, within half a year or so of the *Second Advice*)
but also speaks of Bristol as his "Ancient and Honourable Friend."

If Wase is supposing here that Denham went mad out of a jealousy caused by the Duke of York, it is a sheer act of faith on his part that the strains that cracked Denham's sanity should have left his loyalty, especially to the Duke, intact. When all contrary indications are examined, Denham seems still the most probable real author of the *Second Advice to a Painter*.[20]

---

[20] The authorship of the *Second Advice* (and also of the *Third*) is discussed in a series of articles in *BNYPL*: George deF. Lord, "Two New Poems by Marvell?" *ibid.*, 62 (1958), 551–570; Ephim G. Fogel, "Salmons in Both, or Some Caveats for Canonical Scholars," *ibid.*, 63 (1959), 223–236, 292–308; Lord, "Comments on the Canonical Caveat," *ibid.*, 63 (1959), 355–356. To these articles has been added a further contribution by Ephim G. Fogel, "On 'Multiple Rhymes': Some Clarifications," a typescript of which he has kindly allowed me to examine. It is planned to reprint all these articles together, with others, in a volume of essays on the problem of attribution to be edited by David Erdman and Ephim G. Fogel. In the initial article in this series Lord revives the thesis that Andrew Marvell is the real author of the *Second* and *Third Advice* as well as of *Last Instructions to a Painter*. His assertion is based upon "many bits of evidence of different kinds," which, while he concedes that "examined separately, [they] may not be very impressive," yet, he insists, "they amount to a strong probability when examined together" (*BNYPL*, 62 [1958], 551). Consequently the complete refutation of Lord's contention is a tedious, futile, and thankless task. If an objector demonstrates that each and every bit of Lord's evidence, examined separately, is not very impressive, he has demonstrated no more than Lord concedes at the outset. Thereafter, discussion is reduced to metaphysical speculation on the number of grains of sand required to make a binding rope. Professor Fogel raises only a comparative few of the many possible objections to Lord's stand, but to my mind Lord fails completely in his subsequent rejoinder to answer any of them satisfactorily. It seems therefore the more unfortunate that Lord should with so little apparent hesitation have printed both the *Second* and the *Third Advice* under Marvell's name in his edition of *Poems on Affairs of State: Augustan Satirical Verse, 1660–1714*.

A number of the considerations that make Marvell's authorship of the *Second Advice* improbable may be mentioned. For one thing, the obliqueness of the reference to Lady Denham contrasts markedly with Marvell's open and callous references both to Denham's madness and to his cuckoldry. For another, the poem fails to mention some of Marvell's favorite targets of attack, e.g., the "two Allens" (Sir Allen Apsley and Sir Alan Brodrick) who, though hangers-on of Clarendon, were both on good terms with Denham. (For contrast see Marvell's *Last Instructions*, line 212, and *Clarendon's House-Warming*, stanza xiii.)

The unkind reference to Waller's need to do penance for "Cromwell's Epitaph" as his motive for writing the original *Instructions to a Painter* may also suggest Denham rather than Marvell. Marvell had also written his own "Cromwell's Epitaph," but was not likely to consider the act one that required penance. Denham, however,

The case for Denham's authorship of the successor *Third Advice to a Painter* is very much weaker than that for his authorship of the *Second Advice*. The arguments in favor are almost all of a negative nature: the *Third Advice* continues the discussion of the Dutch War from the point at which the *Second Advice* ended, the replacement in the naval command of York and Sandwich by the Dukes of Albemarle and Cumberland. Additionally, the glancing allusion to Lady Denham in the opening line of the *Third Advice* — "*Sandwich* in *Spain* now, and the Duke in Love" — is even more tangential than the reference in the *Second Advice*, and so might bespeak Denham's tenderness on the point.[21] More-

---

might wish to score off Waller if he knew Waller to have written the poem disparaging his marriage to Margaret Brooke. An almost gratuitous reference to "*Petty's Double-keel'd Experiment*" in the last line of the *Second Advice* may also betoken Denham's presence behind the poem. Sir William Petty, F.R.S., inventor in 1663 of a double-keeled sea boat that sank in the Irish Sea, was Denham's counterpart, surveyor-general in Ireland. (By the same token, the "Sir William's Isle" of Wase's *Divination*, line 180, which Lord is unable to gloss, may very possibly be Ireland.)

[21] To a considerable extent the plausibility of Professor Lord's contention that Andrew Marvell is the author not only of the *Last Instructions to a Painter* universally conceded to him, but of the *Second* and *Third Advice* as well, depends upon the assumption that the two *Advices* are self-evidently the products of a single pen. So deeply is Lord committed to this assumption that, directly in the face of Professor Fogel's specific denial of a common authorship for the *Advices*, he can nonetheless write, "the two *Advices* are so intimately related in thought, structure, style, metaphor, and attitude that they must unquestionably [*sic*] be the work of one man" ("Comments on the Canonical Caveat," *BNYPL*, 63 [1959], 361). The convenience of this assumption to Lord is very great, since it enables him to regard the two *Advices*, for comparison with *Last Instructions*, as constituting essentially a single work. Thus he can say that "in their treatment of Clarendon, Coventry, Sandwich, Albemarle, Clifford, Arlington, the Duke and Duchess of York, Waller, Henry Brouncker, Sir John and Lady Denham, etc., the *Advices* and *Last Instructions* often agree in the smallest details" without ever really considering whether the *Second* and *Third Advice* agree between themselves in their treatment of these persons. This hasty amalgamation overlooks the facts, for instance, that Clifford, Waller, Brunker, Denham, and Lady Denham are mentioned in the *Second Advice* but not in the *Third*, and that Albemarle is named but once in the *Second Advice*, three lines from the end, and is treated of only in the *Third Advice*. The treatment, therefore, in the *Advices* of six of these twelve persons, which is to be compared with their treatment in *Last Instructions*, is a treatment confined to only one of the two *Advices*. In these six cases there is, then, the grossest kind of discrepancy between the *Second Advice* and the *Third Advice*.

over, Denham's probable insanity at the time of the events satirized in the *Third Advice* (June 1666) cannot be used as evidence against his authorship. The poem was certainly written later than the *Second Advice* and designed as a sequel to it, and Denham's

---

But even without considering the extent of disagreement between the *Second* and the *Third Advice*, Lord's major assertion must be severely qualified. In some instances the uniformity of treatment he postulates as between the *Last Instructions* and the *Advices* is inevitable regardless of unity or multiplicity of authorship; in other instances the uniformity does not exist. Of the first kind, obviously, is the treatment of Clarendon, the target of everybody and of uniform and public charges; the "Fourth" and "Fifth Advice," which nobody would pretend are by Marvell, belabor him in the same terms as the other poems. The entire sequence of painter poems may be defined as attacks upon the Chancellor within the campaign that culminated in his impeachment and downfall. Marvell was neither the architect of that downfall nor its sole poet; in the sequence of poems, however, it may be noted that *Second Advice* is mildest in its animosity toward Clarendon, Marvell's genuine work the most virulent. Of a somewhat similar nature is the abuse of Sir William Coventry, the second name on Lord's list; he also is a universal target, referred to slightingly by Pepys and alluded to in the "Fifth Advice" as well as in the poems in question. Yet his treatment is not uniform: in *Second Advice* he is mentioned scatteredly for his venality, in *Third Advice* only once, for the same offense (for which the *DNB* notes that he was notorious); yet in *Last Instructions* the notorious venality is scarcely so much as glanced at, and Coventry, who was York's secretary, is depicted as a conniver and betrayer of trust between the King and his brother. As for the Earl of Sandwich, the very reverse is true, and Lord's assertion has no force whatsoever, because Sandwich is neither mentioned nor alluded to at all in either *Last Instructions* or (Marvell's) *Clarendon's House-Warming*. His sole extended treatment occurs in *Second Advice*; in *Third Advice* he is only briefly and retrospectively alluded to.

George Monk, Duke of Albemarle, in the *Second Advice* is named only once, three lines from the end. In *Third Advice* he is at the center of attention, depicted as a courageous but coarse bumpkin, and seen largely through the eyes of his coarser wife. There is much broad gibing about a wound in his arse, characterized as the Rump's revenge. In *Last Instructions*, on the contrary, Albemarle is presented through the sympathetic eyes of the poet, who sees him as a doughty, devoted, overburdened, and frustrated defender of English honor. The contrast in treatment as between the two poems is far more striking than any similarity. Clifford, likewise, is mentioned only in *Second Advice* and *Last Instructions*. In *Second Advice* he is depicted as a venal bungler; in Marvell's poem he is only alluded to, not named, in a comical simile that compares his appearance carrying the white rod with that of a "tall louse" seen on a hair under a magnifying glass. Arlington, secretary of state, is mentioned in both *Advices* and in Marvell's *Instructions*, but in different terms on each occasion. In the first poem he is an engrosser of prize money and a pimp who marries a bastard of the house of Orange. In *Third Advice* he is an inept in-

recovered sanity in the latter months of 1666 would certainly have allowed him to learn what public events had taken place during his disability. But no sufficient motive appears why Denham should have wished to plod on through the whole Dutch War as he had

---

telligence chief and a seller of secrets to his Dutch wife's compatriots. In *Last Instructions* he is more mildly represented only as feckless and confused about geography, and as false to his former employer the Earl of Bristol, initiator of the parliamentary attack on Clarendon.

The Duke of York, hero of Waller's poem and consequently chief butt of the *Second Advice*, by virtue both of his initial prominence and of his relationship to Clarendon, might reasonably be expected to receive fairly uniform treatment throughout these poems even with a multiplicity of authors, so that it is the more surprising that the reverse is the true case, and Lord's assertion lacks even that unimpressive solidity. Although central to the *Second Advice*, the Duke is scarcely mentioned in the *Third*. In the opening line of the latter poem he is dismissed as "in love," and is later passingly alluded to as Clarendon's son-in-law. More critical for Lord's assertion, however, the *Last Instructions* reduces the Duke still further to mere errant husband of his Duchess. The fact that all three poems show some awareness of the Duke's affair with Lady Denham is scarcely treatment agreeing "in the smallest details," for the affair was common knowledge. The treatment of the Duke among these poems in fact is uniform only in the very broadest and most commonplace details. The Duchess of York likewise is mentioned in all three of these poems, as well as in Marvell's *Clarendon's House-Warming*, but about the Duchess the first thing to remember is that she was Ann Hyde, daughter of the hated Chancellor and popularly regarded as his instrument to gain control of the royal succession. Nevertheless, in *Second Advice* she is represented only as the Duchess, visiting the Duke in the fleet at Harwich and recipient later of gifts of seashells. In *Third Advice* she is much more darkly viewed as having connived with her father in her marriage to the Duke and of having somehow encompassed the deaths of her royal in-laws, the Duke of Gloucester and the Princess Mary. In *Last Instructions* she is accused in similar terms of duping the Duke (but this allegation was common; see *DNB*, "Clarendon") and, for the first time in these poems, of poisoning Lady Denham. The treatment, then, of the Duchess is markedly different as between the *Second Advice* and *Last Instructions*, and similar as between *Last Instructions* and *Third Advice* only in a matter of common gossip.

As for Waller, the assertion is empty. All mock *Advices* are to some extent allusions to Waller, regardless of who wrote them — the "Fourth" and "Fifth Advice" as much as those here in question — but only *Second Advice* and *Last Instructions* actually name Waller. *Second Advice* opens by alluding to Waller's *Instructions* and toward the close ridicules Waller for writing a "penance" for his elegy on Cromwell; the attitude of *Second Advice* toward Waller is distinctly satirical. *Last Instructions*, on the contrary, though deprecating Waller's foolish poetic venture, treats him sympathetically as a patriotic, "Country-party" M.P. A very different person, treated also only in *Second Advice* and in *Last Instructions*, is Henry Brunker, about whom rela-

dealt with the Duke of York's campaign of 1665. The butt of the *Third Advice* is the Duke of Albemarle, and to some extent his Duchess, but Denham seems to have had no particular animosity against that homely couple. On balance, then, the *Third Advice*

---

tive unanimity might have been expected even from separate authors, but who in fact is treated quite differently in the two poems. In *Second Advice* Brunker is the confidant of the Duke of York who, by a cowardly misrepresentation of orders from the Duke, was responsible for the English failure to destroy the Dutch fleet after Lowestoft. This charge was no secret, and it led to Brunker's dismissal from Commons in 1667. Yet *Last Instructions* scarcely alludes to the charge, and represents Brunker only as a pimp, a characterization supported by Pepys, among others.

Finally, and of greatest present concern, may be considered the treatment of Denham and his wife throughout these poems. Denham himself is mentioned in *Second Advice* only once, and as a poet, as a gainsayer of Waller. In *Third Advice* he is not mentioned at all. In *Last Instructions* he is mentioned directly only as a wittol, not as a poet. That hardly constitutes identity of treatment. To extend the discussion it may be remarked that he is mentioned also in Marvell's *Clarendon's House-Warming*, this time as having been demented by a blow from a brick. Lady Denham is likewise mentioned only in the same three poems ("the Duke in love" in the first line of *Third Advice* is scarcely an allusion to Lady Denham, still less a treatment of her). In *Second Advice* she appears as "the Duke's mistress . . . Madam l'Edificatresse," an allusion so roundabout as to obscure her relationship to Denham, who is mentioned (as a poet) only four lines previously. In *Last Instructions* she is mentioned as the Duke's mistress and then as victim of the Duchess' revenge; in *Clarendon's House-Warming* the Duchess is once more accused of poisoning her. Uniformity of treatment therefore prevails only between the two undoubted Marvell poems; reference to the Denham-York *affaire* is all that connects *Second Advice* with the two Marvell poems, and that was common knowledge, as Pepys testifies. In "small details," however, the treatments are markedly different.

Having demonstrated at length the nullity of Lord's major assertion about the relationship between the two earliest *Advices* and the undoubted Marvell poems there is little further point in demonstrating the discrepancies between *Second Advice* and *Third Advice*. It has been shown already that only six of the twelve persons named by Lord are really "treated" in both *Advices*. Of these, Sandwich is not treated at all in the Marvell poems, and is scarcely treated in *Third Advice*. Of the others, the similar treatment of Clarendon is insignificant, and the treatments of Coventry, Arlington, and of the Duke and Duchess of York have already been shown to be different as between the two *Advices*. Part of Lord's difficulty with these two poems comes from a kind of hypnosis under which he follows Banks in the assumption that both *Advices* proclaim themselves to be Denham's work. But the pieces themselves identify no one as their author. Denham's name was first publicly attached to the *Second Advice* by the unscrupulous printer of the 1667 edition, and to the subsequent printed *Advices* only in continuation of that precedent. That the ascription to Denham was not the product of Marvell's malice, and was not an in-

to a Painter would appear to be the work of another hand. As for the successor poems, the *Directions to a Painter* written and published later in 1667, they express a deeper general hostility to the government than Denham is likely to have felt and do not

---

trinsic part of any *Advice*, is readily demonstrable. Pepys, although he received manuscript copies of both *Advices*, offers no conjecture as to their authorship, and drops no hint that either manuscript ascribed the poem to Denham or to anyone else. At the other end of the process, the *Second, Third*, "Fourth," and "Fifth" *Advices* were all printed together as by Denham, along with Marvell's *House-Warming* poem, which was attributed to "an unknown author." The ascription is clearly the work of the printer (not a "blind" as asserted by Lord); *Clarendon's House-Warming* is not ascribed to Denham because it is not an *Advice* poem. Marvell did not arrange for the publication of the five-poem volume, nor for the inclusion of his *House-Warming*. The latter came to the printer by manuscript circulation, as did, no doubt, the "Fourth" and "Fifth Advice." If Marvell were behind the publication he might as well have ascribed the *House-Warming* to Denham, if it is assumed he had previously fathered the *Second* and *Third Advice* upon Denham; and he might as well have published his own *Last Instructions* rather than the inferior but parallel "Fourth" and "Fifth Advice" — the risk to him would have been equal. But Lord is quite secure that Marvell had nothing to do with this volume, although he fails to consider its implications. He seems to think that perhaps the author[s] of "Fourth" and "Fifth Advice" are responsible, using Denham's name as a blind — but why did they not also ascribe *Clarendon's House-Warming* to Denham? And of what utility was Denham's name as a "blind"? Would not "anonymous" serve the purpose as well?

Clearly the printer attributed "Fourth" and "Fifth Advice" to Denham because the preceding volume containing *Second* and *Third Advice* had attributed those to Denham; and that volume attributed those poems to Denham because the *Second Advice* when published alone had been attributed to Denham. Why that publication was so attributed is the only essential question, but there can be hardly any doubt that the person responsible was not the author of *Second Advice*, Denham, Marvell, or another, but the printer. And his motive was either purely commercial — exploiting Denham's name as a lure for buyers — or an honest but callous belief that Denham was in fact the author. Such a belief, in turn, would derive either from knowledge, rumor, or an allegation on the manuscript.

Since, aside from the ex post facto attribution to Denham, the *Third Advice* contains no reference whatsoever to Denham, Lord is totally unwarranted in glossing the remark of the Duchess of Albemarle in line 262 of that poem, "but he thinks I'm mad," as a slip on the part of the poet, who has "momentarily forgotten that the Duchess, and not Denham, is speaking" (*Poems on Affairs of State*, p. 79). But since Lord does falsely imagine that the *Second* and *Third Advice* do purport to be by Denham, and since *Last Instructions* certainly makes no such claim, it is strange that he does not regard that apparent discrepancy as an obstacle to his thesis of common authorship for all three poems.

227

read much like his authentic work. Most probably they can safely be excluded from Denham's canon as mere imitations of the *Second* (and the *Third*) *Advice*, parallel to Marvell's *Last Instructions to a Painter*, which also commences immediately where the *Third Advice* ends, and which covers the entire sweep of events from late summer of 1666 until August or September of 1667.[22]

---

[22] Marvell's *Last Instructions to a Painter* is a very long poem (990 lines), which proclaims itself at the outset a successor to the *Second* and the *Third Advice:* "After two Sittings, now our Lady-State / To end her picture, does the third time wait." Thus in a manner it is a rival production to the two pieces of unknown authorship, the "Fourth" and "Fifth Advice," included with the two earlier *Advices* in the volume called *Directions to a Painter.* To some extent *Last Instructions* reviews the entire course of the Dutch War, from 1665 until July 1667, though it concerns itself chiefly with the session of Parliament from September 18, 1666, until February 8, 1666/7; with Clarendon's effort to escape blame for the war and its failures; with administrative inefficiency and corruption; with the Parliament hastily summoned on July 25, 1667, and as hastily prorogued on July 29 upon the government's patching up of the Treaty of Breda; and of course with the national disgrace of the Dutch invasion of the Medway.

The poem is a valuable commentary on the political world inhabited by Denham, and it proceeds through the narration of events in which Denham was involved with a remarkable observance of chronological contemporaneity. Thus in lines 65–78 the Duchess of York is shown as jealous of Lady Denham and as meditating poison. At line 151 a catalogue of the leading members of the House of Commons commences, under various classifications: lines 151–154 describe Sir John Denham as the leader of the wittols. The wittols are followed by "old Courtiers . . . That sold their Master, led by Ashburnham" (lines 155–156), a raking up of the old scandal concerning Charles I at Carisbrook, and some distance later by the procurors, including "Brouncker, Love's squire" (line 175). By the time the Parliament is prorogued in February 1666/7 it has become appropriate to associate "fair Denham" with "mortal chocolate" (line 342), she having died in the meantime. When later events of 1667 are described, the Denham scandals recede into the past and are no longer mentioned.

Marvell's authorship of *Last Instructions* is unquestioned, but when Lord attempts to associate *Last Instructions* directly with the *Third Advice* on the ground that in both poems Ann Hyde, Duchess of York, is accused of poisoning, he is on false footing. In the first place, the *Third Advice* mentions Ann only obliquely, by a pun on her name, and does not accuse her of poisoning, only hinting that the Duke of Gloucester and the Princess Mary died because they were in her way; she is not linked in any way with Lady Denham. In *Last Instructions*, on the contrary, she is directly accused of poisoning, and specifically of poisoning Lady Denham. Lord seems to think, or to have thought, that this charge was an exclusive prejudice of Marvell's, for he says explicitly that "Ann was not among the suspects" in the death of Lady Denham (*BNYPL*, 62 [1958], 561), whereas, of course, as we have seen, she was the only

If Denham then really wrote the *Second Advice to a Painter* he may be said to have done so by way of mental therapy. By striking back under cover at the public possessor of his wife he could reestablish his inward composure, and the entire record of 1667 suggests that Denham throughout the year enjoyed peace of mind, all passion, perhaps, being spent. Copious records of his business as

---

contemporary suspect. In any event, the accusation establishes no link between *Last Instructions* and *Second Advice*, and this particular line of argument is not presented in Lord's *Poems on Affairs of State*.

In final consideration of the kind of reasoning Professor Lord employs in attempting to show that Marvell wrote the *Second* and *Third Advice* as well as *Last Instructions*, one consecutive chain of arguments he presents in his rejoinder to Professor Fogel ("Comments on the Canonical Caveat") may profitably be examined. The first link in Lord's chain is the argument that the author of *Last Instructions* (Andrew Marvell) must also be the author of an anonymous prose pamphlet, *Flagellum Parliamentarium*, published in 1678 but probably written around 1671–72. These two works, written from an Opposition viewpoint, list the names of M.P.'s who formed the hard core of supporters of the court: the lists coincide on twenty-two names. Therefore, Lord says, Marvell is "beyond a reasonable doubt, the author of *Flagellum Parliamentarium*." This kind of argument supposes either (*a*) that the hard-core Royalist faction in Commons was a private delusion of Marvell's, so that no other Oppositionist would be capable of agreement with him in naming twenty-two of its members, or (*b*) that Marvell was the sole member of the Opposition, and therefore the sole person capable of viewing with hostile eyes twenty-two leading members of the court group. Either supposition is nonsense. Marvell might be the author of *Flagellum Parliamentarium*, but on the evidence so might any number of other people.

From this shaky basis Lord goes on to note that both *Flagellum Parliamentarium* and the *Second Advice* concur in applying the epithet "halcyon" to the Earl of Sandwich. From this fact he deduces that both works must have a common author, and, since he thinks he has proved Marvell to have written *Flagellum*, he can conclude that Marvell must likewise have written *Second Advice*. But the coincidence of the phrase "halcyon Sandwich" between *Second Advice* and *Flagellum* is susceptible of many explanations. Perhaps the author of *Flagellum* had read *Second Advice* (an overwhelming probability) and become captivated by the adjective. Or must we suppose that one author (Marvell) had a monopolistic patent on the word (as also on the names of the royal faction in Commons)? But the fact that two separate anonymous seventeenth-century documents, written six years apart, both refer to the same man as "halcyon Sandwich" is precisely the sort of evidence from which a biographer of Sandwich might deduce that his subject was *called* "halcyon Sandwich." The nickname (equivalent perhaps to "Fairweather" Sandwich) might have been acquired in naval service, or it might even refer to Sandwich's part in the successful transportation of Charles II home from Holland at the Restoration. (It is perhaps not without significance that Dryden in *Astraea Redux*, describing the then Montagu's ships on that

surveyor of Works survive from all but two months in that year, March and November. March is the only month for which all records fail, for in November Denham was involved with House of Commons affairs. He was called in several times to advise the Treasury Lords; he was deeply engaged in the continued construction work at Windsor and Greenwich; he made several new arrangements about Portland stone; he arranged to borrow shipping from the Navy to transport building materials; he set about drawing up plans for the new customhouse, ultimately to be built by Christopher Wren, to replace the old one destroyed in the fire. On August 26 a payment of £530 was ordered to Denham for repair of demolitions effected on his house in Scotland Yard at the time of the fire; the wording of this order suggests that Denham allowed part of his buildings to be torn down during the conflagration on the King's express promise to pay compensation. Since the Great Fire broke out on September 2, 1666, the implication is that Denham at that time was already sane — likely enough, in view of his appearance at the House on the 18th.[23]

---

occasion, should refer to halcyons: "Secure as when the halcyon breeds, with these / He that was born to drown might cross the seas.") Certainly Lord is far from having proved common authorship of *Flagellum Parliamentarium* and *Second Advice* on so flimsy a basis as the sharing of an epithet.

The last part of Lord's argument is the assertion we have already noticed (n. 21, above), that the two *Advices* "must unquestionably be the work of one man." This is nothing but bold assertion, and will not in the least withstand analysis. Therefore Lord's entire sequence of arguments is worthless. Although Marvell is the author of *Last Instructions*, there is no proof that he is also the author of *Flagellum Parliamentarium*. Although Marvell just might be the author of *Flagellum* there is no ground worth speaking of for believing that the author of *Flagellum* is also the author of *Second Advice*. Finally, though common authorship of the *Second* and the *Third Advice* is not utterly impossible, the lack of real cohesion between the two, as well as certain arguments of style (touched on by Professor Fogel), make separate authorship of the two on balance the more convincing hypothesis.

[23] S.P. Dom., ser. 44, Vol. 18, p. 257: "His Maty remembers well his promise of repairing w[t] was demollished in S[r] John Denhams buildings at y[e] time of y[e] fire & accordingly is pleased to recommend it to y[e] Rt Honble y[e] Lds Comrs of y[e] Treasy to give direction for y[e] assigneing the sum . . ."; S.P. Dom., ser. 44, Vol. 23, pp. 358–361: "CHARLES &c To Our Trusty & Wellbeloved S[r] Charles Herbert Knt Surveyor Grall of Our Lands, S[r] John Denham Knt of y[e] Bath, Surveyor of Our Workes . . . Whereas

When Parliament resumed its normal session on October 10 Denham was promptly returned to the Committee on Elections and Privileges, and was named to three other committees in the same month. Also, on the 26th, he was appointed to a delegation "to attend the Lord General, to advise with him, for securing the Highways against Thefts and Robberies." [24] On November 9 the House instructed Denham and Sir Charles Harbord, by name, "to put the Laws in Execution against Hackney Coachmen." [25] On December 2 and 14 he was named to two more committees. [26] This session of Commons was a portentous one: it was the session that impeached the Earl of Clarendon. Denham does not, however, appear in the record as active one way or the other in the impeachment process. His sympathy with the Earl of Bristol may, however, be taken as indicative of the way he cast his vote.

Neither Denham's activities as surveyor general nor as Member of Parliament are his acts of greatest interest in 1667. Sometime during the summer he visited "the Wells," either Tunbridge or Epsom, and there, by his own testimony, he recommended the serious writing of poetry. [27] When he went to the Wells, or for how long, is difficult to say, for he can be found at business in

---

by ye late deplorable fire wch happened in Our Citty of London, Our Custome house there is demolished . . . prepare a draught or modele of a New Custom house to bee erected" (Feb. 22, 1666/7); S.P. Dom., ser. 29, Vol. 198, no. 120, f. 212: signed financial statement, dated "Greenwich Aprill 1667," of expenditures and receipts in building Greenwich Palace; S.P. Dom., ser. 44, Vol. 25, f. 10: warrant dated May 10, 1667, to Denham and other officers of the Works to survey Windsor Castle, to certify Mordaunt's repairs, if commensurate with his expenditures "according to your judgment"; S.P. Dom., ser. 29, Vol. 199, no. 17, f. 29: a holograph request to the Navy commissioners to transfer to the Office of Works Christopher Onsiloy and Nicholas Weymouth so that they may be more closely supervised, with a request that they be paid their arrears; S.P. Dom., ser. 29, Vol. 202, no. 132, f. 200: draft request to the King that the City of London use Portland stone granted on the surveyor's warrant rather than having "free liberty to fetch from Portland what stone soever & out of what quarries soever they please" (see *C.S.P.D.: 1666–1667*, p. 525; *1667*, pp. 65, 69, 88, 140, 153, 334, 417, 510; *1667–1668*, pp. 128, 145; *C. Treas. Bks.: 1667–1668*, pp. 20, 24, 32, 44, 50, 51, 61, 67, 70, 139, 161, 181, 183).

[24] *Commons Journal*, IX, 2, 3, 6, 8, 9, 17.

[25] *Ibid.*, p. 17.   [26] *Ibid.*, pp. 28, 38.   [27] See n. 3, above.

London at various times during May, June, July, and August, and
at the beginning of September he went to inspect Windsor Castle.
His holiday, then, could only have been brief. It is difficult to say,
also, exactly which poems were written in this year, and how many,
although concerning two there is absolute certainty. On July 28
Abraham Cowley died at Chertsey. His body was floated down
the Thames and buried amidst pomp and magnificence in Westminster Abbey on August 3. On the 15th of August Roger
L'Estrange licensed for publication a folio sheet entitled *On Mr.
Abraham Cowley His Death, and Burial amongst the Ancient
Poets*, written by the Honorable Sir John Denham.[28] This speedy
poetic response to the loss of Denham's former-day Paris correspondent is by no means a perfunctory performance. On the contrary, the ninety-eight lines of this tribute are among Denham's
most polished, even though he elected to compose in tetrameter
couplets. By a miracle he avoids the "whisking" effect of this
kind of verse cautioned against by Hobbes and used for burlesque
by Butler and Swift. The effect achieved by Denham is in fact
at times reminiscent of Ben Jonson, as in the epigrammatic opening:

> Old *Chaucer*, like the morning Star,
> To us discovers day from far,
> His light those Mists and Clouds dissolv'd,
> Which our dark Nation long involv'd;
> But he descending to the shades,
> Darkness again the Age invades.
>
> (lines 1–6) [29]

The ending also has something of Jonson, playing in an early
seventeenth-century manner on a more typically Augustan theme.
From line 63 to the end the talents and careers of Vergil and Cow-

---

[28] The date and circumstance of the license are set forth below the title of the poem
itself in its folio edition.

[29] Printed by Banks, *Poetical Works*, pp. 149–152.

ley are closely paralleled, a feat by Denham which probably accounts for something of the high esteem in which this elegy was long held, and the concluding ten lines may serve as a characteristic sample of the whole:

> Both by two generous Princes lov'd,
> Who knew, and judg'd what they approv'd:
> Yet having each the same desire,
> Both from the busie throng retire,
> Their Bodies to their Minds resign'd,
> Car'd not to propagate their Kind:
> Yet though both fell before their hour,
> Time on their off-spring hath no power,
> Nor fire, nor fate their Bays shall blast,
> Nor Death's dark vail their day o'recast.

(lines 89–98)

Also without doubt a product of 1667, and of only slightly less certain a date, are Denham's translations of two of a set of four fifteenth-century Latin verses on the cardinal virtues. The originals are by Dominico Mancini, and Denham rendered into English "Of Prudence" and "Of Justice." [30] Both translations are couched in heroic couplets, the first occupying 262 lines, the second 120. Denham first published these verses in his *Poems and Translations* of 1668 prefaced by a note in which he explains the circumstances of the translation:

Going this last Summer to visit the *Wells*, I took an occasion (by the way) to wait upon an Ancient and Honourable Friend of mine, whom I found diverting his (then solitary) retirement with the Latin Original of this Translation, which (being out of Print) I had never seen before: when I looked upon it, I saw that it had formerly passed through two Learned hands, not without approbation; which were *Ben Johnson*, and Sir *Kenelme Digby*;

---

[30] *Ibid.*, pp. 189–201.

but I found it, (where I shall never find my self) in the service of a better Master, the *Earl* of *Bristol.* . . .[31]

The translation of Mancini was probably not the solitary product of the resurgence of creativity Denham encountered at the Wells. At the beginning of the following year his *Poems and Translations* appeared, and that volume contained a number of pieces never previously published which it is difficult to assign to any earlier year.

The first that is heard of the projected publication of Denham's poems in a single volume comes, like so much else, from Samuel Pepys. On August 10, 1667, that man-about-town heard surprisingly for the first time the news of Cowley's death, as well as other literary news, on the occasion of a visit to the bookseller Henry Herringman, who kept his shop at the Blue Anchor in the Lower Walk of the New Exchange. Pepys recorded in his *Diary*: "Abroad and to the New Exchange, to the bookseller's there, where I hear of several new books coming out — Mr. Spratt's History of the Royal Society and Mrs. Phillips's poems. Sir John Denham's poems are going to be all printed together; and among others,

---

[31] This mention of a visit to the Wells is the second in the 1668 volume (the other is in the dedication "To the King"). Bristol's house in 1667 was at Wimbledon; the fact adduced by Banks (*Poetical Works*, p. 190n) that Bristol "was again in Parliament July 30, 1667," indicates nothing as to the time of summer when Denham visited him and, by consequence, the Wells. Actually it was on the 29th that the Earl was at the Lords' House, but for only one day. An emergency session of Parliament was called on Thursday, July 25, and upon convening it was immediately adjourned until Monday the 29th. Bristol was not present on Thursday, but appeared on Monday, when Parliament was promptly adjourned until October 10, the date originally set for its regular meeting. Presumably Bristol then went home again. Banks's introduction (*Poetical Works*, p. 26) also contains the misprint 1668 for 1667 as the date of the Mancini translation, the Cowley elegy, and the visit to the Wells.

Sir Kenelm Digby was the Earl of Bristol's first cousin, with whom he maintained a heavy correspondence, which resulted in the Earl's conversion to Roman Catholicism. The fact that Ben Jonson was a still earlier owner of the Mancini copy is of interest in view of the Jonsonian manner of Denham's August elegy on Cowley. Denham's open avowal of respect and "Ancient" friendship for Bristol has his customary timeliness, for when the tribute was finally published the Earl had had the satisfaction of seeing his enemy Clarendon impeached and banished.

some new things; and among them he showed me a copy of verses of his upon Sir John Minnes's going heretofore to Bullogne to eat a pig. Cowley, he tells me, is dead; who, it seems, was a mighty civil, serious man; which I did not know before." [32] Herringman was a trifle beforehand with his information: not until August 19 does the Stationers' Register record the transfer to him from Ann Moseley, widow of Humphrey Moseley, of the rights to "Coopers Hill, a Poem. The Sophie, a Tragedy, The Destrucčon of Troy, being a Translation of the Second Booke of Virgills Eneiads into Englishe." Preparation of the volume took some time, and Herringman did not register *"Poems and Translations wth the Sophy*, written by the Honorable Sr John Denham Knight of the Bath," until February 9, 1667/8.[33] Undoubtedly actual publication took place close to this date. The volume is a peculiar production, and many surviving copies contain a bound-in errata sheet. *The Sophy* and *The Destruction of Troy* have separate title pages, and each carries the imprint date 1667, although the general title page is dated 1668. *The Sophy*, moreover, has separate pagination, but *The Destruction of Troy* is paginated continuously with the rest of the volume.[34] This state of affairs arose partly, no doubt, from the fact of the book's being prepared at the turn

---

[33] Pepys, *Diary*, VII, 62–63. Sprat's *History of the Royal Society* requires no comment. "Mrs. Phillips" was Katherine Phillips (d. 1664), the "Matchless Orinda," with whose literary remains Denham shortly was to be connected, possibly at the instigation of Herringman. Pepys's informant here I take to be Herringman, not Denham himself, as some have read the entry (e.g., A. H. Nethercot, *Abraham Cowley: The Muse's Hannibal* [London, 1931], p. 277).

[33] The date February 9, 1667/8, appears to embody an error of some sort, as that date (i.e., February 9, 1668) fell on a Sunday.

[34] Unwary bibliographers and librarians, seduced by the separate title page and pagination, sometimes catalogue detached copies of *The Sophy* (1667) as a distinct issue from that contained in *Poems and Translations*. Wing, for instance, gives it a separate listing (D1010). All copies I have seen, however, are identical with those bound into the complete volume. *The Sophy* may perhaps have been sold separately, but it was never registered by Herringman as a distinct book in the Stationers' Register. It is named in the general title of *Poems and Translations*, is listed in the table of contents, and was obviously always intended to form part of that volume, which, as Pepys shows, was planned by Herringman as early as August 10, 1666.

of the year, and issued during the intercalary period before March 25. The *Poems and Translations* contained a total of twenty-five poems, in addition to *The Sophy*, fourteen of which were apparently printed for the first time.[35] Of the previously published works, *The Sophy* was somewhat cut and slightly rewritten from the 1642 edition; *Coopers Hill* contained four lines not in the first "B" text edition of 1655, as well as a number of revisions from that edition. Of the previously unpublished poems, aside from those already discussed and assigned a known or conjectural date of composition, three or four may tentatively be considered further products of 1667. These are "Friendship and Single Life against Love and Marriage"; the translations of "Sarpedon's Speech to Glaucus in the 12th of Homer" and "Martial. Epigram: Out of an Epigram of Martial"; and, if not the entire "The Progress of Learning," at least the Preface to it.

"Friendship against Love" is a playful composition in thirty-four octosyllabic triplets, quite free of the bawdiness typical of Denham's playful verses of the 1650's. The topic might well be a congenial one to a man recently liberated from the yoke of a galling marriage. The poem reflects the skeptical antirationalism and contrast between beasts and men which in the Restoration became a fashionable import from France. Denham was less bitter than Rochester, less scathing than Swift, more playful than Pope (of *An Essay on*

---

[35] The previously unpublished poems were: "On the Earl of Strafford's Tryal and Death," "On my Lord Crofts and my Journey into Poland," "On Mr. Tho. Killigrew's Return from his Embassie," "To Sir John Mennis, Being Invited from Calice to Bologne," "Natura Naturata," "Sarpedon's Speech to Glaucus in the 12th of Homer," "Martial. Epigram: Out of an Epigram of Martial," "Friendship and Single Life against Love and Marriage," "A Dialogue between Sir John Pooley and Mr. Thomas Killigrew," "An Occasional Imitation of a Modern Author upon the Game of Chess," "The Passion of Dido for Aeneas," "Of Prudence," "Of Justice," and "The Progress of Learning." The previously published poems were: *Coopers Hill*, "A Song" (from *The Sophy*), "News from Colchester," "A Speech against Peace," "To the Five Members," "A Western Wonder," "A Second Western Wonder," "On Mr. John Fletchers Works," "To Sir Richard Fanshaw," *On Mr. Abraham Cowley his Death, The Destruction of Troy*. Several of these had been previously published only in such collections as *Rump Songs* (1662).

236

Man), though influenced by the same philosophy also reflected in those three writers, when he composed these final triplets:

> But Love may Beasts excuse, for they
> Their actions not by Reason sway,
> But their brute appetites obey.
>
> But Man's that Savage Beast, whose mind
> From Reason to self-Love declin'd,
> Delights to prey upon his Kind.[36]

It is very difficult to believe that these lines could have been written much before 1667.

The *Iliad* translation likewise connects Denham forward with the major Augustans, for the same speech of Sarpedon was among Pope's earliest efforts at Homer, and Pope on two separate occasions generously acknowledges the merit of Denham's translation, asserting its strong influence upon his own. No clue, however, ties this to any definite year in Denham's life prior to 1668. Perhaps the translation was made during the stay at Wilton in 1653 and 1654, but most likely it too belongs to 1667. This translation is notable as Denham's only attempt at rendering Greek, if indeed the translation comes directly from the original. The whole speech in Denham's version is concluded within twenty-nine lines, eight more than the twenty-one hexameters of the equivalent passage of the original (*Iliad* XII.307–327). The translation from Martial (*Epigrams* XI.104), on the contrary, is backward looking, to the *Epigrammes* of Ben Jonson. Nevertheless the deliberate Jonsonism may be construed as additional evidence that this exercise belongs to Denham's new creative period of 1667. Pointing in the same direction is the fact that this essay, although in fact somewhat bawdy, lacks the gaminess of Denham's original creations of the 1650's, displaying instead a rather archaic air of Tribe of Ben freshness and innocence, as the following excerpt may instance:

---

[36] Banks, *Poetical Works*, pp. 96–99.

Why so many Bolts and Locks,
   Coats and Smocks,
And those Drawers with a Pox?
I could wish, could Nature make it,
   Nakedness, Nakedness
It self were naked.[37]

Finally, the Preface to "The Progress of Learning" is openly the statement of a man conscious of his old age, and serenely accepting it. As such it may be associated both with Denham's translation of Cicero's *Cato Major*, which he probably did not complete until 1668, and with his newly won equanimity. The "Progress of Learning" itself is a discourse on one of the themes set forth in *Coopers Hill*, and may possibly be, as has been suggested, a product of the Wilton period. But Denham reviewed *Coopers Hill* again for the *Poems and Translations* edition, and therefore might just as well have been moved to write the entire "Progress" in 1667. The emphasis placed by the poem on religious zealotry, however, while not definitive, suggests the earlier time. But the preface almost without question was written in 1667, and deserves quotation both as it reflects Denham's state of mind that year and as it provided a verbal inspiration to Alexander Pope:

My early Mistress, now my Antient Muse,
That strong *Circaean* liquor cease to infuse,
Wherewith thou didst Intoxicate my youth,
Now stoop with dis-inchanted wings to Truth;
As the Doves flight did guide *Aeneas*, now
May thine conduct me to the Golden Bough;
Tell (like a Tall Old Oake) how Learning shoots
To Heaven Her Branches, and to Hell her Roots.[38]

---

[37] *Ibid.*, pp. 180–181.
[38] The "Progress of Learning" is printed in *ibid.*, pp. 114–121. The Preface is on p. 114. With lines 3–4 of the Preface (above) compare Pope's "not in Fancy's Maze he wander'd long, / But stoop'd to Truth, and moraliz'd his song" (*Epistle to Dr. Arbuthnot*, lines 340–341).

The poems contained in *Poems and Translations* do not exhaust Denham's literary productivity in 1667. Three years before, the estimable poetess Katherine Phillips, the "Matchless Orinda," had died, leaving behind among her other works a translation of three full acts and five scenes of Corneille's *Horace*. Henry Herringman, just beginning his career as a major literary publisher, brought out at about the same time as Denham's *Poems and Translations* (as he informed Pepys) the collected works of Mrs. Phillips, including the truncated *Horace*.[39] But in a subsequent edition, that of 1669, Herringman printed *Horace* with the remaining sixth and seventh scenes of Act IV and all of Act V supplied by Sir John Denham. This dramatic translation was also a product of 1667, for in the theatrical season of 1667–68 (and also in 1668–69) the play was presented at the Theatre Royal. John Evelyn saw a performance on February 4, 1667/8, and Pepys saw it the following year, on January 19, 1668/9, when he judged it to be "a silly tragedy."[40] In 1667, therefore, Denham had also resumed dramaturgy, on however small a scale, and so had the opportunity again to hear words from his own pen declaimed upon the stage.

During this miraculous year of 1667 Denham is also connected, by anecdote at least, with a literary event of really major proportions: the first publication of *Paradise Lost*. The story is one that presents new difficulties at every reexamination, but needs to be taken up again. It first appeared in Jonathan Richardson's *Explana-*

---

[39] POEMS / By the most deservedly Admired / Mrs. KATHERINE PHILIPS / The matchless / ORINDA. / To which is added / MONSIEUR CORNEILLE'S / POMPEY / & TRAGEDIES. / HORACE, / With several other Translations out of / FRENCH. / LONDON, / Printed by *J.M.* for *H. Herringman*, at the Sign of / the *Blew Anchor* in the Lower Walk of the / New Exchange. 1667. (Wing P2033.) This was actually the second edition of Mrs. Phillips' *Poems*, the first (Wing P2032) having been published by Richard Marriot in 1664, which establishes the earliest possible date at which Denham might have translated the end of *Horace*. Most likely, however, his translation was made between 1667 and Herringman's 1669 edition (Wing P2034), which contains it.

[40] The accounts of the performances are presented by Philip Webster Souers, *The Matchless Orinda* (Cambridge, Mass., 1931), pp. 229–230.

tory Notes and Remarks on Milton's Paradise Lost, published in 1734, in this form:

Sir George Hungerford, an ancient member of Parliament, told me, many years ago, that Sir John Denham came into the House one morning with a sheet, wet from the press, in his hand. What have you there, Sir John? Part of the noblest poem that ever was wrote in any language, or in any age. This was Paradise Lost. However, 'tis certain the book was unknown till about two years after, when the Earl of Dorset produced it. . . . My Lord was in Little Britain, beating about for books to his taste. There was Paradise Lost. He was surprised with some passages he struck upon dipping here and there, and bought it. The bookseller begged him to speak in its favour if he liked it, for that it lay on his hands as waste paper. . . .[41]

The classical objections to the veracity of this narrative were first formulated by Edmund Malone and adopted with modification by David Masson, and they compose a two-pronged attack.[42] One line of attack objects to the inconsistency between the two parts of the story: if Denham "discovered" *Paradise Lost* at the time of its printing, why was it "waste paper" two years later, requiring rediscovery by the Earl of Dorset? Banks has little difficulty parrying this thrust, showing from Masson's own account that *Paradise Lost* had in fact sold over 1,300 of the first 1,500 copies by the time of Dorset's supposed rediscovery, so that Denham's praise of the poem cannot be discounted as ineffective.[43] The other prong of the attack is aimed at Denham's share of the anecdote, and is the product either of perversity or sheer ignorance, consisting as it does of three objections: (1) Denham could not have acquired one of Milton's proof sheets; (2) he was mad when *Paradise Lost* was going through the press; (3) he was not a Member of Parlia-

---

[41] Printed and discussed by Banks, *Poetical Works*, pp. 32–35.
[42] The arguments are summarized in *ibid.*, pp. 32–33, nn. 162, 163.
[43] *Ibid.*, p. 34.

ment, and so could not have brought the sheet "into the House." Banks properly shows the perversity of the first objection, pointing out that the anecdote says nothing about proof sheets. In a seventeenth-century printer's or bookseller's Denham might certainly have found unbound sheets of a book, whether hung up to dry in a printer's, as Banks suggests, or merely lying unbound prior to sale. The second and third objections are obviously the products of ignorance, and Masson already realized that Denham was no longer mad by August 1667, when *Paradise Lost* was printed. In fact, of course, his sanity had been restored for a full year by then. As to why Malone and Masson agreed that Denham was not a Member of Parliament there is no telling.

But refutation of the classical objections fails to leave the story unchallenged. For one thing, if the story as a whole is true, the detail of the sheet "wet from the press" must be discarded. It might be possible to concoct an explanation for the arrival at the Houses of Parliament of a still wet sheet fetched from Samuel Simmons' shop in Aldersgate Street, several miles away.[44] Much more difficult to explain, however, is the arrival of a newly printed sheet at the House of Commons in the month of August. Parliament was not in session, and by the time the House convened on October 10 one would expect sheets printed in August to have had ample time to dry. An alternative way of accepting the story, of course,

---

[44] Perhaps rain, or mere smudginess, might be conjured up as an explanation for the description. Actually, the first of the eight title pages of the first (ten-book) edition of *Paradise Lost* does not bear Simmons' name, asserting rather that the copies are "Printed, and are to be sold by *Peter Parker* / under *Creed* Church near *Aldgate*; And by / *Robert Boulter* at the *Turks Head* in *Bishopsgate-street*; / And *Matthias Walker*, under St. *Dunstons* Church / in *Fleet-street*, 1667." Walker, at St. Dunstan's-in-the-East, was perhaps the closest to the Parliament House in Westminster, but still not very close. Although Simmons' name does not appear until the fourth title page, dated 1668, it seems probable nevertheless that he was the actual printer. It was in the name of "Master Sam. Symons" that the Stationers' Register received on August 20, 1667, the entry of "a booke or copie intituled *Paradise lost A Poem in Tenne bookes by J. M.*" It had also been with Simmons that Milton had concluded arrangements for printing and copyright on April 27, 1667, and whatever the vending agreements Simmons worked out, a "wet sheet" probably could come only from his establishment.

is to eliminate the House of Commons, and substitute perhaps a coffeehouse. This would have the advantage of allowing Denham to see a sheet freshly printed, in August, and, assuming the coffeehouse to be convenient to the printshop, to come "into the House one morning with a sheet, wet from the press, in his hand." But the tale cannot be swallowed whole without trimming, and how far the necessity for trimming invalidates an anecdote is perhaps a matter for the individual conscience to decide. Almost all such anecdotes prove, when proof is possible, to contain some grain of truth, and so it may properly be acknowledged to John Denham that he saw *Paradise Lost* in the year of its first publication, and had the perspicuity to recognize and to praise its unparalleled excellence. Certainly *Paradise Lost* was sincerely admired by all the later, more eminent Augustans, and it is impossible to believe that Denham, with his rather sober frame of mind and his intense respect for Vergil, would not extend his admiration to the new English epic.

The year 1667 also affords a last, and quite authentic, personal view of Denham. On September 26, 1667, Lord Lisle (afterward Earl of Leicester) wrote to Sir William Temple an account of the current social season and of some of its figures:

poor Sir John Denham is fallen to the ladies also [i.e., like Edmund Waller]. He is at many of the meetings at dinners, talks more than ever he did, and is extremely pleased with those that seem willing to hear him; and from that obligation exceedingly praises the Duchess of Monmouth and my Lady Cavendish; if he had not the name of being mad, I believe in most companies he would be thought wittier than ever he was. He seems to have few extravagancies, besides that of telling stories of himself, which he is always inclined to. Some of his acquaintances say, that extreme vanity was a cause of his madness, as well as it is an effect.[45]

Denham's continuing reputation for madness, to which this letter

---

[45] *The Works of Sir William Temple, Bart.* (London, 1814), I, 459.

testifies, is at the same time revealed to have no basis outside of gossipy prejudice. He does appear, however, at the age of fifty-two, to have become definitely an old man; his falling "to the ladies" is obviously not anything in the way of new sexual adventures, but just the contrary. He has become the garrulous, sexless elder, the perennial fourth hand at cards with the ladies, a sort of honorary old lady himself. Unfortunately nobody has recorded the stories about himself with which Denham bored his company, though possibly some of the stock Denham anecdotes (his witticism on Wither, for instance) may first have been retailed by Denham himself to some of his feminine auditors. It seems extravagant, nevertheless, to characterize Denham at this time as "noticeably eccentric." [46] He was merely becoming a premature old gaffer. Such was his state a year and a half after his own affliction, nine months after the death of his wife.

Despite the marks of encroaching old age, Denham entered upon the year 1668 with much of the vigor that had characterized his life during 1667. He received an assignment of money from the King on January 10, and returned to Parliament for its session that resumed on February 6.[47] On February 4, as has been noticed, he might have seen his part of the translation of Corneille's *Horace* at the Theatre Royal, and about February 9 his *Poems and Translations* probably came out. On February 19 and again on February 26 he was asked to serve on committees of the Commons.[48] On the 12th of March, and also on April 10 and 21, he was named to additional committees.[49] On March 10, 1667/8,

---

[46] Banks, *Poetical Works*, p. 23.

[47] *C.S.P.D.: 1667–1668*, p. 176; *Commons Journal*, IX, 43, 49. A roll call was taken of the House on Thursday, February 13; the name of Sir Denham does not occur in the list of fifty-four members absent without excuse. Since his name likewise fails to occur in any of the records of members requesting permission to absent themselves, the inference follows that he was present that day. At no time during his service in Commons is Denham recorded to have requested leave, or to have been absent during a "calling over" of the membership.

[48] *Commons Journal*, IX, 53, 56.

[49] *Ibid.*, pp. 65, 78, 84.

he was requested in writing "to recommend some one to the place of Master Carpenter, in the place of Mr. Davenport, deceased."[50] On March 18 his name is joined with the names of the other officers of Works in a petition about the disposal of funds; on April 13 he was issued a money warrant for his fees for one year, and on April 18 he received the payment of £530 due the artisans rebuilding his lodgings in Scotland Yard.[51] On May 21 Denham was asked to make a report on a paper drawn up by the Lord Great Chamberlain; on June 1 he was asked to certify bills for payment by the Treasury; on June 30 he presented a royal warrant for applying some tiles from Greenwich to the repair of his own house in Scotland Yard.[52] On July 14 and 16 he was again involved in money matters; on the latter date his expenditures "for repairing the roof and buildings called Sir John Denham's buildings, in Scotland Yard, which the King in the late fire had commanded to be uncovered and defaced for preventing the further spreading thereof," hitherto always referred to as £530, were specified as exactly £527 6s. 1d.[53] The subject of quarries came once more under Denham's purview in a petition submitted on Friday, July 24, by one William Ellesden.[54] Ellesden's petition, about a lease of the stone in Portland, was read by the Treasury Lords, together with Denham's report on the petition, on September 9: "Mr. Ellesden says none can dig but by the King's warrant from Sir John Denham. Lord Ashley says any may dig. Mr. Ellesden to attend on Monday hereon with Sir John Denham and Mr. Oliver, the city surveyor."[55] On Monday, the 14th, the Treasury books record, "as to the business of the Portland stone, Sir John Denham says that the quarry is the King's property. Lord Ashley says none can dig but a tenant or by the King's warrant. Sir John Denham is to state the King's title to the quarries."[56] With this note the

---

[50] *C. Treas. Bks.: 1667–1668*, p. 272.

[51] *C.S.P.D.: 1667–1668*, pp. 297, 345; *C. Treas. Bks.: 1667–1668*, p. 546.

[52] *C. Treas. Bks.: 1667–1668*, pp. 330, 338, 366.

[53] *Ibid.*, pp. 381, 598.   [54] *Ibid.*, p. 395.   [55] *Ibid.*, p. 435.   [56] *Ibid.*, p. 438.

obscure drama of the Portland quarries apparently fades finally out of Denham's life, for no more is recorded on this topic.

On August 28 "Sir John Denham's buildings" were mentioned in another money warrant, and on September 14, at the same time he submitted his report on Ellesden's petition for a lease of Portland stone quarries, Denham also testified to the Treasury Lords the necessity for maintaining a shelter for fire engines in Scotland Yard.[57] On September 16 he sent up for the King's signature a warrant for £500 for the Works, and on October 7 moved for liberty to take possession of his renovated lodgings in Scotland Yard.[58] On Friday, November 20, Sir Charles Harbord, Sir John Denham, and Hugh May were ordered to attend on Monday the Lords of the Treasury "about the business of re-building the Custom House," and on the Monday Denham was asked "for an estimate of the charge of building that part of the Custom House which is reserved for His Majesty's use by the models agreed upon April 27 last."[59] Harbord and Denham on December 1 were requested by the Treasury Lords "to return a list of all the King's houses and lodges which are not His Majesty's houses of residence, and which they conceive are to be kept in repair by the parties enjoying lodgings &c. in them."[60] A Treasury warrant was issued to Denham as surveyor general on December 11, "to make bricks in the Great Park at Richmond and to cut furze and ferns there for burning same."[61] Many other documents of a similar nature, some lacking specific dates, also survive to testify to Denham's business activities in 1668.

The Parliament in which Denham had sat in the spring adjourned on May 9 until August 11. Denham probably reappeared in the House on that day, but the sole business transacted then was the issue of warrants for elections to fill the seats of dead or removed members, after which the House adjourned until November 10,

---

[57] *Ibid.*, pp. 424, 438.   [59] *Ibid.*, pp. 489, 491.   [61] *Ibid.*, p. 641.
[58] *Ibid.*, pp. 440, 452.   [60] *Ibid.*, pp. 498–499.

without recorded roll call or appointment of committees. The meeting of November 10 was likewise immediately adjourned to March 1, 1668/9, but it is quite unlikely, though not impossible, that Denham attended in March. In any case, on March 1 the Parliament was prorogued until the following October 19 (1669), by which time Denham was dead.[62] Therefore the spring session of 1668 was his last real service as a Member of Parliament.

But in 1668, despite the publication of his collected *Poems and Translations*, Denham continued to write poetry. To his own copy of *Poems and Translations* he made, sometime between its publication and his death in 1669, copious manuscript additions. Some of these, such as the transcripts of six of his anonymous contributions to *Certain Verses by severall of the Authors Friends to be reprinted with . . . Gondibert*, represented earlier work that had been omitted from the collection. Perhaps the intention was to include these in a projected new edition. Very likely of equal origin with these six were the other two poems of the same kind also added, "As I came from Lombardy," and "Sir William's no more a Poet," although neither of these had been previously printed. But the last of the Davenant poems is clearly a product of 1668, and so was written after the publication of *Poems and Translations*. This is a fifty-two-line "Elegy on Sir William D'avenant," still in a mocking vein but at the same time touched with gentle affection. Sir William died on April 7, 1668; Denham attended his funeral in Westminster Abbey. John Aubrey also attended, and reported: "He had a coffin of Walnutt-tree; Sir John Denham sayd 'twas the finest coffin that ever he saw." Two stanzas of the "Elegy" may be quoted, as indicative of both the humor and the affection Denham could display:

> Cowley a Fayre appartement keepes
> Receiving him with ioy he weepes

---

[62] All relevant entries occur in *Commons Journal*, IX, 97.

Into his bed Sir William creepes
And now in Abrahams bosome sleeps . . .

And yet I feare thy want of breath
Will prove the English Stages death
Could I to thee new life bequeath
No other head should were the wreath.

Of a more ambivalent nature are passages marked for insertion into other poems. It is impossible to know, for instance, if eight new lines marked for insertion into Denham's translation of Mancini's "Of Prudence" represent a postpublication afterthought or an inadvertent omission from the text printed in *Poems and Translations*. A similar situation prevails with the six new lines marked for insertion into *Coopers Hill*. The text of *Coopers Hill* printed in 1668 already contained four lines never previously printed, as well as several textual revisions from the 1655 edition, so indicating that Denham was active on the text of *Coopers Hill* just before publication. The four lines newly printed in 1668 and the six lines added in manuscript thereafter all occur within the same passage of *Coopers Hill*, so again leaving optional the inferences that the six lines were accidentally omitted, or that they were the product of a revisory process protracted past the publication of *Poems and Translations*.[63]

Late in 1668 Denham published for the first time, with an introduction and preface, a free translation in verse of Cicero's dialogue on old age, which was printed as *Cato Major of Old Age: A Poem*. The poem appeared as an octavo published by Henry Herringman, bearing the imprint date 1669. The imprint is puzzling, however, for the first number of the *Term Catalogues* (then just

---

[63] This discussion of Denham's manuscript additions to his own copy of the 1668 *Poems and Translations* is derived from James M. Osborn, "New Poems by Sir John Denham," *Times Literary Supplement*, Sept. 1, 1966. The additions to *Coopers Hill* are for the first time embodied in the text in my edition of the poem in *Expans'd Hieroglyphicks*.

beginning) lists as printed and published in Michaelmas Term, 1668, "*Cato Major*: Of Old Age. A Poem. By Sir John Denham, Knight. In Octavo. Price 6d." [64] The poem therefore seems to have been in print by November 1668. Sometimes it has been erroneously asserted that this translation belongs to Denham's youth, and had been published before in 1648, but Banks is quite correct in believing the poem to be in Denham's late manner. [65] The misconception arises from the existence of a book called *Cato Major*: *or, the book of old age*, printed for William Leake in 1648, but that translation is not Denham's. [66] In his version, running

---

[64] The first of the *Term Catalogues* appeared under the title of *Mercurius Librarius, or A Catalogue of Books Printed and Published in Michaelmas Term, 1668. Cato Major* is listed under the general heading of "Histories."

[65] Banks, *Poetical Works*, p. 202n. George Sherburn, in a review of Banks's edition (*MLN*, XLIV [1929], 194–196), challenges Banks on this point: "One might wish that we might have had more complete bibliographical descriptions. One wants to know, for example, if *Cato Major* of 1669 is a 12mo" (p. 194). It was in fact an 8vo, but the source of Sherburn's inquiry is apparent in his further contention (p. 195): "Apparently the last statement in the important but (to this reviewer) unconvincing note on page 202 is a slip. It asserts that *Cato Major* was first printed in 1669; but the poem appears in the 1668 *Poems* from which Banks seems to have reprinted it. Anthony Wood's manner of listing this poem makes one feel that he probably saw a 12mo edition dated 1648." Wood indeed does list as by Denham "*Cato Major*, of old age, a poem. *Lond.* 1648. in tw, in 4 parts, &c." and states further that *Cato Major* appeared in *Poems and Translations* of 1668, but in both regards he is mistaken. As the text above makes clear, the *Cato Major* of 1648 was not translated by Denham, and Denham's actual translation did *not* appear in the 1668 *Poems and Translations*. Banks is correct in asserting that the edition dated 1669 is the first printing of Denham's *Cato Major*, and his claim of that edition as his own copy text is buttressed to the extent that there was no earlier text for him to have printed. Perhaps a certain apparent scholasticism in Banks's presentation of his case for the dating of this translation (he attempts by reasoning alone to refute the recorded assertion of Sir James Ware that Denham produced *Cato Major* in 1648) provoked Sherburn into an equally scholastical attack on his accuracy. Neither attempts to settle the facts about the 1648 edition, which either might have done by reference to the Stationers' Register, the *Transcripts* of which had been published (1913–14) well before the time of the dispute.

[66] Wing C4288. This little book seems to be scarce, Wing listing only four holders of copies: Bodleian, Dulwich College, Yale, and the Clark Library. Leake's entry in the Stationers' Register (on March 2, 1647/8) reveals the name of his translator: "a booke called *Cato maior, or, the booke of old age, written in Latyn by* Mar. Tull: Cicero *in praise of the same & englished by* Wm Austen, Esqre." The title page of the Clark Library copy reads: "Cato Major: or, the book of old age. First written by

---

to almost a thousand lines of verse, Denham is seen once more in contemplation of old age, which seems to have preoccupied his thought throughout these last two years of his life.

Another effort at the end of Denham's life, on a minor scale, was his thirty-two-line prefatory poem "To the Honourable *Edward Howard Esq*; Upon his Poem of the British Princes." Howard's *British Princes* was published in 1669 with Denham's poem attached.[67] Presumably Denham wrote this set of verses on request, for the occasion, and therefore this may be the last poetic product of his pen. If so, the fact is rather a pity, for Denham undoubtedly had his tongue in cheek in fulsomely praising Howard's poem that everyone else ridiculed. Denham may have grown charitable at the end, but he otherwise shows no decline in his ability to discern quality in poetry.

Sometime also in 1667 or 1668 Denham undertook a more ambitious project, and one expressly designed to be his final work: a paraphrase of the Psalms. Denham's *Psalms* were not published until 1714, but there can be no doubt that they are authentically his work. They were transmitted to Heighes Woodford, the 1714 editor, by Denham's grandchildren, and were printed with a preface by Denham quite in his valedictory manner of 1667 to 1669. He speaks of "My old Master Virgil" and "My new Master David," and of "the Change which Age and many Infirmitys had made in me," and by his example advises "no Man to dishearten himself by the Sense of Age, or Decay of Strength." A reference to Cowley faintly suggests that the poet was already dead at the time of writing: "I cannot but mention with Honour my Friend Mr. *Cowley*, who was the first who of late offer'd to redeem

---

M. T. Cicero. And now excellently Englished by William Austin . . . London, Printed for Wm. Leake, 1648."

[67] Howard's poem is listed in the third number of the *Term Catalogues* as having gone on sale during the Easter term of 1669: "The Brittish Princess [*sic*]. An Heroick Poem. Written by the Honourable Edward Howard, Esq. In Octavo. Price, bound, 2s. Printed for H. Herringman at the Anchor in the New Exchange." Perhaps the request for complimentary verses came to Denham from Herringman.

[Poetry] from that Slavery, wherein this deprav'd **Age** has prostituted her to all imaginable Uncleanness." The conclusion of the preface is of interest as showing Denham in the mood of a Christian rendering his account of the spending of his talent:

... the inclination which I have to [Poetry], came to me by Nature from my Infancy, before Reason cou'd direct: Yet as I cam early to it, so early I laid it by in pursuance of other Inclinations, it may be less innocent. So that if in my self I make the Proverb good, *That Age does repuerascere, and often relapses into the In-clinations of Youth*, I shall not repent, if the end prove good. . . . And as I hope [God] will take it in part of repayment of that Talent which I have so long mispent [*sic*], so I beg that it may favourably be look'd upon by Him to whose Service it is devoted, the World's Great Saviour, his only Son; and receiv'd as a Mite of that large Debt which he has paid for me to his Eternal Father.[68]

These paraphrases of the Psalms, "fitted to the tunes used in churches," are not to be judged by the ordinary canons of poetry. Although prior to their publication it was possible to hope that Denham's *Psalms* would "answer the Authours great name, and talent in pöetry," their purpose was not to compete with the poetry of the Authorized Version, but to provide more singable versions than the traditional doggerel of Sternhold and Hopkins.[69]

---

[68] A / VERSION / OF THE / PSALMS / OF / DAVID, / Fitted to the TUNES Used / in CHURCHES. / By the Honourable / Sir *JOHN DENHAM*, / Knight of the *Bath*. / LONDON, / Printed for J. BOWYER at the Rose in *Ludgate-* / *street*, H. CLEMENTS at the Half-Moon in *St.* / *Paul's Churchyard*, T. VARNUM and J. OSBORN / at the *Oxford*-Arms in *Lombard-Street*. 1714. Woodford explains that Denham's holographs came to him from Bishop Morley, Denham's cousin, and that he had returned them to Denham's descendants, "from whom I receiv'd them again, by my Honour'd Friend William Morley Esq" (Denham's grandson, the younger son of Denham's daughter Anne and her husband Sir William Morley) "with Commands to transcribe them for the Press." William Morley was Denham's principal heir, desig-nated to take the surname Denham, but he died prematurely; perhaps his death had something to do with the obvious delay of publication. The volume was dedicated to the Earl of Derby and his "Excellently Pious Consort, Grand-Daughter of" the poet, that is, Mary, youngest and last surviving child of Sir William and Lady [Anne] Morley, and ultimately last survivor of Denham's line.

[69] Two surviving letters, both from September 1710, indicate that publication of

The quality of Denham's version may be judged by his rendition of the familiar 23d Psalm:

My Shepherd is the living Lord; / To me my Food and Ease
The rich luxuriant Fields afford; / The Streams my Thirst appease.
My Soul restor'd he'l gently lead / Into the Paths of Peace;
To walk in Shades among the Dead / My Hopes, not Fears, increase.

His Rod and Staff are still my Guide, / He stands before my Foes:
For me a Feast he does provide, / My sparkling Cup o'er-flows.
He with sweet Oil anoints my Head; / His Mercy, Grace, and
    Praise,
Have me into his Temple led, / Where I will end my days.

Thirty-five years before their publication, Denham's *Psalms* were complimented in print, in *A Paraphrase upon the Canticles* by Samuel Woodford, published in 1679.[70] Woodford was the fellow collegian of the young John Denham who had been at Wadham College in 1653, and he printed along with his version of *Canticles* some "occasional Compositions in English verse." Among these occurs, dated 1668, a poem of sixteen quatrains "To the Honourable Sir *John Denham* upon his New Version of the Psalms," which indicates that Woodford saw Denham's manuscript in that year.

Denham's *Psalms* was expected at least four years before its appearance. Both letters are in the Ballard Collection of manuscripts in the Bodleian Library. On September 7 George Hickes writing to the Reverend Dr. Arthur Charlett observed, "Sir John Denhams Psalmes will be much valued, if they answer the Authours great name, and talent in pöetry" (Vol. 12, no. 115, ff. 180–181), and on September 15 Jo: Johnson, "a poor Country Vicar," writing to the same Dr. Charlett, who was master of University College in Oxford, says, "I shall rejoice to see Sᵣ J. Denham's version. Tate, & Brady are certainly liable to many objections. I have not yet seen Bp Beveridges Vindication of Sternhold, & Hopkins . . . ," and he remarks of the latter that their poetry is contemptible (Vol. 15, no. 52, ff. 96–97).

[70] A / PARAPHRASE / UPON THE / CANTICLES, / AND SOME / SELECT HYMNS / OF THE / NEW and OLD TESTAMENT, / With other occasional Compositions / IN / English VERSE. / By *Samuel Woodford*, D.D. / *LONDON*, / Printed by *J. D.* for *John Baker*, at the three Pidgeons, / and *Henry Brome*, at the Gun in St. *Paul's* / Church-Yard, 1679. The verses "To the Honourable Sir JOHN DEN-HAM" occupy pages 146–149; the date 1668 appears at the end of the poem.

Interestingly enough, the courtesy must have been mutual, for Denham in his preface alludes to Woodford as a biblical paraphrast, although Woodford's work was not published until more than a decade later. Presumably Samuel Woodford and Heighes Woodford, Denham's 1714 editor, were in some way related.

Only one remaining poem of Denham's canon cannot with security be fitted into any particular period of his life. In *Chorus Poetarum or Poems on Several Occasions*, published in 1694, appeared for the first time in print a twenty-line poem, "To His Mistress," ascribed to Denham. Since this did not appear in *Poems and Translations*, and is not included in the manuscript additions to Denham's personal copy, there is no way to date it. It seems unlikely for one of Denham's late poems, although it is free of bawdry; perhaps it dates from his courtship of Margaret Brooke, perhaps it is earlier; perhaps it is not Denham's. If Denham wrote the poem, it is noteworthy as the only love poem of his entire career.

At the beginning of 1668/9 much less information than usual about Denham appears in the records. On January 16, 19, and 21, the translation of Corneille's *Horace* with Denham's fifth act appeared again at the Theatre Royal, but nothing is heard of the poet himself during that month. On February 3 a document reveals incidentally that Denham, among his other titles, apparently bore that of commissioner of streets and highways. On that day he joined with the Earl of Craven and Sir P. Howard, also dignified with the same titles, in a commendation of William Heart, the new paviour general.[71] On March 5 a Treasury warrant was issued to Denham concerning the building of the custom house, "the said building process to be directed by said Denham, Hugh May, Comptroller of the Works, Philip Packer, Paymaster of the Works."[72] This reveals a change in the personnel of the sur-

---

[71] *C.S.P.D.: 1668–1669*, p. 181.
[72] *C. Treas. Bks.: 1669–1672*, p. 196.

veyor's office; what happened to Francis Wethered does not appear. At some time not easily specified Denham had strengthened his own control over his bureau of Works, as his will reveals, by having his "faithfull servant" Henry Cooper appointed clerk of Works at Hampton Court. A more drastic revolution was completed on that same March 5 when Denham wrote to Lord Arlington: "by my patent I have power to make a deputy, during my life. . . . I have appointed Dr. Christopher Wren my sole deputy. I know of no verbal deputations, and if Mr. May or anyone else pretends thereto, it is without my knowledge or consent." Thus were Hugh May's ambitions finally crushed. The next day, March 6, a grant was issued "to Dr. Chris. Wren, LL.D., of the office of Deputy Surveyor of Works in the Tower, and other the King's residences, at request of Sir John Denham, Surveyor, on account of his weakness." [73]

Denham apparently foresaw the end of the weakness that led him to ensure Christopher Wren's succession to his office, for on March 13 he made his will.[74] Reports agree that it was at his office in Whitehall that death finally seized Sir John Denham, probably on Friday, March 19, 1668/9.[75] The event took place almost with-

---

[73] *C.S.P.D.: 1668–1669*, pp. 224, 227.

[74] *The Marriage, Baptismal, and Burial Registers of . . . Westminster*, ed. Joseph Lemuel Chester, Publications of the Harleian Society, X (London, 1876), 170. Denham's will is reproduced in *Wills from Doctor's Commons*, ed. John Gough Nichols and John Bruce (Westminster, 1863), pp. 119–123; it is dated "this thirteenth day of March, in the yeare of our Lord one thousand six hundred sixty and eight, and in the one and twentieth yeare of the raigne of King Charles the Second." The 21st year of the reign of Charles II began in January 1668/9, on the anniversary of his father's death.

[75] Both date and place are reported by Manning and Bray, *Hist. Antiq. Surrey*, III, 250. Nichols and Bruce, in *Wills from Doctors' Commons*, p. 119, give the date, as from the register of Westminster Abbey. Banks (*Poetical Works*, p. 26), following Sir Thomas Pope Blount (*De Re Poetica: or, Remarks upon Poetry. With Characters and Censures of the Most Considerable Poets* [London, 1694], p. 66), who himself takes directly from Gerard Langbaine (*An Account of the English Dramatick Poets* [Oxford, 1691], I, 127), gives March 10 as the day of death, but that is impossible because of the date of the will. Both Langbaine and Blount say Denham died "at his House near *White-hall*," which is to say, in Sir John Denham's Buildings, his home and

out public notice, but Denham nevertheless achieved the honor of burial in the Poets' Corner of Westminster Abbey, "near Mr. Chaucer's monument," on March 23, 1667/8.[76] There appears, however, to have been little of pomp or ceremony at the funeral, and Denham's end went not merely unremarked in the daily records of his contemporaries, but unsignalized by the outpouring of elegiac verses which often accompanied the death of a celebrated poet — which had accompanied, for example, the death of Abraham Cowley. It is against this poetic neglect that the single voice of Christopher Wase, Denham's old friend and admirer from the quiet days at Wilton, protested futilely in his *Elegy upon Sr John Denham, Knt of ye Bath, lately deceased*:

> What means this silence, that may seeme to doome
> Denham to have an undistinguished tombe?[77]

In the sense intended by Wase, Denham's tomb remained undistinguished. No elaborately inscribed monument marked the resting

---

office. Aubrey says, "He dyed . . . at the house of his office (which he built, as also the brick-buildings next the street in Scotland-yard)," and Wood says much the same. Neither gives a specific date. No contemporary seems to have recorded either the cause or the circumstances of the death, but clearly Denham had been anticipating it when it came, and had been of sound mind within the preceding week. Almost certainly, then, his fatal affliction was not a paretic attack.

[76] *The Marriage, Baptismal, and Burial Registers of Westminster*, p. 170. Other accounts specify "near the grave of Spenser," or "amongst those Noble Poets, *Chaucer, Spencer*, and *Cowley*."

[77] Printed by Banks, *Poetical Works*, p. 26, as from S.P. Dom, ser. 29, Vol. 270, p. 182. Banks interprets these lines as referring to "some hesitation as to the disposition of [Denham's] body," which he believes was resolved by the burial in Poets' Corner. Such a line of thought no doubt arises from his necessary assumption that Denham lay unburied for thirteen days: from death on the 10th until burial on the 23d. But Denham did not die until the 19th, and so was buried within four days, hardly long enough for much controversy to arise over the disposition of his body, or to generate such a poem as Banks imagines Wase's tribute to be. Wase, moreover, complains specifically of "silence," and surely the proper interpretation of his poem is that suggested in the text above: to lament the poetic silence that accompanied Denham's death, that his tomb should be undistinguished by its due meed of melodious tears. Sir Sidney Lee records (in *DNB*) another exception to this silence: an epigram in Denham's honor which appeared in William Speed's *Epigrammata* (1669), p. 82.

place of his bones as one belatedly ornamented the repose of Cowley; nor could his grave begin to approach the splendor of Waller's, although the latter had to lie outside Westminster Abbey. Denham's monument, such as it was, was of his own construction: the reputation of his poetry, particularly of *Coopers Hill*; his influence upon English Augustan "numbers"; his esteem in the hearts and minds of poets such as John Dryden and Alexander Pope.

Denham's death was followed by the customary legal adjustments through which the vacancy caused by the loss of a man in public life is rapidly filled up. Christopher Wren passed smoothly into the office of surveyor of Works which he was to adorn with such splendor, and the disappointed John Webb resigned from the public service in indignation.[78] Hugh May likewise retired into private life, consoling himself with a promised pension and reflections on the current unprofitableness of the surveyorship, in the present straitened condition of the royal finances.[79] On the 17th of November, after some dispute, Sir Eliab Harvey was declared elected to the seat for Old Sarum vacated by Denham's death, and another gap was closed. Denham's will was proved on May 9, 1670, by his unmarried daughter Elizabeth, whom he had named as executrix. The notion promulgated by a few writers that he died in poverty is, needless to say, absurd. Among his benefactions was "that noble and pious work," the rebuilding of St. Paul's, toward which he left all the fees he had himself received for the work (20s. per day), plus the sum of £100. Denham's daughter Anne, married to Sir William Morley, had at least five children in all, two sons and three daughters, of whom the sons and one daughter are named in Denham's will. Denham provided

---

[78] *C.S.P.D.: 1668–1669*, p. 132. Webb protested that he had had a grant in 1660 of the reversion after Denham of the surveyorship of works (see above, chap. vi, p. 157 and nn. 4, 5), but that Denham had opposed its passing the Great Seal. Webb added that he "cannot now act under Mr. Wren, who is by far his inferior."

[79] Pepys, *Diary*, March 21, 1668/9 (see chap. vi, p. 171 n. 40, above).

generously for the elder boy's education, and left land to the younger, William, with the proviso that he assume the surname of Denham.[80] But Morley's older son, John, died unmarried in 1683, and William,

---

[80] Denham's will gives some sense of his affairs at the time of his death. He had three chief properties to bequeath: his lease on his grounds and buildings in Scotland Yard; a moiety of a lease of land in "Bedford Levell Fennes, not farre from Peterburgh," of which the other share belonged to his longtime friend William Ashburnham; and a moiety of a lease for seventy years of lands "to be regained from the sea between the peninsula of Selsea and the contiguous parts of the county of Sussex," of which the other moiety belonged to his son-in-law Sir William Morley. Only the Bedford Level lease was encumbered, to the extent of £500 borrowed by Denham from John Ashburnham, William's brother (also an old companion). In addition, Denham had "three judgments or statuts . . . upon the manor of Thorpe, in the county of Surrey, late the estate of Wolley Leigh, esquire," relics of the money-raising campaign Denham and Leigh had undertaken in 1642, prior to joining the King in the Civil War, which Denham sardonically bequeathed to his infant granddaughter, Mary Morley, with the comment "which judgments or statuts are all the satisfaction I am like to receive for diverse great sumes of money which I have paid for the said Wolley Leigh."

Denham left both the Scotland Yard and Bedford Level leases to his daughter Elizabeth, but charged her with a number of expenses on the income. These included minor bequests of £10 per annum each to his servants Mathew Bosworth and Henry Cooper. Denham notes that he has already provided for the accommodating Cooper both "the office of Clearke of his Majesties Works at Hampton Court" and the post of "Harbinger to the Queens Majestie." Out of the income from Scotland Yard Elizabeth was instructed to provide for Denham's elder grandson, John Morley, the sum of £50 per annum toward his maintenance "att some good grammer schoole" from the age of six to the age of fourteen; thereafter, "if he be then found fitt," the sum of £100 per annum during his residence in the university of Oxford "if he continue there three yeares at the least"; and lastly, £200 yearly "to travell into foraigne parts . . . not exceeding two yeares."

The lease at Selsea Denham left to his younger grandson, William Morley, "provided the said William Morley the sonne doe take and keepe the name of Denham for his sirname; and if the said William Morley the younger shall dye without issue, then I give that my said moiety to his next younger brother, upon the same termes and condicion of takeing and beareing my sirname as aforesaid." (In the event, all the Morley children predeceased their father, save only Mary, who became Sir William's sole heir in 1701.)

Denham named as overseers of his will his friends Sir John Birkenhead and William Ashburnham, with Elizabeth Denham as executrix. His signature was witnessed by Birkenhead, by Denham's servant Mathew Bosworth, and by one Ambrose Ward. The will was proved at Exeter House before Sir Leoline Jenkins, on the 9th day of May 1670, "by the oath of Elizth Denham, daughter of the decd, and executrix in the will named."

never having assumed the name Denham, died *sine prole* ten years later. Of Anne's three daughters, Anne and Cicely died unmarried, while Mary, born only in 1667, married the tenth Earl of Derby and had as sole offspring one son, William, Lord Stanley, who died as an infant. Thus Denham's progeny disappeared in the third generation. Mary, Countess of Derby, died in 1752, the last survivor of her grandfather's line.

Later in 1669 than Denham's own death occurred that of his former patroness of the Louvre, the dowager Queen Henrietta Maria. On February 6, 1670/1, in settlement of the late Queen's affairs, a Treasury warrant was issued for the payment of certain debts and wages that she owed. The fifty-seventh name on a list of fifty-eight persons to whom the sum of £10 was to be paid, "by moieties in order as they stand and when one moiety is paid to all then the other moiety to be paid," was that of Sir John Denham.[81] To whom the money was actually paid the record does not show. This was the last official cognizance of Sir John Denham in the public records of England. The fifty-eighth name on the list was that of "Dr. Christopher Wrenne."

---

[81] *C.Treas.Bks.: 1669–1672*, p. 780.

Appendix A

DENHAM'S ACTIVITIES
FROM OCTOBER 1642 UNTIL APRIL 1643:
DEGENERATION OF THE ACCOUNT
THROUGH SUCCESSIVE BIOGRAPHIES

(For details of what Denham really did and suffered during this six-month period, see pp. 55–61, above.)

ACCOUNT 1

Aubrey, *Brief Lives*:
Anno . . . (I ghesse 1642) he was high-sheriff of the countie of Surrey.
At the beginning of the civill warre he was made governor of Farnham-castle for the king, but he was but a young soldier, and did not keepe it. In 1642/3, after Edghill fight, his poeme called *Cowper's Hill* was printed at Oxford. . . .

ACCOUNT 2

Wood, *Athenae Oxonienses*:
he was prick'd High Sherriff for *Surrey*, and made Governour of *Farnham Castle* for the King: But he being an inexpert soldier, soon after left that office, and retired to his Maj. at *Oxon*, where he printed his poem called *Coopers Hill*. . . .

ACCOUNT 3

Johnson, *Lives of the Poets*, "Denham":
He was after that picked for sheriff of Surrey, and made governor of Farnham Castle for the King; but he soon resigned that charge, and retreated to Oxford, where, in 1643, he published *Coopers Hill*.

ACCOUNT 4

Manning and Bray, *Hist. Antiq. Surrey*, III, 250:
In 1642 he was designed for Sheriff of *Surrey*, and was made
Governor of *Farnham Castle* for the King; but finding himself
unqualified for such a post, he resigned it, and retired to the King
at *Oxford*, where, in 1643, he published his Poem called *Cooper's
Hill.*

Aubrey probably had some sense of the realities behind his
remarks, but as always he is very weak on dates. His guess of 1642
for Denham's appointment as sheriff of Surrey is correct, but Wood
is cautious about Aubrey's dates, and Manning and Bray probably
worked out the year for themselves. It may have been delicacy
that caused Aubrey to word his record of Denham's inept defense
and ignominious surrender of Farnham Castle in so ambivalent
a way, or it may have been Aubrey's own carelessness or unsure-
ness of the facts. Whatever the cause, the results are ludicrous.
Aubrey passes completely over Denham's subsequent period as a
prisoner of war in London, and with his next sentence removes
him (with typical confusion about dates) to Oxford. Wood, with
his instinct for tidying the narrative, inserts a factitious transition
from Farnham to Oxford. Aubrey's note that Denham was "but
a young soldier" is given precision (and, as it happens, accuracy)
by Wood's statement that he was "inexpert." But when Wood
altered "he . . . did not keepe it" — by which Aubrey covered the
blunt reality that Denham *lost* the castle — into "he . . . left
that office, and retired to . . . *Oxon*," he went far beyond his evidence and so brought about Johnson's illusion that Denham *resigned* his office, and ultimately misled Manning and Bray, who,
by combining Wood and Johnson, at last present as an act of
grave and judicious self-appraisal on Denham's part what was in
fact an event mingled of bravado, incompetence, and pusillanimity.

As for the publication of *Coopers Hill*, Aubrey is correct insofar
as the poem did come out at Oxford early in 1643 (probably in
April). But his formula "In 1642/3, after Edghill fight" could
have come from Aubrey alone. Edghill fight occurred on October 23,

1642, before Denham's occupation of Farnham Castle, and more than a month before his ultimate surrender. The period designated 1642/3 (January 1 through March 24, 1643, by modern reckoning) commenced more than two months after Edghill, and the association of dates is therefore misleading. The Oxford *Coopers Hill* bears an imprint date of 1643, which almost certainly indicates it was printed after March 24, and Johnson probably determined the date from a copy of the poem. Aubrey appears to have been unaware of the existence of the earlier London edition of the poem, in August 1642, and so throughout this succession of writers the 1643 publication is always assumed to be the first edition of *Coopers Hill*. Pope's friend Joseph Spence was under the same impression, and seems to have used a copy of 1643 for his analysis of the alterations between the "A" and "B" texts of the poem.

Appendix B

A REVISED CANON
OF THE WORKS OF JOHN DENHAM

The works are listed chronologically within categories by date of probable composition. Date of first publication, if any, is then given, and dates of subsequent publication if within Denham's lifetime. Inclusion in Denham's collected *Poems and Translations* of 1668 is designated by *1668PT*.

A. Works either incontestably by Denham or never contested:

Date of composition	Title or description	Date of publication
1636?	Partial translation, *Aeneid* II–VI	Still unpublished
ca. 1636–1639	*The Anatomy of Play* (prose)	1651
1641	"On the Earl of Strafford's Tryal and Death"	*1668PT*
1641	*Coopers Hill*, Draft I	1969*
1641	*The Sophy*	1642; *1668PT*
1641–42	*Coopers Hill*, Draft II	1969*
1642	"Elegy on the Death of Judge Crooke"	1790
1642	"To the Five Members of the Honourable House of Commons: The Humble Petition of the Poets"	1662; *1668PT*
1642	*Coopers Hill*, Draft III	1642, 1643, 1650

---

* In *Expans'd Hieroglyphicks*.

262

1642/3	"A Speech against Peace at the Close Committee" (*Mr. Hampdens speech . . .*)	1643, 1662; *1668PT*
1643	"A Western Wonder"	1662; *1668PT*
1643	"A Second Western Wonder"	1662; *1668PT*
1644–45	"To Sir Richard Fanshaw upon his Translation of *Pastor Fido*"	1648; *1668PT*
1647	"On Mr. John Fletchers Works"	1647; *1668PT*
1649	"An Elegie upon the Death of the Lord Hastings"	1649
1650?	"Natura Naturata"	*1668PT*
1651–52	"To Sir John Mennis Being Invited from Calice to Bologne To Eat a Pig"	*1668PT*
1651–52	"A Dialogue between Sir John Pooley and Mr. Thomas Killigrew"	*1668PT*
1651–52	"On My Lord Crofts and my Journey into Poland, from whence we Brought 10000 L. for his Majesty by the Decimation of his Scottish Subjects There"	*1668PT*
1651–52	"On Mr. Tho. Killigrew's return from his Embassie from Venice, and Mr. William Murray's from Scotland"	*1668PT*
1651–52	At least six of the satires in *Certain Verses by severall of the Authors Friends* [on *Gondibert*], viz., 1. "Upon the Preface" ("Room for the best of Poets heroick"); 2. "Upon the Preface of Gondibert" ("As *Martials* life was grave	1653

and sad"); 3. "To Sir W. Davenant" ("After so many sad mis-haps"); 5. "The Author upon himself" ("I am old Davenant with my fustian Quill"); 6. "A Letter sent to the good Knight" ("Thou hadst not been thus long neglected"); 14. "Canto 2" ("Rais'd by a Prince of *Lombard* blood")

1652	"An occasional Imitation of a modern Author upon the Game of Chess"	*1668PT*
1652	"As I came from Lombardy"	Still unpublished
1652	"Sir William's no more a Poet"	Still unpublished
1653–54?	"The Progress of Learning" (without the Preface)	*1668PT*
1653–54	*Coopers Hill*, Draft IV	1655; *1668PT*
1653–54	*The Destruction of Troy*	1656; *1668PT*
1653–54?	"The Passion of Dido for Aeneas"	*1668PT*
1659	"News from Colchester" (*A Relation of a Quaker* . . .)	1659; *1668PT*
1667	*On Mr. Abraham Cowley his Death and Burial*	1667; *1668PT*
1667	"Friendship and Single Life against Love and Marriage"	*1668PT*
1667	Preface to "The Progress of Learning"	*1668PT*
1667	"Sarpedon's Speech to Glaucus in the 12th of Homer"	*1668PT*
1667	"Martial. Epigram: out of an Epigram of Martial"	*1668PT*
1667	"Of Prudence"	*1668PT*
1667	"Of Justice"	*1668PT*

1667	Translation of Corneille's *Horace*, IV, vi, vii; V	1669 (performed 1668, 1669)
1667–68?	Four-line addition to *Coopers Hill*	*1668PT*
1667–68?	Six-line addition to *Coopers Hill*	1966
1667–68?	Eight-line addition to "Of Prudence"	1966
1667–68?	*A Version of the Psalms of David*	1714
1668	"Elegy on Sir William D'avenant"	1966
1668	"To the Hon. Edward Howard Esq; upon his poem of *The British Princes*"	1668 (not in *1668PT*)
1668	*Cato Major, of Old Age*	1668 (not in *1668PT*)

B. Works of uncertain authorship attributed to Denham and not improbably written by him:

1665?	"To his Mistress"	1694
1666	*The Second Advice to a Painter**	1667

C. Works attributed to Denham but almost certainly not written by him:

1655	"Verses on the Cavaliers Imprisoned in 1655"†	1890
1659/60	*A Panegyrick on His Excellency, General Monck*†	1660
1660	*The Prologue to his Majesty* †	1660
1667	*Third*, "Fourth," and "Fifth" *Advice to a Painter*	1667
1668	*The Battel of the Catts*	1668

---

* Excluded by Banks from Denham's canon.
† Included by Banks in Denham's canon.

265

Index